THE SUPERCHIEFS

*To the memory of Helen Heller (1903–1992);
my most faithful reader*

Other books by Robert Heller

Superman
The Naked Manager
The Supermanagers
The New Naked Manager
The Age of the Common Millionaire
The Supermarketers
The Best of Robert Heller
The Decision-Makers
Unique Success Proposition
Culture Shock

The Complete Guide to Modern Management
   (editor – published annually)

The Superchiefs

The People, Principles and Practice
of the New Management

Robert Heller

MERCURY

Copyright © Heller Arts 1992

The right of Robert Heller to be identified as author of this work has been asserted by him in accordance with the Copyright, Designs and Patents Act 1988.

All rights reserved. No part of this publication may be reproduced, stored in a retrieval system, or transmitted in any form or by any means, electronic, mechanical, photocopying, recording, or otherwise without the prior permission of the publishers.

First published in 1992
by Mercury Books
Gold Arrow Publications Limited,
826 Garratt Lane, London SW17 0NB

Setting produced from Authors Disks by TecSet Ltd, Wallington, Surrey
Printed and bound in Great Britain by
Mackays of Chatham PLC, Chatham, Kent

This book is sold subject to the condition that it shall not, by way of trade or otherwise, be lent, re-sold, hired out or otherwise circulated without the publisher's prior consent in any form of binding or cover other than that in which it is published and without a similar condition including this condition being imposed upon the subsequent purchaser.

British Library Cataloguing in Publication Data is available
ISBN 1–85251–146 X

Preface

This book began as a return to the ground covered by *The Once and Future Manager*, a philosophical study of management's future commissioned by that great headhunter, Per Berndtson, in the 1970s. As the project developed, though, it became clear that, in the hard and testing conditions of the 1990s, a harder and more prescriptive approach was essential – and the always perceptive Truman Talley, my publisher at NAL/Dutton, strongly urged me in that direction.

It happily coincided with my work, in collaboration with Edward de Bono, on the monthly newsletter, *Letter to Thinking Managers*. The combination of Edward's unique insights into the thinking process, and my investigation of new management ideas in practice, mirrors the immensely productive union of 'soft' and 'hard' concepts in what I've called 'the new management'. In addition to the *Letter*, another important source of material was the series of management articles expertly commissioned from me for the magazine *Business Life* by William Davis and David Taylor.

I am very grateful for their support, and for that of Philip Beresford, editor of my former magazine, *Management Today*, who gave me the opportunity to comment on the vital management issues of the day in a monthly column. The reviews I was asked to write for *Business Solutions*, the Unisys magazine, and the columns commissioned by George Littlejohn for *Professional Investor*, have also widened by horizons. In a world more frenetic than fast-moving, journalism is invaluable for picking up new trends and, even more important, for testing ideas against the only measure which counts: the reality of unfolding events and results.

That applies to other people's journalism as well as my own. Nobody can stay sufficiently informed in this field without reading *Business Week, Fortune, The Wall Street Journal*, and the *Harvard*

Business Review in the US, or the *Financial Times* and *Management Today* in Britain. I owe a great debt to the editors and journalists of these publications for the superb quality of the factual and analytical material that is fully acknowledged in the text. The *Los Angeles Times* and *New Yorker* have also thrown searching light on important issues raised by the book.

It draws, too, on the contributions of many original minds which have remade the map of modern management. Peter Drucker is, of course, the ultimate source of most of the new wisdom in general management. My thinking has also been profoundly influenced by the work of W. Edwards Deming. I have been greatly enlightened by several other writers and speakers, mostly met through our mutual work at seminars and the like: including Harvard's Rosabeth Moss Kanter and her husband, Barry Stern; Igor Ansoff; Xavier Gilbert of IMD in Lausanne; David Norburn of the Management School at Imperial College; Ben Tregoe of Kepner Tregoe; Sir John Harvey-Jones, late of ICI; Warren Bennis; Francisco Gomez, met through Denis Bourne of the Management Excahange; and Robert Waterman, Jr.

One seminar organiser in particular, José Salibi Neto of HSM Cultura & Desenvolvimento in São Paulo, has made a major contribution, not only by making me organise my thoughts for his Brazilian audiences, but by introducing me to the work of a star-studded list of speakers – for example, Ron Zemke of Performance Research Associates, whose work on service quality is outstanding. The bibliography lists my indebtedness to books by some of the above and by other authors, to all of whom I am extremely grateful.

Many business leaders have contributed knowingly or unknowingly to these pages. I should particularly like to mention and thank Robert W. Galvin of Motorola; Ben Rosen of Savin Rosen; Floris Maljers of Unilever; and David O'Brien, chief executive of the National & Provincial Building Society, who found Peter McColough's remarkable talk for me when at Rank Xerox (UK). Victor Lewis, managing director of Cornhill Publications, has my warm thanks for introducing me to the European Foundation for Quality Management, and thus to Hansjörg Manger of Robert Bosch and Karel Vinck of Bekaert.

My admiration for the intelligence and information of management consultants has been reinforced by the work I have drawn on – notably that of Korn/Ferry International on boards of directors, and of CSC Index on channel strategy. I have particularly benefited

PREFACE

from my association with the Kalchas Group, the London-based strategic consultancy. My conversations with the partners, and our work on presenting the results of Kalchas's research, have been very helpful in shaping some of the concepts in this book.

Michael de Kare Silver of Kalchas is among the many authors (some close friends), who have contributed to the four editions of the management annual that I edit for Sterling Publications, republished by Mercury Books as *The Complete Guide to Modern Management*. It has been a privilege to edit their work and to learn so much while doing so. Several others have helped invaluably during an unusually long gestation period: I must especially thank three excellent secretaries, Gillian Riley, Sandra Willis and Elli Petrohilos.

This book resembles what I describe in its pages as the 'management consensus' in really being the work of many minds. I observe in an early chapter that the great majority of managers don't yet practise what the consensus preaches. They will.

Robert Heller

Contents

PREFACE v

INTRODUCTION: WESTWORLD LTD xiii

PART ONE: HOW TO INVEST IN LEADERSHIP 1
1. The Right Stuff 3
2. Compaq: The Soured American Dream 9
3. RJR Nabisco: The American Nightmare 15
4. The New Order Cometh 19
5. Xerox: The Broken Breakthrough 25
6. The Corporate Entrepreneur 29

PART TWO: HOW TO ADD POWER TO RESPONSIBILITY 35
7. General Electric: The Kraken Wakes 37
8. The Liberators' Ball 41
9. Deming: The Un-American American Way 47
10. The New Age of Management 50
11. Hanson: The Big Pay-off 56
12. The Reagan-Thatcher Write-off 59

PART THREE: HOW TO TEACH SUCCESS 65
13. British Airways: The Flying Business School 67
14. What Managers Need to Learn 70
15. Nintendo: The System Game 76
16. What Managers Need to Know 79
17. General Foods: The Jump in Jell-O 85
18. The Genie of the IT Lamp 88

PART FOUR: HOW TO MAKE TOP MANAGEMENT RIGHT — 95
19. Campbell: Deep in the Soup — 97
20. The Once and Future Chief Executive — 100
21. Sony: The Magic of Morita — 106
22. The Nine-Yes Chief — 109
23. Chrysler: The Cult of Iacocca — 115
24. The Boss and the Board — 118

PART FIVE: HOW TO CREATE THE SUPER STRUCTURE — 125
25. Ford: The Plutocrat's Puzzle — 127
26. The Direction of Thrust — 130
27. Guinness: A Tale of Two Boards — 135
28. The Non-Executive Nonentities — 138
29. McDonalds: Eating its Words — 144
30. Why the Matrix Lost Merit — 147

PART SIX: HOW TO GENERATE STRATEGIC POWER — 152
31. Philips Electrical: The Light that Failed — 155
32. The Figures That Don't Count — 158
33. Toshiba: The Hidden Agenda — 164
34. The Everlasting Strategy — 167
35. Berkshire Hathaway: Buffett's Beating — 173
36. The Right Measure of Management — 176

PART SEVEN: HOW TO MASTER THE NEW MODES — 183
37. Robert Bosch: The Founding Obsession — 185
38. Quality's Total Impact — 188
39. Coca-Cola: The Mightiest Mega-Brand — 194
40. The Old Magic of Marketing — 197
41. Levi Strauss: The Humanity of Haas — 203
42. The Value of Values — 206

PART EIGHT: HOW TO WIN PRIME PERFORMANCE — 213
43. United Technologies: The Carrier Bag — 215
44. Against the Organisation — 218
45. Time-Warner: The Rich Rewards of Ross — 224
46. The Right Kind of Company — 227
47. Harley-Davidson: The Kick Restart — 233
48. Managing Out of Recession — 236

CONTENTS

PART NINE: HOW TO ACHIEVE THE IMPOSSIBLE   243
49. Apple: The Hard Core   245
50. The World-Class Manager   248
51. The Washington Post: What Katy Did   254
52. A Regiment of Women   257
53. Merck: The Magic Pill   263
54. Motivating Beyond Money   266

PART TEN: HOW TO UNIFY ORGANIC STRENGTH   273
55. Toyota: The Legacy of Ohno   275
56. An Age Created by Japan   278
57. Motorola: The Impossible Win   284
58. The Era of Innovation   287
59. IBM: The Biggest Crossroads   293
60. The Right Management   297

EPILOGUE: WINNING IN THE GLOBAL MARKET   304

BIBLIOGRAPHY   308

INDEX   311

Introduction:
Westworld Ltd

Western management is at war. The great corporations headquartered in the US are locked in a struggle for world markets with counterparts from Western Europe and, above all, Japan. Equally plainly, the battle has been carried to American soil, again with the Japanese in the van. Faced by this dual onslaught, very few US industries or companies have been able to preserve, let alone enlarge, their shares of the key world markets. It's hardly surprising that British counterparts have fared no better.

Less obviously, Western management is at war with itself, and the outcome of this hidden battle will determine the result in global competition. The West has won some famous commercial victories in the second half of the twentieth century, from Boeing's domination of the civil airliner market and Silicon Valley's leadership of the electronics revolution to Germany's triumphs in executive cars. But even these brilliantly won positions are under threat because much of the West has in practice fallen behind where in theory the US still leads the world: modern management.

The internal struggle is between the deep knowledge imbibed by or available to energetic managers and the forces of inertia – institutional and personal – that prevent managements from applying that powerful know-how consistently and decisively. The prime duty of the chief executive is to resolve that conflict in overwhelming favour of change, progress, innovation, speed, adaptability, achievement – all the essential attributes to which more and more managers aspire. Their frustration is ultimately the chief executive's failure. It arises because the forces of inertia bear especially heavily on the people in this often lonely position.

It shouldn't be lonely. The sum of a corporation can be no greater than that of its human parts, working in combination. That truth applies as much to the chief executive as anybody else. The boss can (and must) make the unilateral decision that the company will be managed in the new ways described in this book, jettisoning the old and outworn for ever. But that decision can be translated into action multilaterally only in a management system where people, from the chief executive downwards, are never more than *primus inter pares*, first among equals – and where the equality has far more weight than the being first.

Without a deep and wide change in management practice, the competitive war will continue to be lost, not in one overwhelming defeat, but in one local battle after another. A front cover of *Business Week* in June 1991 referred to 'The Battle for Europe' and observed, with dead accuracy, that: 'The world's largest market is up for grabs. While the Europeans and Americans are losing ground, the Japanese are coming on strong'. In cars, communications, computers, consumer electronics, tyres, office equipment, machine tools, construction equipment and semiconductors, the story was the same – coming on *very* strong.

That's only to be expected. After the Second World War, American companies did exactly the same, seeking to enlarge their sales by building markets and plants across a fast-growing European economy. And the Europeans returned the compliment, fighting back in their domestic markets and pushing for US and global share as well: the huge inroads made by the Airbus into Boeing's market are symbolic of that European revenge. The Japanese are attacking the same task more effectively, which means that today's challenge for Western management is greater by far.

Many of the companies locked in this competitive war are fighting essentially defensive actions, responding (sometimes belatedly) to attack and hoping, at best, to preserve their existing market shares. Very few have turned the tables, coming back from defeat to seize leadership from the overseas challengers to become once again the cynosures, the companies which set the pace and the standards in all respects – technology, market penetration, innovativeness, continuous improvement and all-round management skill.

It can be done, as proven by the story of one Western business and its boss. The reverse suffered at the hands of Asian competition had been especially humiliating: morale at all levels had collapsed before the clear evidence that massive spending had been ill-directed, and that, under fumbling management, the company was unfit to face fierce competition. A market which had been thought vital was lost

INTRODUCTION

completely – just as a great Japanese company, Sony, virtually lost the VCR market it had created.

Like Sony's Akio Morita and his cohorts, the new Western management refused to accept its calamitous setback as final. First, with full backing from its financiers, the firm invested enormously in world-beating and state-of-the-art technology, the product of intensive and brilliantly successful R & D. Second, the people working the excellent technology were intensively trained to the highest standards: that showed, not just in effectiveness, but in their restored morale. Third, their managers, carefully trained, qualified and selected, only reached the top after much full-time education, technical and general.

Equally important is the organisational structure in which these people operated. The general manager in charge of the turnround had full delegated power to run his operation his way. His instructions from above were absolutely clear, and his full-time chairman, a man of obvious command and mastery, gave total support. The same writ ran downwards: once allotted their role by the boss, the subordinate managers made their own plans – and were expected to execute them decisively.

They weren't very keen when the boss proposed a daring strategy to sweep past the competition. The operating managers gave the classic response: 'it can't be done'. Their belief that he had lost his marbles only encouraged the general manager. Wouldn't the rival management be saying exactly the same thing? That a grand slam assault, like the Japanese attack on Detroit, could never win?

That preconception exposed, not just an Achilles heel, but a yawning gap in the market, which the company exploited at merciless speed. The boss had performed one crucial role of the leader: he turned the negative into a positive, by insisting that his managers had to achieve the 'impossible'. They only agreed, though, after the distribution chief had pledged in writing that everything would be in place for the launch – everything. That, too, is an elementary and elemental management principle: give people the tools if you want them to finish the job.

There's much more to the story, of course. Those running the company are masters and developers of the most modern techniques (including logistics) and are also deeply immersed in the lessons of history (including those of failures, above all their own). The leaders, and everybody below them, also have an enormous supply of three vital elements: *information*, *planning* and *communications*. They come in that order, because nothing can be effectively planned without efficient information, and neither information nor planning is any use without communication.

But the planners and the information experts aren't disembodied backroom boys in this company: they are an integral part of all its efforts. The distinction between line and staff is meaningless in modern high-tech circumstances: the best staffers are ex-line managers, and this company draws its staff largely from the latter, who are often moved right back into the line. As the Japanese have demonstrated, line and staff roles must be inseparable and interchangeable in the drive for global markets.

In the outcome, success was as total as the previous failure. True, the general manager was lucky in his opposition: his chief opponent, a dominant chairman and chief executive who delegated nothing and ruled by fear, had recently made a large, rash and doomed takeover bid. QED: *quod est demonstrandum*. That description can be applied to too many chief executives in the West. The truth is that this great turnaround depended on utterly logical and powerful courses of action that happen to highlight some contrary patterns in much of big Western business today. For utter contrast, consider what the new management did:

1. It *invested* to win leadership in the technology of product and process.
2. It gave effective *power* to people with clear responsibility.
3. It *trained* and educated everybody, from top to bottom, all the time.
4. It led a management *collective* that collaborates, cooperates and consults.
5. It created the *superstructure* of success by assigning the right roles to the right people.
6. It used the fullest possible *information* for the most ambitious possible strategy.
7. It mastered and developed the new *techniques* of hard and soft management.
8. It linked responsibility, status and rewards to prime *performance*.
9. It acquired the means of achieving the *impossible*.
10. It unified *organic* strengths to win exemplary success.

Any chief executive, any management, any business can obey these ten fundamental principles or precepts: although my example isn't,

INTRODUCTION

in fact, a business. The general manager was a general, Norman Schwarzkopf, and the company, Desert Storm, Inc., was one in which British military management played a notably effective part – following exactly the same ten principles. What was demonstrated by the organised body of men and machines known as an army can be emulated by the organised body of men (which in both cases now includes women) and machines known as a business.

The ten sections of this book, each summarised at the end, set out those demanding but rewarding fundamentals with the illustration of real-life case histories, both good and bad – frequently in the same case. Perfection isn't given to man, certainly not to business, and every success carries within it, not only the seeds of its own decay, but current examples of corporate rot. That wondrous economic phenomenon, Westworld Ltd., is no exception. But if I'm right, and corporate setbacks result from negative behaviour, the correct, positive response in peaceful, warlike competition is clear, and its successful outcome is certain.

PART 1

HOW TO INVEST IN LEADERSHIP

CHAPTER 1

The Right Stuff

Consider this picture of one nation's management. It is gaining ground against global competitors as its firms, large and small, make great advances in productivity, management, quality and cost control. Forcing their way into new markets abroad, they are seizing market share from other countries. The top companies are actually enlarging their lead over world rivals. Moreover, this competitive supremacy is continuing to mount, because the enormous acceleration of recent years has created further payoffs whose prime benefits are still to come.

Then consider this savage indictment of a nation's management. Its manufacturing prowess has been eroded, in older technologies, notably cars, and in new, including computers. Lack of effective domestic competition has opened the door to massive import penetration. Several major manufacturers have been taken over by foreign companies, raising the question of whether the country will 'increasingly become a branch-office colony' for Japanese and other foreign owners.

The falling national interest in manufacturing hasn't, however, been matched in the shops. There, consumers have been spending more and more on manufactured goods which have had to be imported. So a one-time surplus in trade in manufactures has become a huge, apparently incorrigible deficit. And there's little sign of improvement. In higher technologies – chemicals, aerospace, computers, telephone equipment, semiconductors, machine tools, even pharmaceuticals – the trend line in national share of the world market points ominously downwards.

The Super-economy sounds like Japan: who else? The Wimp-economy reads like Britain: that condemnation of managerial sin could have been shot at British industry almost any time after the

Second World War. But the two nations are one and the same: the USA, the mighty land that once led the world, virtually unchallenged, in all the industries mentioned above. The two accounts of the same economy appeared in the same magazine, *Fortune*, one in 1989, the other in 1990. It's the later one that depicts a rake's progress bearing an uncanny parallel to the infamous decline in British manufacturing. Nor, though it tried hard, did the article offer much hope that the US tide – let alone the British – will be turned.

This book does offer that hope. Today's knowledge of how to manage is better and deeper than managers of the past possessed, and the vast majority of that knowledge stems from the West. What's more, it is virtually unanimous. The arts and sciences of management are no longer controversial. There's no debate, great or small, about rights and wrongs. No matter what managers read, or where they read it, no matter where they study or who they hear, the lessons and the sermons are on the same track. They overlap, they dovetail – and they all make perfect sense.

From the wise to the merely fashionable, the teachers speak the same tongue. They speak of cooperation and collaboration, tolerance and teamwork, devolution and delegation. Their context is the non-stop search for competitive advantage in the holy war to provide the customer, who always comes first, with the best in quality and service. This is the humane language of competition and contribution together, of firmness and kindness combined. Today's management rests not on enforced coercion, but on intelligent agreement.

If this great and convincing chorus is right, how can *Fortune*'s indictment be equally valid? There's a problem with consensus. It's generally wrong. (That verdict doesn't apply to 'consensus' in the meaning used by apostles of the new management. Their kind of consensus, inside the firm, arises when colleagues agree mutually on the best course of rational action.) Historically, broad consensus is disproved time and again – when the conventional wisdom overwhelmingly alights on one dominant view. When all men agree, all men are probably wrong.

In business, 'everybody' in Europe once believed that the major threat to European industry came from 'the American challenge' – when the real threat was to America, first from Europe, then (and more formidably) from Japan. Many ideas to which Western managers are still enslaved trace back to that era when the US was wrongly identified as both danger and ideal. But today, as a great prophet of the new management, W. Edwards Deming, has observed, 'we are in a new age created by Japan' – and the new management thinkers are strongly influenced by their common perception of that age.

Their many books resonate with each other. Yet in finance, fortunes are usually made not by Establishment figures, who generally agree, but by 'contrarians', who never join the pack, but always and deliberately move in the opposite direction. They observe, for example, how central bankers regularly convince 'everybody' that their view of the right and proper level for a currency (usually the dollar) will prevail. The Bank of England and its friends have never been right, save by accident. Those who believed them lost money: the contrarian few who didn't are still counting their gold.

Personally, I've never felt happy in a consensus. Show me a piece of conventional wisdom, and I look at once for its enshrined folly. My first book, *The Naked Manager*, was heretical, a hatchet job on the old consensus view that management had become almost a scientific discipline. The best brains, on this theory, only had to apply the best techniques in the best way (which the brains had mastered) and any business, any managed organisation, from the Pentagon to a petfood company, would respond to the magic touch.

That touching faith has been debunked as thoroughly as Marxism. Yet the new management consensus comes near to that misplaced faith in certain respects. It strongly implies that there's one 'right way' in which to manage. Where the most misled pundits of the Sixties pointed, believe it or not, to the conglomerates, the Nineties can nominate (with much better reason), the Japanese. That has led to a new formula.

Japan broke through to competitive success by harnessing adapted Western ideas to national cultural norms. *Ergo*, the West can marry adapted Japanese methods to its own culture. The theory may not be explicit: many Britons and Americans are still unwilling to accept that the Japanese may simply show superior management skills and application. But in essence the objective of the new management is to out-Japan Japan. Given the competitive circumstances, it couldn't be anything else.

The task is tough, but the elements are humble enough: or maybe the word should be 'humbling'. The consensus calls for the chief executive to share power all the way down; to reach decisions jointly and severally, rather than singly; to delegate authority more than he (or possibly she) assumes it. Only in that way can the company become the competitive, adaptive, responsive learning organisation that is mandatory for success in a modern world where only high achievement wins.

The theory has many corollaries – for instance, the need to pay exceptionally only for exceptional achievers. But just look at the villains of the British manufacturing scene in the many industries whose share of the domestic and global markets has been shrinking. Shrinkage is not the word for the pay of those presiding over the contraction, for the pay of UK top executives accelerated notably over the 1980s in a process topped only by the Americans. A report in *Fortune* noted that in 1976 long-serving chief executives earned only 34 times the average factory workers' pay 14 years before. That multiple was now *130–fold* – thanks largely to stock options and the like. Plainly, the best US rewards lie not in manufacture and marketing, but in negotiations with the compensation committee of the board. J.Peter Grace, for bad example, liked to average $4 million a year (200 times the workers' basic) for heading W.R. Grace, a mediocre corporation whose earnings per share struggled up by 1.7 per cent annually over the decade to 1989. Berkeley professor Graef S. Crystal calls all this 'the Marie Antoinette school of management'.

There's alarming evidence to show that, as in the France of Louis XVI, too large a gap between top and bottom has a direct and damaging effect on morale throughout. That's no surprise to modern psychologists. Their work is one of the best-supported elements of the consensus, resting on real-life studies that, unlike the cases in the management best-sellers, are scientifically rigorous, have been repeated many times, and are evidently sound. One of my friends is a brilliant exponent of this convincing material. I wanted to know how many in his general audiences (very enthusiastic) put all his preaching into practice.

The answer was none. I had my clue to what was wrong with the consensus, and I speak as a paid-up charter member of the new school of management: hardly anybody does what it teaches. The management experts all agreeing with each other could well be right in theory: because, in practice, they are heretics, contrarians, iconoclasts. The true (or untrue) consensus is how managements actually behave: and that bears little relation to the theory.

To use a political analogy, management in the West is too Stalinist. But a great gulf yawns between the aspirations of the managed society which managers lead and the practice of those leaders. Because the leaders control the apparatus of the managerial state, they seem impervious, indomitable, immovable. But beneath this surface appearance, the mountain is moving. Only the dead hand of the past stops the mountain – or should it be the Wall? – from crumbling.

One thing is certain right now. The manager who manages in the spirit of the contrarian consensus has nothing to lose. The few maverick companies which, at least in part, have sought to manage in the new 'right' way (like Nike, the athletic shoe company, or Apple Corporation in personal computers), have had bad commercial breaks (and Apple, for sure, will have them again): but they've been resilient in adversity in a way that contrasts well with the Stalinist norm.

Maybe that's one ray of hope. Another is that, while Stalinist and neo-Stalinist managements don't practise what is preached, they often preach it themselves. One day lip-service could turn to service and release the organisation from its biggest burden: a heavy, massive inertia that is deeply rooted in the need of human beings for order, position, permanence, authority, rules, power – all the classic features of bureaucracy.

To remove deep roots requires radical action, and that demands radical men and women. As never before, the manager must be a revolutionary, confident that anything and everything can be changed – and for the better. If this sounds Utopian, an impossible dream, consider what one organisation achieved. Devastated in its home market, it decided to go global, though all the required resources were in short supply, and its managers lacked market knowledge of the target areas (whose languages and distribution systems differed profoundly from their own).

What little reputation they had overseas was bad. Now the firm's subsidiaries control half of one world market, a quarter of another, 90 per cent of a third (which the company created from scratch) and 70 per cent of a fourth (in which their subsidiaries comprehensively overtook the lead of the industry's creators). In the process, the organisation became the richest in the world. It is, of course, Japan, Inc., the industries being colour television, cars, VCRs and memory chips: there are many other examples, and they are increasing all the time.

In scores of Japanese companies, paradigm organisation men have performed prodigies of entrepreneurial creativity and marketing, forming enterprising *ad hoc* groups within highly effective functioning bureaucracies. Not only have they kept abreast of accelerating change, they have generated much of the acceleration. At root, this achievement has been founded on a total professionalism which accepts that how things are done now gives no guide to how they *should* be done – now or in the future.

That's the right stuff of management: and it works in any culture, any society, any country. It created, in the US, the world's mightiest industrial machine. It can replenish that might – if the new managers tear down the Stalinist monuments, and win the conflict between positive and negative demonstrated so dramatically by the contrasting pictures with which this chapter began. Anyone can be a chief: but it's the many fewer Superchiefs who are leading management into the most dynamic era it has ever known.

CHAPTER 2

Compaq: The Soured American Dream

The great dream of American capitalism is the successful start-up whose rocket-like launch and second-stage boost end in stratospheric orbit. It can still be done. What Apple Corp. did in the 1970s, Compaq did in the 1980s – and more. The Houston-based company soared from zero to 1990's $3.5 billion of sales in just eight years. As Polaroid, Xerox Corporation and many others have found before, though, the super-start brings with it an eternal management problem: sustaining success.

That sobering thought has fatally eluded many star managements. It didn't escape Rod Canion, Compaq's chief executive in the years of glory that took it from infinitesimal start to global status. Back in 1983, 'We began to look for the things that would bring Compaq down'. That may sound defeatist. It actually sums up a careful philosophy that maintained growth, as Canion noted before his removal in late 1991, past milestone after milestone, one potential 'stumbling point' after another. Compaq didn't stumble over its own growth, partly because each new phase had been anticipated: but in 1991 it fell flat on its face over what had never been foreseen – the non-growth of general and specific recession.

Typically, the runaway entrepreneur stumbles, even crashes, over the transition from gung-ho, undisciplined growth to the necessary disciplines of the large, professionally managed corporation. Compaq was guided past this potential crisis by an engagingly shrewd New York venture capitalist, Ben Rosen, and it began life as it meant to continue – in the professional mode. As Rosen says, though, the results went 'well beyond' anybody's wildest dreams. Yet in 1991, as the company moved from sharply reduced profits to actual loss, the financial results went beyond any of their nightmares.

In late 1990, the survivors of the super-starting days wrongly felt that the strategy, basically still that of those early years, was good for the next five – if not ten. Their mistake wasn't vainglory or intellectual laziness, but the outcome of analytical, factual, numerate judgment applied in a situation that was about to change more radically than the judges knew.

At super-starts numerate analysis always poses a tricky problem anyway. In 1985, when Compaq (at record speed) broke into the *Fortune* list of the 500 largest US corporations, sales only just passed through half a billion dollars. Multiplying at the 1985–90 pace would have taken turnover to $24.5 billion in 1996 and $171.5 billion early in the new century, or getting on for three times the 1990 size of IBM. Computers' prices were tumbling as their power soared, so that degree of growth was surely impossible. Even half that pace would still have been phenomenal: but the Theory of Relativity (Heller's, not Einstein's) means that it wouldn't be seen as such.

Accelerate growth from 5 per cent annually to 15 per cent, and you will be hailed as a managerial hero. Descend from 30 per cent to 15 per cent, and the feet turn to clay. According to Rosen, however, the stock market rating had shown scepticism about the company 'since Day One'. In 1990 Compaq overall (when it grew by 24 per cent) was 'very close to plan': 'we couldn't have executed better', yet the share price was on a roller-coaster. It hardly mattered: $1,000 invested in IBM in December 1983, when Compaq when public, would still have been $1,000 seven years later: a similar investment in Apple fetched $4,000: but money in Compaq multiplied tenfold, or double the market average.

For so stunning a super-start, the 1990 performance wasn't enough to dispel doubts: witness the headlines over a prescient *Business Week* article: 'Doing unto Compaq as it did unto IBM? Rivals are seeking ways to exploit the PC maker's weaknesses'. Weaknesses? In a company that had expanded sales sevenfold in six years? But that is the other half of the super-start problem. It isn't only the mathematics that make slowing down inevitable. As the success piles up, the competition piles in.

Apple's growth spurred IBM into the personal computer business, with unexpected but enormous impact on IBM, the market and a great many companies which took advantage of IBM's open architecture to produce 'compatible' clones. The all-time champion of the latter is Compaq. It had to pay the price of facing clones of its own, led by aggressive companies that attacked where it hurts most – margins.

The assault was directed at Compaq's policy of offering better products at a 'competitive' price (but never the cheapest). Its basic business equation for maintaining super-margins (44 per cent gross and 14 per cent net in 1990) was to reduce prices, driven by the underlying chip technology, but not so fast as it cut costs: and so long as that equation worked, the most deliberately brilliant, nothing-left-to-chance start-up of them all could still work its magic. But Compaq had planned on price reductions of only 15–20 per cent annually: the price collapse in 1991 turned the magic to misery.

As Canion articulated the previous necromancy, getting product leadership was essential – but in computers, though high technology holds the key, that's the easiest of three necessities: the other two being distribution (harder) and, hardest of all, reputation. In technology, according to Rosen, Compaq 'led the world into the new generation' with the 386 chip. There was high risk involved, but it 'totally changed the perception of the company'.

From then on it was seen as a leader, pushing the technology. Other critical decisions were *not* to introduce products. The company's brief annals include some that were taken 'all the way up', but just fell short. A once 'almost impeccable record of new product development' was thus like the almost impeccable quality of final production in a Japanese plant – the rejection took place down the line, not in the market. But almost imperceptibly Compaq was losing that capacity to lead the world – and its customers noticed, fatefully.

In marketing, too, Compaq was a pioneer of a philosophy – dealers only – that was only good so long as it lasted. That policy not only avoided conflicts of interest, between dealer and supplier, but met economic necessity: PCs don't fetch high enough prices or margins to support a direct sales force. In the 1990s Compaq had to invest large money and effort in support and back-up for the authorised dealers; and building its own 'complementary' operation was essential to selling the large-scale, complex systems to which the big customers are moving; but, fatefully again, it didn't protect Compaq against moves by others to alternative methods, like mail order.

Until 1991, the distribution philosophy remained effective in the US, and in Europe, where 82 per cent of PC sales were shipped through dealers. The European drive was headed from the start by Eckhard Pfeiffer, who in 1991 first moved to the US as chief operating officer, and then displaced Canion at the helm. Europe had become the major driving force behind continued growth: in all, overseas sales expanded by a phenomenal 50 per cent in 1990. Again, forethought paid off. Just as it thought like a major company while still a venture capital start-up, so the two-year-old Compaq began thinking multinational when it hardly counted nationally.

Starting from scratch, Pfeiffer had the concept of a 'European company', even though it was 'physically impossible and legally impossible'. Year by year the bounds of impossibility shrank, while Compaq's global reputation simultaneously enlarged ('much beyond what we thought we could have achieved', in Canion's recollection). The rise in reputation was partly and deliberately the result of a massive advertising spend, again from the start.

By the same token, Pfeiffer didn't think it enough just to become the 'strong, solid No. 2', to IBM in Europe. The company, which manufactures 65 per cent of sales locally in Scotland, needed to be reputed 'a European PC vendor' as well. That inspired, among much other communicating, its first sports sponsorship, 1990's Grand Slam Cup, which gave 19-year-old Pete Sampras $2 million for playing four games of tennis. Beyond Europe, where sales soared over the $1 billion mark even faster than in the US, lies the rest of the world market – meaning above all Japan.

Compaq has laid careful plans for Japan, too. If they come off, in a sense, this will be a counter-attack, since the original portable leader was led in laptops by the Japanese. Technologically and in the market, the Houston company fought back – with an 8 lb. 'notebook' computer that, while a technological *tour de force*, is in fact Japanese, made by Citizen Watch. The company which beat IBM to the 386 chip by seven amazing months, though, depends on being both best and first – for it's that alone which provided the ability to sustain the 'competitive' prices'.

That's the beautiful combination which first slipped in 1990 and came completely unstuck in 1991. The year before *Business Week* had argued that other makers, from IBM downwards, were beating Compaq to the technological punch, and undercutting its prices by up to 35 per cent. Thus the old, old story was replayed in this new, new company. True, when IBM announced a product with the 486 chip first, and Compaq was actually last, the wonder-chip wasn't ready. When full supplies began, 'Compaq had 75 per cent of the market. It started when we began to ship', in Canion's claim. Fully-fledged competition from IBM wasn't announced until the end of 1990 – 'a year late', he noted triumphantly.

Denting Compaq's confidence and self-esteem has never been easy, which is typical enough of super-starts, and has its grave dangers. Once a management takes the Panglossian view, that all's for the best in the best of all possible companies, it's probably done for. One frequent sign of Panglossism is an unchanging guard: the Compaq leaders saw the relative stability of their management as a strength in an industry where managers have traditionally been as volatile as their markets. But the upheavals of 1991, with long-time executives, led by Canion, leaving in droves, shattered the image.

The founders' Texan backgrounds and common upbringing in Texas Instruments had helped bind together a culture much less frenetic than that of Silicon Valley. The culture was every bit as entrepreneurial, open and quick to the draw on decisions. But, in Canion's phrase, it was marked by a 'very conservative philosophy of managing risk'. Through the 1980s, he and his fellows proved remarkably adept at getting the best of both worlds, keeping alive the entrepreneurial culture and competitive challenge – while taking advantage of the economies of scale in manufacture, marketing and global branding.

But Rosen's warning, before the deluge, was that a $3 billion company has to 'guard against ossification', and Canion himself noted that 'once you've lost effectiveness and spirit, getting back is a whole lot harder'. The truth was that the threefold strength of Canion's technology-marketing-reputation platform had weakened at the very time when it needed reinforcement to face an unavoidable future: fighting hard for share across the broadest product line in the business in a fragmented market of mounting volatility.

It was no longer a matter of only out-manoeuvring IBM, whose much pressured profits handsomely led Compaq's total *sales* in 1989. The one-time Texan upstart now has a massive weight of many-sided competition to push against. Ben Rosen's six basic necessities of start-up success (good people, good products, a marketing strategy, financial resources, world presence and excellent execution) suddenly needed reworking, rewriting and reform.

The company has been caught up in a continuing revolution. To Rosen, the decade's mega-change to open systems (in which purchasers can combine purchases from several different suppliers) from proprietary ones (anything you like, so long as it's ours), is generating something like 'what Eastern Europe has been going through'. Management must be equipped to exploit this revolution, both strategically and psychologically: and the necessity doesn't only apply to Compaq and its PC rivals.

'You use technological change, or you fight it', says Canion. 'We designed the company around change'. The design proved so robust that, had the founders created their PC miracle inside their *alma mater*, Texas Instruments, the latter would have been 50 per cent larger in sales in 1989 – and twice as profitable. Only, the miracle wouldn't, and maybe couldn't, have happened inside the latter-day TI, once a great super-start itself.

The writing appeared on Compaq's own wall because that immense lesson was being forgotten or ignored at the very time when the founders were reassuring themselves (and everybody else) that it couldn't happen to them. It's a lesson that every would-be Superchief should ponder: for, to a critical extent, every business is a start-up now.

CHAPTER
3
RJR Nabisco: The American Nightmare

The change round which Rod Canion claimed to have built Compaq was deliberately pursued, not in reaction to untoward events, but as a proactive means of achieving strategic goals. In the frenetic world of the 1980s, the imperatives of change became more obvious by the hectic minute: so the spotlight turned on this deliberate 'management of change'. It's a tautology – for any manager worthy of the name has to cope with change all the time.

There's one school of management practice, very different from Canion's, which makes a virtue of this necessity. You won't find any management thinker advocating a chaos-driven culture, but there was once a practising manager named Tony Peskett who had 'a lifelong belief in the creative uses of chaos' and a firm conviction that 'the minute you establish an organisation, it starts to decay'. Peskett operated on a small stage, a Canadian department store chain. But he found a disciple who took this philosophy to Broadway, so to speak.

That was F. Ross Johnson, who carried 'a love for constant restructuring and reorganising' into 'every business he ever ran'. The quotes come from *Barbarians at the Gate*, in which two *Wall Street Journal* reporters, Bryan Burrough and John Helyar, mercilessly anatomise Johnson and the battle he launched (and lost) for the ownership of RJR Nabisco, the seventeenth largest corporation in the US. Since Johnson, after a late start, rose at lightning speed to chief executive first of Standard Brands, then Nabisco, then RJR Nabisco, the Peskett philosophy plainly worked well – but mostly for him.

There's little evidence that constantly stirring up the organisation triumphed in the market place. On the contrary, the disruption inflicted on the Reynolds tobacco business speeded up its decline relative to Philip Morris. Yet this and other Johnson failures can't be separated from his clear faults as a manager: in the *Barbarians* version, he threw money at everything and everybody (including himself) without any sign of planning or forethought.

A system of management by chaos might work, if operated by a manager of real ability and application: but so can a system of law and order. Another consumer goods company, with a better record than any Johnson achieved, has combined the two in a pungent action philosophy: the company is PepsiCo, and the injunction is 'Ready, fire, aim'. My management audiences usually laugh at the inversion of fire and aim, without paying too much attention to the most important word: 'ready'.

Moving sharply into a new market, or launching a new product without waiting for exhaustive test results, is a powerful antidote to the disease of excessive checking and analysis. But the 'fire, aim' policy will be suicidal if the company hasn't built permanent resources which guarantee, so far as human possibility allows, that the technology will work, the distribution system will set the product or service before every potential customer, and the marketing machine will provide an effective promotional and sales back-up.

Johnson certainly had a 'ready, fire, aim' philosophy: but judged by the results, the readiness doesn't seem to have been especially brilliant. In 1987, when it was ranked among the five tobacco-led companies in the *Fortune* 500, RJR Nabisco was fourth, third and third in net return on sales, assets and equity, and last in earnings per share growth over a decade. The much-admired Philip Morris led the company on every score. Set among food companies, RJR Nabisco looked much brighter, true, but only because of inherently high margins on tobacco.

All that had become academic by 1990. Still a giant, the 24th largest company in America, RJR Nabisco was shrinking as assets were sold off (including parts of its multinational empire): and the loss of $1.15 billion represented a *negative* return on shareholders' equity of 92.9 per cent. That equity had itself become meaningless as the result of the super-colossal debt that financed the company's $25 billion takeover.

It's a deeply disturbing story which really began over a century before Johnson put his giant conglomerate 'in play' by proposing the biggest management buyout in history. In 1875, the young R. J. Reynolds opened the factory that, by his death in 1918, was the world's greatest tobacco company, built on hard work, thrift, innovation and paternalism: Camels swept the US market, propelled by brilliant advertising and an innovative corporate culture, which later led both in filter and menthol cigarettes.

In 1898, a Chicago lawyer named Adolphus Green made an equivalent mark in the baking business. His National Biscuit Company, with Green personally engaged, produced the Uneeda Biscuit. The soda cracker was brilliantly advertised by N. W. Ayer, the same agency that Reynolds used so successfully for Camels. Green followed Uneeda with Oreo, 'the best-selling cookie in the world', and his successors did even better with the Ritz cracker. Like Reynolds, Green embodied the Great American Dream, or rather its reality: the creation of great businesses by true corporate builders who combined marketing enterprise with long-term vision and lasting management genius.

The depressing feature of *Barbarians at the Gate* is that hardly any of the cast who hurtle through its hectic pages appear to fit any part of that description. The plan unveiled to a startled board wasn't a true management buyout. The executive coterie led by Johnson wasn't a group of ambitious managers eager to take control of their business and improve its performance. They already had absolute control, weakly surrendered by a board that had been carefully and cheerfully led along by the chief executive's 'free spending'.

Only the spending wasn't 'free': somebody else paid. Spending other people's money is always pleasant: spending it without let or hindrance, for men of no conscience, is marvellous. The coterie wanted to preserve their company apartments, the fleet of planes stigmatised as a 'private air force', country club memberships, sporting connections, exorbitant incomes, and grotesque provisions for their own capital gains. The buyout would advance the process only through financial engineering: by buying RJR Nabisco cheap and selling most of it dear (the only management ability Johnson undeniably had), the clique stood to share an unheard-of $2 billion in capital gains.

The key wasn't management, but cash flow – the billion a year spewed out by a tobacco business which was steadily losing ground in the marketplace to Philip Morris. Apart from a bloody and costly victory in the soft cookie wars, Johnson had advanced, not through outside engagements, but through successful boardroom infighting in all three of his employing companies. But *Barbarians* gives no indication that he was much interested in either marketing or management – only in the power that preserved, financed and enhanced his extravagant lifestyle.

Paradoxically, putting the company 'in play' risked everything. As the book tells in meticulous detail, Johnson set off a Wall Street power struggle whose participants, like him, were uninhibited: it wasn't their money, either. The billion dollars of fees, and the bankable consequences of winning or losing, drove the Wall Streeters on in a frenzy of hunger. Amidst all the frenetic conduct and misconduct, one character, John Greeniaus, stands out: the head of Nabisco actually enjoyed managing the business. Naturally, he was excluded from the Johnson clique.

The good work of Greeniaus is one reason why, after a massive refinancing, the fate of RJR Nabisco, long in the balance, began to look brighter a year after the tumult. Can the same be said about major US corporations as a whole? Johnson took to excess some common characteristics of the period, notably the pursuit of rich remuneration (and the rich life) by professional chief executives and their minions, in which the ideals and objectives of the founding fathers were abandoned.

Corporate behaviour in Britain and, to a lesser extent, in the rest of Western Europe, has been following in this jetsam-strewn wake. Given the departure of Western business *mores* and motives from the famous footsteps of the past towards self-seeking, basically corrupt paths, poor performance against Japanese competition becomes easier to explain. Corrective forces have now destroyed Drexel Burnham Lambert, one of the vultures at the corporate feast, along with many companies (such as the Maxwell empire and Polly Peck) that shared the table. If the correction is taken as far as it needs – which is much further – the Great American Nightmare will fade: and it will be time again for the Dream.

CHAPTER 4

The New Order Cometh

F. Ross Johnson tackled the ever-mounting jobs in his progress to the summit of RJR Nabisco in the spirit of a turnround man, who doesn't have a 'ready' system, but must first remake the company. The evidence is overwhelming – since it's happened to so many of them – that organisations, large or small, can be changed, to all intents and purposes, overnight: though often the change agent has to be a stranger to the company, even to the industry, as Johnson was first to food, then to tobacco.

Study of turnrounds reveals a recurring pattern, which consists of eight fundamental elements:

1. Leadership is the fulcrum.
2. Nothing is sacred.
3. Decisions are taken firmly when and where they must be made.
4. Necessary action is taken equally decisively and rapidly.
5. What is being done, why, and with what results is clearly communicated.
6. The change is facilitated and strongly symbolised by unmistakable actions.
7. The basics of the business, starting with the management of cash, are executed and improved with the greatest achievable efficiency.
8. The future lies ahead.

The last line, taken from one of comedian Mort Sahl's albums, means that management must look beyond present objectives, however pressing and indispensable, to future aims. That applies no matter how hopeless the present abyss may seem. In some respects – though not in the last – Johnson epitomised the turnround culture. The leadership was certainly there, for a start: it can be that of a single leader (most likely) or of a tightly knit group of like-minded people. Johnson oscillated between the two modes.

Certainly, nothing was sacred to him: jobs, products, factories, routines, philosophies, offices – they all went without argument. He was often decisive, believing that to veto projects proved who was boss. An excellent communicator, he persuaded *Fortune* that he was America's top marketing man. Nothing could have been more symbolic of his intentions than moving the headquarters of Reynolds from its homeland in Winston-Salem to the comforts of Atlanta.

But basic efficiency doesn't seem to have interested Johnson any more than vision. Failure to look far enough ahead often explains the loss of steam in large turnrounds (and probably accounted in part for the lagging stock price that spurred Johnson into his buyout bid). In that eight-point turnround programme, the other principles are all essential if you want to achieve the sixth: successful change itself. It won't be achieved without somebody giving a lead.

First, is top management prepared to alter its own style, methods, role or personnel both to symbolise and effect change? If the answer is No, don't expect anything more affirmative lower down the organisation. Second, is it prepared to tackle the written and unwritten rules which are the cement of organisations? The only way to prevent the cement setting hard is to keep on changing and breaking the rules – but not capriciously, *à la* Johnson.

What you're after is a state of continual turnround. That sounds dangerously close to the Peskett/Johnson philosophy of stirring things up for the hell of it. But good turnrounds are always extremely tightly focused on very clear objectives: the aims of Johnson, other than the largest possible fortune and the richest possible lifestyle, were difficult to discern.

The management of change starts with the managers at the top, and ends with their willingness to share their powers and responsibilities. That may be the most difficult psychological effort of all. But it must be made if you want to master the forces of turbulent change. They have been working and swelling away ever since the oil price doubled in 1973. That most shocking post-war discontinuity put the world economy and the great corporations into incipient crisis. It only began to clear during Ronald Reagan's second term, a decade later. Then the second blow fell: the Greatest Crash.

To some, the sudden sinking of equity markets is still as mysterious as ships disappearing in the Bermuda Triangle; actually, the biggest credit bubble ever inflated simply burst. Anyway, the managers of the businesses whose market value fell floorwards carried on as usual – except that business will never be usual again. It isn't only oil, the world's basic commodity, and the financial markets whose foundations have shifted. Management itself has lurched away from established lines of development.

Traditional concepts of managing men and machines and markets are under urgent challenge. The necessary reign of hierarchy, the supreme power of economic scale, the invincibility of market leadership – all these and other ideological lynchpins, tried and found wanting in the world's first general post-war recession, have broken loose. The change is permanent, and will affect managers in every kind of organisation, from lilliputian to large.

In key industries, from finance and cars to chemicals and food, the largest giants still dominate output. The top five competitors in these sectors control an overwhelming 60 per cent of world markets. If these economic overlords were owned by individuals, they would be among the most powerful men on earth. But today's colossus, owned by largely anonymous institutional investors, no longer throws up Masters of the Universe – Tom Wolfe's acid phrase from *Bonfire of the Vanities*.

Significantly, Wolfe's Master belonged to a former managerial underclass, a bond dealer. The individual entrepreneur, dealer, manager, technologist, designer, creator, and specialist has been rising at the expense of the Organisation Men. These professional business executives, the hired hands, still run the show: but as the century ends, these men (far too few executives, even as late as 1992, are women) face massive disturbance.

The monoliths they mostly serve are tending to weaken, and the careers of the successors rising beneath haven't been spent safely in monolithic service. There are few hero managers any more, and no hero corporations: the few apparent exceptions usually prove Andy Warhol's dictum that anybody can be famous for fifteen minutes. The epitome is the overnight disappearance of Drexel Burnham Lambert: one minute among the mighty powers of Wall Street, the next gone in a puff of smoke, along with the ashes of Michael Milken's all-conquering reputation.

Could Milken and the other creators of the junk bond extravaganza be called managers? The conventional definition has been cracked, notably by the rise of 'staff' people lacking any 'line' command over others. Their growth expresses another reality of management. After a relatively brief time, what Peter Drucker has called the 'knowledge industry' – to which the Drexel gang belonged – may already be the dominant life-form. Many managers now work in specific knowledge industries, from computer software to market research. And all managers, no matter where they work, are in the knowledge business.

The acceleration of high technology is pushing aside old concepts of products and processes in all businesses and all environments, from shops and offices to warehouses and plants. Simply to stay competitive in their own businesses and functions – and their careers – today's managers need more know-how (and more 'know-why') than their predecessors. They need competence in the technicalities of their own business, and beyond that they must master matters once left to specialists.

For several years, I've edited on annual guide to some seventy aspects of modern management, under the headings of strategy, performance, financing, information technology, communications, human resources and logistics. There's not one aspect which a would-be wholly effective manager can safely ignore: and not one aspect, either, where practical knowledge doesn't change and develop fast from year to year.

The paragons expected to master this vast and shifting body of knowledge must also cope with rising aspirations and qualifications of workers below management level. People in charge of robotic equipment are different in kind from people who are mistreated as robots. Levels of service have become decisive in winning customers: so the treatment of those who serve is also decisive – it has to become more personal, supportive and collegiate. That necessity applies just as strongly to treatment of managers, of all grades.

The rise of the young demands no less. Better educated, bred in less authoritarian homes and schools, less respectful towards their elders, encouraged to seek self-expression from birth, each new generation is simply less manageable and more managing. So there's internal pressure on the old, natural superiority of managers who are senior in years as well as status: and still more severe threat from the outside, in the marketplace.

Much of today's competitive pressure stems from the upsurge of Japan, supported by other Asian economies, the 'little dragons'. Coupled with the excess Western capacity created by recession and slow growth after the two oil price shocks, the Asian effect has been inescapable. The competitive forces unleashed have become self-perpetuating. In a crucible of competition, the security of management – top, middle and bottom – has melted down.

The heat has been highest for top managements blasted by the new predators of the 1980s. The mechanism of widely held equity capital, which used to protect and virtually guarantee survival for entrenched managements, was turned against its beneficiaries. By offering premiums above market value, the predators – some financial raiders, some corporate empire-builders, some other corpocrats – cut the ground from beneath sitting managements.

Their reputation was inevitably stained by the predators' attacks on managerial competence. The sitting tenants were sitting ducks. Their assets really had been undermanaged. Attackers like Lords Hanson and White, or Sir James Goldsmith, or Carl Icahn, the raider of TWA, or T Boone Pickens, the scourge of the oil giants, weren't perhaps the best-qualified people to criticise big-time corporate managements. But their self-serving criticism of complacency and wastefulness in the typical large company was founded on the same realities which explain Japanese inroads into markets at home and overseas.

Attacks on such undeserving incumbents, from Asian competitors, investment banks, or the rival businessmen backed by the bankers, made it much harder for big-time management to argue that father knows best. It's easier to argue that management's fathers don't know their business at all. That can't be true. Yet these boardroom sitters plainly aren't the people to turn round the too-typical Western corporation, throw away its counterproductive traditions, and create a new kind of a company capable of trading blows with Japan's best – and beating them.

The proof is that, at the moment of writing, few of the Anglo-American giants have climbed this Everest. Some on the Continent, especially in West Germany, are in stronger shape: but that owes as much to institutional forces – notably protection by bank shareholdings – as to the less flashy, long-termist policies of Continental corpocrats. So far, too, the Continentals have enjoyed more artificial protection against the Japanese. Their most testing times lie ahead, as the Single Market and the break-up of East European Communism redraw an economic map on which Japan's leaders are staking large claims.

The best of managements can't easily accomplish swift corporate revolutions in an environment which is sometimes unhelpful; the Europeans have to contend with many obstacles as they limp towards their own equivalent of the US. The US itself is hamstrung by a perverted reward system that, as at RJR Nabisco, diverts corporate energies from future horizons to present cash-boxes. In the best of circumstances, modern management is a complex task, full of fluctuating difficulties, but also of boundless opportunities.

In grabbing those chances, the trade-offs between costs and benefits are more complicated than ever before – and more numerous. Knowledge, appreciation and manipulation of the constraints, always an essential part of the equipment of any manager, are now decisive. These constraints will not lessen with time, any more than they have in the past decade. Rather, the constraints and the pressures have intensified and are still increasing as these words are being written or read.

Managers are in a race with their times; it is important for the times, as for managers, that they should win. But they will lose unless the consensus of the great and good management teachers – the right management – becomes the practice, as opposed to the mere preaching, of managers who themselves have the right stuff. Those who stick mentally in the past will be stuck there for ever. Those who accept the imperatives of the continual turnround will own the future. Provide vision and leadership, meet all challenges with decisiveness and speed, define and communicate objectives with clarity, and improve the basics perpetually: the turnround formula guarantees powerful, meaningful change and acceptance of change. It works every time.

CHAPTER 5

Xerox: The Broken Breakthrough

A most extraordinary speech was delivered in 1963 by Peter C. McColough, one of the two prime architects of the Xerox Corporation. Addressing an internal 'Talk Leadership Seminar', he asked an arresting question: 'Is it inevitable that such organisations as Xerox should have their periods of emergence, full flower of growth and prestige and then later stagnation and death?'

He tracked the development from a 'new organisation', like the early Xerox, which is 'loose on procedure, unclear on organisational lines, variable in policies', to the mature company which, beset by written and unwritten rules and the 'heavy hand of custom', becomes 'less venturesome' as it accumulates 'possessions, stature and reputation'. That makes it harder to achieve characteristics that every manager would surely want for the organisation:

1. It is willing to experiment with a variety of ways to solve its problems.
2. It is flexible and open to the lessons of current experience.
3. It is not bowed by the weight of tradition.

These words (McColough's own) are the very characteristics which writers like Tom (*Thriving on Chaos*) Peters are ramming home as the only way for companies to cope with the shifting complexities of a highly competitive era. But how can they be achieved when McColough's description of the mature business is plainly as accurate in 1992 as in 1963?

1. It develops subtle policies and habitual modes of solving problems.

2. It becomes more efficient, but also less flexible, less willing to look freshly at each day's experience.
3. Its increasingly fixed routines are congealed in an elaborate body of written rules.

As McColough pointed out, 'the final stage of organisational senility is that there is a rule or precedent for everything'. That sounds terrible enough. But if it's also true (and it must be) that 'The written rules are often the least of the problem', what hope is there for the mature company – and the mature manager?

The speech described the *unwritten* rules as 'the attitudes and values that accumulate and develop in any organisation'. Some may actually be 'precious assets', like 'standards of excellence, loyalty and high morale'. Others constitute a 'choking underbrush of custom and precedent. There comes to be an accepted way to do everything. Radical approaches from past practices are ruled out. The old hand says "You just have to understand how we do things around here", and what he means is that "how we do things" is sound and respectable and the best way'.

The picture is depressing and familiar. The roots of the disease lie not in the nature of corporate maturity, but in that of human beings. Most people like to think of themselves as experimentally minded, flexible, ready to learn from and adapt to what happens day by day, unshackled by tradition. But equally strong human forces encourage all managers to stick to what they know, stand firm by established positions and past experience, and build procedures which stop them having to think – or rather, to make choices.

One firm way forward in turbulent times is to experiment: to take a limited area of the organisation or its product range, and see what happens. What will usually happen is nothing. Experimenting with the new idea (unless it's their own) will carry an implied criticism of the managers – they have perhaps been missing golden opportunities for years. If the experiment succeeds, that will be even worse: their past sins of omission will be explicitly exposed. So one reason why, in McColough's words, young organisations 'are flexible' and 'willing to try anything once' is that their managers have no past record to defend.

Their *amour propre* is invested, not in the past, but in the future – in making a success of this new thing in which they've invested their careers. That's what every management needs to discover or recover in the 1990s: personal investment in the future. Being 'willing to try anything once' was the key to the success of McColough & Co. with xerography. But he wondered out loud to his audience 'whether xerography would today pass the tests that we now put all new products or ideas through, such as financial analysis, including return on investment, return on sales, technical feasibility, size of market, ability to finance such programmes and so forth'.

McColough talked about 'our far more sophisticated approach to such problems today and our increasing desire to see things more clearly for the future', and he came to a startling conclusion: 'I think there is really a good possibility that we would not have undertaken to do what we actually have done in the xerographic field'. There's plenty of evidence to support that stunning statement in what had actually happened.

The xerography inventor, Chester Carlson, was turned down by, among many others, General Electric, RCA, IBM and Remington Rand. Only funds from the private Battelle Memorial Institute kept Carlson's 'electrophotography' going long enough for Joe Wilson of the small Haloid Company and his chief engineer to see a demonstration – and for Wilson to see at once that here was a miracle in the making. Wilson faced no problems of creativity or communication. But McColough, sitting in Haloid grown large, thought that 'one of our greatest obstacles for future growth and vitality is that our people will not feel that they are in the know' and 'therefore will become inert and ineffective'.

Making a powerful case for creativity, 'trying new things and risking failure' and making 'inevitable mistakes', McColough delivered a grave warning; 'that the only stability possible today is stability in motion'. And that, remember, was delivered in the much slower-moving world of 1963. It is much truer, and more urgent, today.

The story of little Haloid holds the real answer. Wilson saw that demonstration in 1945. The Xerox bonanza wasn't born until 15 years later, when the 914 copier hit the market, and knocked it sideways. McColough's doubts are thus amply justified. How many established managements would have made so instant a commitment to so long, arduous and immensely difficult a development period, with an uncertain payoff – even if resources were abundant? In Haloid's case, the 914 cost more to develop than all the profits earned by the company in the 1950s, and one school of thought would declare this to be right and proper.

This maintains that Haloid-style companies are the only places where Xerox-style breakthroughs can be expected. If that were so, it would be a tremendous indictment of the large corporation. But it isn't true. The creativity of the bigger businesses where most managers work is constrained by people who have the freedom to unleash it – and freedom under discipline is the key that can unlock the latent powers of the Western business. McColough knew this totally: yet his own corporation proved how well-founded were his fears of the opposite.

It was McColough's inspiration to set up the Palo Alto Research Center to take the next stride forward in what wasn't even called 'information technology'. The team brought together at PARC, by serendipity and brilliant personnel selection in equal proportions, identified and solved all the technological and conceptual problems that inhibited the production of the personal computer – as yet an unnamed dream. The PARC team went far beyond the Wang word-processor, whose smash-hit debut in 1976 made it perfectly clear that office machinery, like accounting and scientific equipment before it, was certain to acquire electronic brainpower.

But the PARC scientists didn't know how to cope with the inertia and obstructionism which McColough had feared. In a brilliant study, *Fumbling the Future*, Douglas K. Smith and Robert C. Alexander delineate the awful process which justified their subtitle: 'How Xerox invented, then ignored, the first personal computer'. Demonstrated successfully at a 'Futures Day' at Boca Raton in 1977, that computer, the Alto, was never put on the market – not by Xerox, that is.

In 1979, a very young millionaire named Steve Jobs, the creator of Apple Corp., visited Palo Alto and was deeply impressed. He is supposed to have asked 'Why isn't Xerox marketing this? You could blow everybody away'. In 1983, first with the Lisa, and then with the Macintosh, Apple 'replicated many features invented at Xerox'. It was McColough's vision: he could have blown everybody away, but what was blown away was the chance to create a second business bigger even than Xerox's first breakthrough.

And Peter McColough was in charge the whole way through.

CHAPTER

6

The Corporate Entrepreneur

An ancient Chinese curse, much quoted in editorials and other think-pieces, says 'May you live in interesting times' – the point being that uninteresting times and countries (as Switzerland, for example, is said to be) offer better chances of living to a ripe and peaceful old age. In management terms, the curse should be rewritten: 'may you live in turbulent times'. Which means that every management working today is cursed, for times are surely the most turbulent business has ever known.

Turbulence is not an unmixed curse. It throws up many more opportunities than the steady state. One of the main reasons for the success of the opportunistic Japanese is that established Western rivals were undermined by turbulence which disturbed the foundations of their monopolies and quasi-monopolies. So far, the Japanese have known better how to exploit such turbulent developments as the eclipse of mechanical and electro-mechanical products by electronics, or the lowering of export cost barriers by the containerised transport revolution.

The opportunism they have deployed so successfully is another word for entrepreneurship: the great entrepreneur is someone who sees and seizes a great opportunity. So could the emphasis in management be shifting – in reality, not just lip-service – towards that elusive animal, the corporate entrepreneur? Is the manager of the future the person who has most of the following qualities, isolated in a *Harvard Business Review* study by Geoffrey A. Timmons as the essential attributes of the entrepreneur?

1. A high level of drive and energy.
2. Enough self-confidence to take carefully calculated, moderate risks.

3. A clear idea of money as a way of keeping score, and as a means of generating more money still.
4. The ability to get other people to work with you and for you productively.
5. High, but realistic, achievable goals.
6. Belief that you can control your own destiny.
7. Readiness to learn from your own mistakes and failures.
8. A long-term vision of the future of your business.
9. Intense competitive urge, with self-imposed standards.

If that is the formula for the future manager, that's bad news for most present ones – for it's rare to find anybody in a seminar audience who owns to even six of the nine attributes (so convincing a list that I used them as the foundation for my book *The Supermanagers*). But does increased turbulence really enlarge the need for entrepreneurial qualities?

The important work done by Igor Ansoff on correlating corporate strategy with the degree of turbulence encountered by the firm turns out to have a great bearing on the answer to that question. The closer the fit, Ansoff says, the greater the success. Like the engineer he is, Ansoff has reduced the strategic success formula to sets of clear propositions, starting with the acute observation that return on investment (ROI) is no longer just the product of a couple of financial variables, but of six interrelated functions.

They are production efficiency, marketing effectiveness and socio-political sensitivity (the three determinants of 'competitive effectiveness'), and market profitability, product attractiveness and socio-political acceptability (which determine 'strategic responsiveness'). As Ansoff says, success demands further that you obey two injunctions: 'Strategy must match environment' and 'Capability must match strategy'. In today's markets, that means matching the degree of 'strategic aggressiveness' to the degree of turbulence, which starts from a low point of 'repetitive' and advances through 'expanding, changing, and discontinuous' to the extreme high of 'surpriseful'.

The matching spectrum of aggressiveness is 'stable, reactive, anticipatory, entrepreneurial, creative'. In other words, confronted at the extreme with a surpriseful environment which is discontinuous and only partly predictable, you need discontinuous strategies which are novel and based on creativity. An example would be Minolta shaking up the single lens reflex market, and stealing its leadership from Canon, by introducing the first autofocus product, and thus rescuing itself from market crisis.

Few managers these days are confident of living in other than discontinuous or surpriseful circumstances, which, according to Ansoff, leaves them little choice but to develop entrepreneurial aggressiveness. The formula for that has a familiar ring in its first four phases. You divest businesses which are or will become unattractive. If your potential trouble is unattractive products or services, but in an attractive business, you either drop the old and change your strategy to the new, or get out altogether. And in general you move your portfolio from unattractive to attractive businesses.

The familiarity springs from the resemblance to the portfolio strategy which the Boston Consulting Group made famous with its matrix of stars, wildcats, cash cows and dogs – to be nurtured, developed, milked or put to sleep. There's a fundamental weakness in this approach to the pursuit of competitive advantage. It tends to enshrine corporate *disadvantage*. Once the business is pigeonholed, there it tends to be stuck – even though few other returns on investment match those from turning a dog or a cash cow into a star.

Make very sure, in other words, that you don't, by giving a dog a bad name, create a bad dog. Self-fulfilling prophecies are common in management – deprive the supposed dog of investment, and a dog it will surely be. The portfolios of large companies are full of businesses that would represent riches to entrepreneurial outsiders, but are being milked or starved to death by bureaucratic managements whose capital allocation policies are the reverse of Robin Hood's: they steal from the poor to give to the rich.

But Ansoff goes beyond the matrix approach in one key respect. His fifth element in entrepreneurial aggressiveness is stated as follows: 'If the importance of organisational functions is expected to shift, rebalance functional influences on the firm's strategic decisions'. That makes a crucial point: organisation determines – and to a high degree at that – the limits of success. Get the set-up wrong, or allow the organisation to fall out of step with the strategic need, and the latter will not be met.

For instance, EMI ruined itself after inventing one of the greatest potential money-spinners in medical electronics (the brain-scanner): the company, instead of totally repositioning itself to exploit this wholly new product, stuck it on to an unchanged structure. This was so unaccommodating that managers couldn't even be persuaded to transfer to the new, entrepreneurial operation. Its management, all necessarily imported, encountered endless difficulties even in simple matters like getting enough office space.

On Ansoff's spectrum of organisational responsiveness, this would count as 'stability-seeking – rejects change': the 'efficiency-driven' organisation 'adapts to change', the 'market-driven' seeks the 'familiar', the 'environment-driven . . . seeks related change' and the 'environment-creating . . . seeks novel change'. Change-seeking, naturally, is the policy best matched to a surpriseful degree of turbulence – and that, judged by the managers who attend Ansoff's seminars, is expected by the great majority of companies. Your own positioning in these turbulent seas can be roughly charted by answering True or False, depending on how you see the business, to these propositions:

1. Future demand can be extrapolated from the present.
2. Profits will follow growth.
3. The firm's growth will follow the market.
4. Historically successful strategies will remain successful.
5. Historical strengths will remain strengths.
6. Surprises will be few.

The more times you can answer True, the nearer you still are to what Ansoff calls the *old* ball game. But you're more likely by far to be in the new game, where extrapolating demand is dangerous, profits don't follow growth, the demand for the firm's products or services doesn't follow the market, historical success strategies are suspect, historical strengths become weaknesses, and surprise events are frequent.

Assuming that to be your situation, Ansoff's dictum that 'during shifts in turbulence general management capability becomes critical to success' assumes obvious importance. So what sort of capability do you need? It's crucial to bear in mind the ease with which 'strategic myopia' overcomes management. Forecasts that are discontinuous from the past trigger neglect, rejection and paralysis by analysis. At the lowest level of turbulence, you can get by with the custodian manager who likes to preserve the status quo, suppress risk and play internal politics – but as turbulence rises, so the need moves upwards to controller and growth leader, and then to entrepreneur and finally creator.

Where the custodian sings out 'don't rock the boat', likes stability and focuses his power through bureaucracy, the creator, says Ansoff, is a visionary leader whose key knowledge is that of 'emerging possibilities' and who exercises technological leadership, with his power focus lying in research and development. The entrepreneur, one stage of turbulence behind, is led by profit potential, has a strategic mentality, exerts charismatic leadership, likes to find opportunities, and has the global environment as his key knowledge.

His culture is 'innovate', his success model is strategic position, his rewards are those of entrepreneurship and the focus of his power is general management. So that's the answer to the question posed at the beginning of this chapter. The entrepreneur is indeed the managerial type who best fits Ansoff's reading, the one best able to match the firm's capability profile to the turbulence in its environment, and to achieve the flexibility to go on doing so as turbulence levels shift.

In other words, he is an effective manager of change. That means, among other things, defeating resistance to change. Ansoff traces a familiar pattern: myopia, procrastination, implementation delays, sabotage/cost-overruns/slippages and finally the rolling back of change. Look out for these tell-tale verbiages:

1. 'There is nothing wrong that a cost reduction wouldn't cure' (myopia)
2. 'Tomorrow we'll make a plan' (procrastination)
3. 'This needs more analysis' (leading to paralysis by it, or implementation delays)
4. 'What the boss doesn't know won't hurt' and 'The more we sell, the more we lose' (sabotage, etc.)
5. 'Let's get back to the real work' (rolling back change, or what Ansoff calls 'death in the drawer')

It sent a shiver down my spine when Buck Rogers, author of *The IBM Way*, and a great propagandist for the company whose marketing he used to run, told me that IBM was consulting his book for help in implementing the wish, 'let's get things back the way they were'. That was early in the corporation's continuing and so far frustrating efforts to escape from the change in its environment – a profound change caused by a pronounced shift in turbulence in which the organisation hasn't been able to react with enough speed or success.

As noted in Chapter 3, any organisation can be changed radically overnight – and many have been under the spur of crisis. But the rich cash flows of an entrenched corporation like IBM encourage entrenched frames of mind. Short of crisis, the only high urgency is provided by charismatic leadership, which as Ansoff points out is rare, or coercive management, which generates high resistance. Resistance is minimal if management opts for organic adaptation, but that's slow, and only suitable for situations of low urgency.

With most companies, the urgency is probably greater than the management thinks; they have a change need of medium urgency, the kind that's concealed when companies are riding high. In the case of Xerox Corporation, while still a runaway success story, the seeds of decay were plainly visible in a ratio of interest, payroll and material costs which rose from under 60 per cent of revenues to nearly 70 per cent in only three years. Such ratios are the giveaways, and they need especially careful watching when the other signs are all apparently hale and hearty.

That's where the entrepreneurial manager shows his true mettle. In the list of qualities mentioned at the start, the ones that seize the imagination are the dynamic ones: the drive and energy, the risk-taking, the leadership, the high ambitions, the man's belief in his own destiny, his long-term vision of the future, his intense competitive urge. People too readily ignore the less apparently dynamic, safety-first qualities: the careful calculation behind the apparent risks, the clear-headed use of money to keep score, the readiness to learn from mistakes and failures and, above all, the self-imposed standards.

Those are the defensive qualities which get swamped by success in aggressive entrepreneurs who either never make the transition to corporate management or, having done so, blow up the boat by the kind of misbegotten strategy that prevented the great work at Palo Alto from creating a second business even greater than Xerox's first. The company's environment was becoming more turbulent than it knew, above all because of new competition in the core business of copiers. But mismatched strategies create inner turbulence, too: and that is the ultimate bomb.

The ultimate manager, though, very probably is the corporate entrepreneur. He's difficult to find, but quite easy to create – if the environment of the firm, as well as its strategy, is matched to the turbulence outside. The catch is that it requires entrepreneurial management to see that need and act accordingly. Only disaster looms ahead if the catch becomes a Catch-22: a vicious circle that can't be broken. But that will never happen, if you know that the circle can be broken and act to turn that possibility into virtuous achievement.

PART 2
HOW TO ADD POWER TO RESPONSIBILITY

CHAPTER 7

General Electric: The Kraken Wakes

For decades now, General Electric has led the changes of fashion in big-time corporate management. In the age of top-down long-range corporate planning, in which top management sought to dictate in entirety the shape of the corporate future, GE was the Big Daddy of them all. Now, in the age of top-down 'empowerment', in which top management seeks to dictate a new, freer style of managerial conduct and success, GE is again in the lead.

In the first stage, according to a *Fortune* profile of GE chief executive Jack Welch, he moved to 'rewrite the book on how to run a big company' by acting to 'empower' and 'liberate' middle managers. Welch, one of the most powerful chief executives in end-century America, wasn't meaning to de-power himself, though: he won his nickname, 'Neutron Jack', for the ruthless decimation of corporate ranks in the pursuit of profitable growth. He has won plaudits, not just from the business press, but from enlightened experts like Rosabeth Moss Kanter of the Harvard Business School (who edits its famous *Review*).

In answer to the question, 'Jack Welch: How good a manager?', once splashed across a *Business Week* front cover, most people would have answered 'very'. Kanter's own interview with Welch, one of the highlights of a most successful business video, concentrates on his continuing efforts to mobilise the strengths of GE's powerful divisions through less formal methods. In her book, *When Giants Learn to Dance*, however, Welch appears only in neutron bomb guise:

'After eliminating a whopping one fourth of General Electric's workforce, CEO Jack Welch understood that the company's ability to attract and motivate people would not come from the promise of job security . . .'.

That qualifies as the managerial understatement of the decade. Instead, says Kanter, Welch turned to 'the attractiveness of opportunities for achievement', saying that 'The job of the enterprise is to provide an exciting atmosphere that's open and fair, where people have the resources to go out and win. The job of the people is to take advantage of this playing field and put out 110 per cent'.

That sounds quite minatory, as does James A. Belasco's praise in another dancing book, *Teaching the Elephant to Dance*. He describes how Welch moves GE 'into new and different areas – gobbling up and then straightening out such huge firms as RCA – with a nimbleness that leaves corporate presidents trembling and wondering whether Jack will land next in their boardroom'. The results of the cutting and gobbling, in any event, have given GE the best record in the most élite group in Western capitalism, the five largest US companies by sales.

In 1989 GE had the largest profit margin (7.1 per cent) of the five and the biggest return on stockholders' equity (18.9 per cent). In growth in earnings per share and total return to investors over a decade, only Ford Motor beat Welch's company – and Ford was heading for the profits débâcle of 1990. But if you take GE's average across all five measures of performance used in the *Fortune* 500, it works out at 166 – almost exactly a third of the way down the list. If that fact indicates anything, it's that bigness is an impediment to business: which is undoubtedly the thought that has inspired Welch's efforts.

They involve a tremendous shift from the type of planning GE once pioneered, from (to quote an executive) 'periodic major data dumps towards more frequent, incremental discussions and decisions' – in other words, from bureaucracy towards *ad hoccery*. The GE top management tries to achieve the best of both worlds by having a formal and highly structured budget process (a 'sacrosanct commitment') that, however, keeps the more informally determined strategic issues 'clearly in mind'.

If that sounds like trying to have your cake and eat it, so it is: but all management involves trying to pitch unavoidable compromises at the highest possible level. The conflict between Welch's aspirations and the fact that they *are* his, and not necessarily those of his underlings, is another example. So is the gap between preaching and practice. For example, Welch's managerial troops are supposedly encouraged to engage in 'spirited repartee', which sounds great.

A former GE executive, now chief executive of another company, followed up the *Fortune* article with a letter about his own experience in GE which darkens this rosy tint. In the unit where he served, 'all decisions – save an individual's preference for lunch – were made by the unit's CEO'. Attempts at spirited repartee were 'viewed as personal affronts to authority'. Change in this unit was 'not really viewed as either necessary or positive... *despite what was happening at corporate*' (my italics).

The answer could well be that it isn't 'despite', but *because* of what happens at corporate that such non-compliance occurs. The negative aspects of central hierarchical control emerge from the failure of GE's business in electrical appliances, as recounted by Christopher A. Bartlett and Sumantra Ghoshal in the *Harvard Business Review*. They chart the 20-year primrose path of GE's 'once formidable position' in this business. The centrally inspired strategy started from a policy that reflected the pure consensus model:

1. *Build 'locally responsive and self-sufficient' mini-GE's' in each market.* Then came the twists and turns:
2. *Develop 'low-cost off-shore sources'.* Then failure to create the desired breakthrough led in turn to wholesale 'international outsourcing', followed and contradicted (in its turn) by...
3. *Focus on 'building concentrated scale to defend domestic share'.*

When that didn't work either the business fell foul of GE's now famous 'one, two or nothing' rule. The company was the father of the 'strategic business unit', the building brick of the modern conglomerate. Under Welch, the model has been ruthlessly applied to build No. 1 and No. 2 positions in growth markets – or quit. While the strategy has achieved unbroken rises in sales and earnings, it has also taken GE out of many businesses where (who knows?) success might have been won under more independent and responsible local regimes.

Throughout the appliance twists and turns, GE abandoned products which couldn't or didn't satisfy its (also arbitrary) criteria on market penetration and financial performance: televisions and small appliances, for example. Whatever else the central management achieved, it certainly made it impossible for local management to manage – that is, in its own terms. Yet Belasco, in his favourable comments on Welch, notes that 'some individuals empower their organisations to execute pirouette-type changes'.

Takeovers like that of RCA are less pirouettes than charges of the heavy brigade, at which the most heavy-footed of chief executives have been reasonably adept (antitrust and monopoly authorities allowing) in recent years. It isn't the elephant or the giant who must dance, but the people and the businesses inside their thick skins. The stirrings within Welch's GE, which in the 1990s developed into a full-scale attempt to 'win by ideas, and not by whips and chains', are tribute to his recognition of this truth. To change monsters, the Kraken wakes: the paradox is that the mythical beast can only realise the chief executive's full purpose by ceasing to be a Kraken at all.

CHAPTER

8

The Liberators' Ball

At first glance, General Electric and the Wall Street firm of Kravis, Kohlberg, Roberts appear to have little in common, except size. Hard to believe, but true, the tiny group of people controlling KKR came to master interests ranking in sales just below the globe-leading GE. True, GE's size would have been larger still but for its disposal, for $2.5 billion, of large portions of its RCA purchase – a buy which at the time, in December 1985, was hailed by both parties as 'creating a company that will successfully compete with anyone, anywhere, in every market we serve'.

The *Financial Times* commented that 'the deal has the potential to strengthen GE's position in the military and consumer markets and industrial electronics'. Much of that potential disappeared with the sell-offs, which left the NBC network as the prime survivor of the deal. In this ruthless dissection of his mega-buy, GE's Jack Welch was acting in a manner which is meat and drink (and caviare) to Henry Kravis of KKR, the emperors of the buyout. The strategy which has made Kravis super-rich is to buy big (the RJR Nabisco deal cost four times the price of RCA), sell bigger, and repeat to taste.

In a curious way, the KKR operation holds out more promise for the future of management than GE's. The emperors have won praise from the highly respected Harvard professor Thomas V. Bonoma, who told *Fortune* that they are 'incredibly good at what they do – just *incredibly* good at what I might call the ultimate transactional behaviour'. Bereft of anything that might be called management capacity, KKR is forced to operate at arm's length from the operating concerns of its acquisitions, confining itself to a few simple orders:

1. Get the debt down as fast as possible.
2. Sell off anything that it makes economic sense to offload.
3. Apply a gimlet eye to capital expenditures and bureaucracies.

No fairy godmother could wish its godchild better – up to a point. That recipe frees the child from the suffocating scrutiny of a can-do central management, but otherwise it is no more than efficient day-to-day housekeeping. It answers no questions about strategy and may actually inhibit the formation of long-term strategic plans that depend on both new capital spending and building up teams of costly people far in advance of any revenues. The day-to-day and the year-to-year take dangerous precedence over the decade.

That wasn't supposed to happen when the buyout first began to gain momentum. No financial technique has mushroomed with such devastating speed in America itself, growing not only in numbers, but in size, so fearsomely as to turn the financial world topsy-turvy, and creating in Michael Milken and his annual jamboree, 'the predators' ball', the abiding image of greed in the 1980s. But at the start the MBO was a peaceful by-way of Wall Street. Some practitioners were attracted to the idea from what sounded almost like benevolence – people such as Royal D. Little, the multi-millionaire founder of the Textron conglomerate, and author of the immortal book title, *How to Lose $100 million and Other Useful Information*.

Little decided to spend his retired eighties really usefully; he and many others have helped frustrated managements to buy out their businesses from purblind employers – very often conglomerates of comparable ilk to Little's own Textron, but of incomparably less distinction.

Like Little, the other players in the early MBO years were outside the Wall Street mainstream, men like the eponymous partners in KKR. No philanthropists they, but this trio, too, passed increasingly lucrative days by putting unhappy managements in happy touch with the four necessities of the buyout: debt, equity, planning and ambition. Fired with the last, incumbent managements were supposed to be galvanised into laying out a persuasive plan for the business and contributing their financial all (if not more) to the small equity, thus encouraging financiers to advance the huge debt required to swing the deal.

If it worked, everybody was gladdened. Vendors shed businesses they didn't want, and which mostly didn't pay, while looking holy; the debt-holders got their interest (usually at usurious rates); and the equity-owners, including the liberated management, the fixers who assembled the deal, and the financiers who swung it, enjoyed a rise in the stock that could be of magical proportions.

Above all, the management took control of its own destiny in what still seems a highly virtuous process. To quote the chairman of one large British enterprise which turned its employees into buy-out millionaires, 'The major change as a result of the MBO was a release of drive, energy and enthusiasm, with everyone feeling that they were working for themselves'. This evident truth can't help but encourage the comment that, if big companies can only release 'drive, energy and enthusiasm' by selling their components, they are ultimately doomed.

Be that as it may, buyout managers have the incentive to work like Trojans for their glittering prizes – or perhaps it should be Spartans: after paying £300 million for Robert Maxwell's printing business, its new buyout boss told the *Financial Times* that 'I am prepared to go without any corporate comforts to drive this business on, and I expect my management to do the same'. This man had a three- to five-year target zone within which to soar above his interest payments and liberate his investors by floating or selling the company.

Genuine MBOs hinge on two principles. First, the management must manage the business so much better than the very same fellows did in the past that the profits do in fact soar above that vast interest. Second, if they do, the simple magic of leverage will transform a tiny equity into a massive profit. The sums won't work out easily, however, unless the vendor is obliging enough to sell out for a suitable song. The sight of enormous gains being pocketed by people who, shortly before, were their subordinates inevitably led corpocrats to bargain harder. The deals got tougher, the targets bigger, the prices higher and the task more intimidating.

But the buyout won't die, because no better method exists, either for off-loading a small division that doesn't fit or doesn't pay (or both), or for elegantly replacing private ownership without destroying the fine old family firm. Selling to the management guarantees both a suitably large pay-off for the shareholders and continuity for a family business in a way that couldn't have been achieved by sale to a public company. The name 'Engulf and Devour', given to a fictitious conglomerate by film-maker Mel Brooks, isn't funny in the context of what has actually happened to some private businesses that have accepted a public embrace.

Not that the buyout, with its release of 'drive, energy and enthusiasm', is necessarily a permanent answer. Recent research has pointed to the real risk that buyout will lead to burn-out. Quite typically, the buyout management outgrows other businesses in the first two or three years, partly because of released energy, etc., partly because of the juicy financial carrots dangling before the management's eyes, and partly because the dead hand of the previous ultimate bosses has been removed from the joystick.

To quote the same chairman as before, the business he sold 'had to carry unnecessary central overheads, its management style was cramped by the central bureaucracy, and its trading approach was limited' by the needs of other, larger divisions. Moreover, when it came to investment, the division 'always had to take third place'. With such an incubus removed, and with the interest payments to meet, managements run very fast along what is actually the easiest part of the course: cutting the excessive costs and correcting the faults that they, as the sitting management, had allowed to develop beforehand.

After a neatly timed financial exit, however, the hard strategic choices have to be made by men who, with millions of carrots now safely tucked away in the bank, are faced with a much reduced monetary incentive and a far bumpier management road. Whether it comes to sell-out or burn-out, most MBOs are a bridge between one management problem and another. To change metaphors, the bought-out management can all too easily step decisively out of the frying pan into the fire.

The chances of making that fruitless exchange were so enhanced by late 1980s trends in interest rates, equities and the real world beyond both that the buyout no longer seemed a viable new solution to the old problem of sustaining business vitality or making corporations more limber. The anxiety about their leaden-footedness is understandable – both on the part of ambitious leaders like GE's Jack Welch and outside the behemoths, among critics who fear the impact on the economy of large leaden feet.

The predators, of course, offered a cure for that condition. The theory was (and, to a somewhat reduced extent, is) that chief executives 'trembling and wondering whether Jack will land next in the boardroom' will shake the lead out of their boots and start to manage more effectively. If they don't, the predator will apply the ultimate sanction, seize the company, expel the failed management and demonstrate the virtues of passing assets from weak hands into strong – and serve the weak right: or so says the former arch-predator Sir James Goldsmith.

At a public forum in London in the spring of 1989, Goldsmith pronounced that 'I've never seen a really good company taken over.

I've only seen bad ones'. The sword (or rather rifle) of Damocles was endorsed by another speaker who declared that 'It is very important that management all the time is under the gun'. Echoing the point, after the trial of Milken, one American columnist opined that the celebrated convict should really have been celebrated for something else: for the enormous benefit he had conferred on the US economy by shattering the too cosy corporate calm.

The logical weakness of this defence is that half of all such deals fail. Moreover, the bigger the target, the likelier the merger is to founder, because of the heavy financial burdens laid on the bidder. Before his final fall, even Milken recognised this hard truth: he piously told the *Wall Street Journal* that 'it was time for some companies to de-leverage, urging a swap of junk bonds for a combination of equity and higher-grade debt carrying a lower interest burden'. That was the horse-thief locking the stable door after the steeds had been stolen. But the financial damage of predatory attacks isn't even half the story.

The most famous of the major Milken-financed deals was the first, the tiny Pantry Pride's raid on Revlon. It took Ronald Perelman from nowhere to the bright lights, which shone down while he brought out 'a plethora of new products, purchased other cosmetic lines, and revived the old Revlon glamour through dazzling ads'. But *Business Week* also reported in the spring of 1991 that Revlon was 'on the block because Perelman is facing hard times'. Under a giant debt load of $3.8 billion, the empire's cash flow had shrunk to virtually nothing (and its value by two thirds).

So, twice within six years Revlon's business and its employees risked the extreme discontinuity of disposal: and no matter whether or not its predator deserved the above good marks for management – higher than you would expect from a breed whose managerial skills are seldom conspicuous. Takeovers just as readily transfer assets, not from weak management hands to strong, but weak to weak. In the process, corporate values are damaged or destroyed to no good purpose: many of the finest firms in the City of London, for instance, have vanished with no trace other than the damage to their purchasers' balance sheets.

The fate is less final if the deal is undone, as many are, by disposal rather than destruction. The takeover argument promptly goes into reverse. This time, the merger isn't the bringer of economic bounty: on the contrary, dismemberment of previous merger creations is overwhelming evidence against the theory that takeovers are good for management and the economy. Instead, the pay-off will be wonderfully provided by *de-merger* as it liberates the energies of the confined managements.

In truth, the seismic reshuffling of corporate assets of the 1980s, which overlapped into the new decade, had nothing to do with either argument. The theorising was self-justifying public relations, nothing more. The mega-buy break-up raiders, like Goldsmith and Lords Hanson and White, were motivated solely by money. As they prowled among the undervalued assets of previous mergers, they often just warehoused corporate properties to feed the fashionable trend: strategic acquisition – and de-acquisition.

For instance, when a desperate Chesebrough-Ponds purchased Stauffer Chemical in a forlorn attempt to render itself indigestible, it set going a chain reaction. The acquiring Unilever offloaded Stauffer on ICI, which in turn rapidly rid itself of superfluous parts. Both had strategic logic to call on: Unilever was only interested in Chesebrough brands like Vaseline; ICI only in building its agrochemicals business into world leadership. The mutual justification is that, to meet global competition, global presence is essential – and that Japanese-style organic growth, on its own, takes too long.

So it will, unless you have strong managements independently developing world-class businesses. That ideal is an idle dream if their horse is liable, at the considered whim of a Jack Welch or the pressured need of a Ron Perelman, to be sold from under the management. Some of today's divisional chief executives have soldiered on through two, three, even four changes of ownership. Their businesses have surely been damaged, both directly and indirectly, by all the consequent shifts in style, uncertainties, reversals and reorganisations.

Ownership is a significant factor in management performance, which is why the genuine buyout can truly be effective: though genuine management buyouts, too, often enough and sometimes sadly, end up as somebody else's strategic acquisition. But the buyout billionaires, in their no doubt perverted way, left two valuable bequests. First, their excesses produced a beneficial backlash against takeovers that will last for quite a while: second, their self-seeking contained the germ of the right idea.

Set the people free from oppressive management, and you free the whole corporation to compete more effectively – on and on, into the foreseeable future. Then it won't be the predators, but the liberated (and their liberators) who will have a ball.

CHAPTER

9

Deming: The Un-American American Way

The history of management thought is overwhelmingly American history. W. Edwards Deming is among the most creative thinkers and, above all, practitioners in that history. Now the hero of two excellent books, *The Deming Management Method*, by Mary Walton, and *The American Who Taught the Japanese About Quality*, by Rafael Aguayo, Deming ended the Second World War in unheroic obscurity: a leading but little-known expert in the use of statistical methods to obtain superior quality of production. But 'for the most part', as Walton writes, the techniques concerned, though of proven and great effectiveness, 'were now regarded as time-consuming and unnecessary, and they faded from use'.

To quote Deming himself, by 1949 'there was nothing – not even smoke'. His talents were turned to helping the US military government in Japan with census work. There in 1950 he gave the first of a dozen standing-room only, unpaid lectures to production people and others on his pet subject – SQC, or statistical quality control. But he had learnt from his American rebuffs that he wasn't talking to the right audience, for 'without pressure from management for quality, nothing would happen'. So he had a dinner arranged with the 21 presidents of Japan's leading industries, and talked to them for a very solid hour.

His message has hardly changed since. 'You can produce quality. You have a method for doing it. You've learned what quality is'. With quality, both in their own operations and those of their suppliers, the Japanese could apply the truth that the consumer 'is the most important part of the production line'. Deming told his audience that by reversing the Japanese image for negative quality 'they would capture markets the world over within five years'. A year ahead of schedule, his prediction had come true, and it has gone on being vindicated ever since.

Note the equally remarkable contribution by Deming's hosts; they swallowed his preaching whole, and put it into practice at once. The very next year, they established the Deming Prize, awarded to 'an individual for accomplishments in statistical theory and to companies for accomplishments in statistical application'. To this day, this has remained Japan's premier management prize, not for dry-as-dust technical work, but for real-life results like those in one camera factory which hearkened to Deming. 'A year ago they made 200 cameras per month; now they are making 400, and hope it will be 500 this month and hereafter, with no increase in workers or hours – simply better control of quality'.

What is this Western magic? And why didn't Western firms fall over themselves to reap the benefits that the East garnered so plentifully? To start with the first question, it isn't magic. Deming makes his seminar audiences play a management game with white beads and red ones, the latter being those which the mythical customers won't accept. He uses this parable to teach, first, a simple lesson in statistical theory: that 'variation is part of any process; planning requires prediction of how things and people will perform – tests and experiments of past performance can be useful, but not definitive'.

That leads on to three decisive points. First, 'workers work within a system that – try as they might – is beyond their control'. Second, 'Only management can change the system'. Third, 'Some workers will always be above average, some below'. It follows that to improve the results you must improve, not the individual worker, but the system: and that is the block over which Western management has stumbled, often disastrously. As Deming has said, 'It takes courage to admit that you have been doing something wrong, to admit that you have something to learn, that there is a better way'. Rather than lose face, too many Western managements have lost markets: that is a very poor exchange.

Deming has enshrined the better way in fourteen now famous points. They start with 'Create Constancy of Purpose for the Improvement of Product and Service' and end with 'Take Action to Accomplish the Transformation'. What's known as the Deming cycle in Japan, and the Shewhart cycle (after Deming's own mentor) in the US, runs simply as PDCA: Plan, Do, Check, Act. Firms don't apply the cycle because they suffer from deadly diseases which are all down to management (blamed by Deming for 85 per cent of all underperformance). The ailments are led by lack of constancy of purpose, followed by emphasis on short-term profits; evaluation of performance, merit rating, or annual review; excessive mobility of top management; and running a company on visible figures alone ('counting the money').

Deming observes that 'Mobility from one company to another creates prima donnas for quick results'. It also reinforces reluctance to institute long-term change programmes (like Deming's), whose results will flow after the incumbent has risen to his next step on the moving staircase. Deming's diseases and the 13 obstacles to quality that he also lists (including 'our problems are different' and 'anyone that comes to try to help us must understand all about our business') must be very powerful retarding forces, for it wasn't until 1980 that the prophet became honoured in his own country.

This came about as the direct result of an NBC television documentary entitled 'If Japan Can... Why Can't We?'. When it appeared, with an immediate and stimulating effect on the demand for Deming's services from companies like Ford Motor and Campbell Soup, the great man was 80 years old, and American industry had largely missed out on the benefits of three decades of wisdom, three decades of deriving the same benefits as the Japanese. But those benefits are still available. Deming won't last for ever. His wisdom will.

CHAPTER 10

The New Age of Management

You couldn't find anything seemingly more remote from chief executive concerns than W. Edwards Deming's 'seven helpful charts': three showing cause-and-effect, flow, and trend; then the control chart, the Pareto chart, the histogram and the scatter diagram. These are very basic statistical tools. But with them, management at any level can manage with the single most important weapon in its armoury: accurate knowledge of the facts, the data.

To quote a Japanese company's manual, 'Views not backed by data are more likely to include personal opinions, exaggerations and mistaken impressions'. That company is Komatsu, the apparently doomed manufacturer of earth-moving equipment which rose from the ashes to give Caterpillar Tractor the fight and the fright of the American company's long, rich life. Like many other US giants, Caterpillar was thus jerked sharply into modernising its management and production methods – and 'modernising' meant in part learning lessons that Deming had been teaching for 40 years.

He is not, be it said, very impressed with the general results. In 1985, Deming observed that he saw 'great advancement in spots'. For every advancing American business, though, 'others remain in the dark ages'. To the extent that competitors ignore them, applying Deming's lessons is a powerful source of competitive advantage. To that same extent, it is a powerful source of national economic weakness. That much is obvious: but so is the muscularity and rightness of Deming's 40-year old lessons.

Why were they ignored so long? The mystery doesn't only apply to quality control. Even when told how to improve operations, not marginally, but by great leaps forward, many managers don't. Even if advised of the virtues of forming a strategy, they don't: even if they do, they don't take the necessary action to match the company's operations to its strategy.

In all this, Western sinners contrast shamingly with the Japanese, as the swift reaction to Deming's speech showed long ago, and as the Kepner-Tregoe consultancy has found to this day: its largest office outside the US is in Japan, reflecting what Ben Tregoe describes as the 'Japanese willingness to take whatever they can get hold of and improve it to obtain increased effectiveness'. The mystery of why this willingness should be an Eastern speciality rears its head every time a management expert speaks or writes in the West.

The problem is that to accept radical change itself demands radical change – for starters. Chief executives may know in their minds and hearts that they can no longer live in the past or manage in the present. They have to manage the future, now. Psychologically, however, they find it more comfortable to persist in believing that yesterday's solutions will solve today's problems. The obstinacy applies, most strongly of all perhaps, to making that start, to changing the mind-set and the management style with all the sinewy rigour of Deming's philosophy.

The greater degree of discomfort lies not in change, but in resistance to change. That overwhelming truth can be seen more clearly in technology than in management, though its consequences are devastating in both. The annals are full of companies which (like RCA when the transistor replaced the thermionic valve) once led their markets, yet lagged in the next evolution of the technology. That compounds two errors: technical blindness and marketing inertia. What couldn't be afforded at a time when technology was moving relatively slowly must be ruinous in an age of accelerating, compressed change.

As the great innovator Konosuke Matsushita once sadly observed, 'today the same day you put a new product on the market it's out-of-date'. That's what managing the future means in the simplest terms: having the next product ready when the new wonder is only being launched. More, it means drastically shortening time-lags, so that, if tomorrow should be needed today, the company can not only cope, but conquer. Both reducing process time and accelerating product programmes demand radically changed attitudes and actions in general management.

You can't manage the future in so positive a way simply by extrapolating the past and the present. Those who try to manage the future that way must miss the benefits of change – for change is not threat, but opportunity. It must be true that, in a market where tastes, buying power, technology and sources of supply are unchanging, opportunities will be hard to come by and still harder to exploit. By the same token, in markets which are changing, or can be made to change, opportunities are inexhaustible.

Nobody can escape the tension inside a business between those who deny reality and those who accept it. The good manager is at odds with the good leader, even inside the same man. The first manages what has always had to be done, while the second tries the new, where the chances of error are greater – and more frightening. Like individuals, organisations easily become victims of habit and inertia. Both vices are readily swept aside by the kind of crisis that has precipitated massive turnaround operations in large companies in every country of the West. But who wants a crisis?

In less threatening circumstances, fear of the unknown and distrust of the unpredictable inhibit acceptance. Sunk cost (the emotional and/or financial investment in the past) is an understandable barrier to adoption of the new. If the sunk cost isn't forgotten, the whole company may sink. It doesn't matter that accepting change implies error. So what if action taken in the immediate past was wrong? So what if the leader shared in, or maybe was wholly responsible for, the obsolete mistakes? In a fast fluctuating world, once correct decisions will be rapidly falsified – and there's no managerial sin in that.

Reluctance to admit to error is a close neighbour to the entrenched self-righteousness which is intensified by increasing age, experience and success. The more you persist in error, though, the worse the position must become. The Watergate style of Management by Cover-up will only work for a while. Its timespan has notably diminished at the same time as the long-term damage from covered-up management has dangerously increased.

Even when change has been successfully completed, its problem can intensify: companies easily backslide into the same complacency and error as before. But if the climate for continual change doesn't exist, the organisation can't manage the future. IBM wanted to call its change programme 'coping with change' – but the very title, suggesting that change could harm its people, rings false. By coincidence or not, IBM has been hard-pressed to achieve the change to which its top management pays ardent service, or lip-service.

'Coping' is fine for the evolutionary, incremental change that will be adapted to and absorbed within the bureaucratic whale: but only revolution – sudden, stark and strongly symbolised change – will defeat the bureaucracy. The latter is bolstered by fear of mistakes, more of which are probable in a situation of flux. That raises two problems for management: how to tolerate error without fatally weakening performance, and how to survive, and succeed, in spite of the errors being made. It isn't a question of damage limitation or averting failure, but of creating success – of succeeding, in part, *because* of errors: mistakes made in the cause of progress.

Systemic error, of course, has no pay-offs. The inbuilt tendency (it seems to have happened at IBM) is for market-led businesses to degenerate into product-led ones, and worse still, for out-of-date methods of producing and managing to be neither challenged nor replaced. Instead of keeping themselves up to date senior managers regress to the roles they knew and loved. These tendencies can be enhanced by job-hopping. Like bees passing from flower to flower, the job-hoppers carry the same ideas, the same attitudes, the same received views from company to company, until the whole industry behaves in the same claustrophobic, short-sighted way.

The pressure to achieve short-term financial results has become a notorious source of short-sighted management: chief executives have intensified that pressure, even though strategic goals and strategic contributions, which may not show up in the short-term numbers at all, are plainly more valuable. But managers lower down can't make a strategic contribution if all strategy is reserved for the corporate summit; which isn't the way they order things in Japan. The essence of the Japanese model is admirably described in his book, *Inside Japan*, by Peter Tasker, a Japanese-speaking financial executive:

'New strategies are usually developed by middle managers, adjusted in discussion with the people involved most closely, then taken to the top for approval and official adoption. Those who disagree or have been disadvantaged can expect compensation the next time round. It is an effective method of procedure, conducive to good morale'.

To set that the other way round, failure to involve middle management is a highly effective way of creating poor morale. As Tasker notes, the Japanese have believed in consensus decision-making for a long time. In the seventh century, writing his famous constitution, Prince Shotuko advised that 'In order to achieve harmony, individual judgments and actions should be forbidden, and discussion at all levels should be respected'. The excellence of the principle is self-evident. Putting it into practice, again, requires the acceptance of what amounts to deeply radical change for the typical Western corporation.

Combined strategic operations are needed to cope with large and growing challenges. All managements, the Japanese no less than those in the West, are faced with saturation in established markets; they all must seek new avenues of future growth by searching for new and different kinds of business. Ben Tregoe says 'that's a new thing' for the Japanese – but it doesn't exactly seem second nature in the West. Indeed, some Western Johnny-come-latelys are still pursuing the former and obsolete Japanese strategy of only improving quality and reducing cost.

As Tregoe says, pursuing the wrong strategic vision efficiently is as bad as inefficiency – a condition that he and Charles Kepner started to analyse 31 years ago, with research into why some managers are more effective than others. Later research, published in 1980, sought to answer a deeper question still. How does top management go about strategic decisions? In many cases it doesn't. 'Strategy is like sex', Tregoe has said: 'When all is said and done, more is said than done'. In addition to total abstinence, potentially dangerous confusions abound: thus, managers equate long-range planning with strategy – 'a recipe for disaster', according to Tregoe, who states that long-range planning is how strategy is *executed*, not devised.

Nor will a 'mission statement do it all'. Like Deming, Tregoe is characteristically blunt; a 'mission statement equals strategy no more than the man in the moon'. He is equally scathing about off-campus strategy sessions: 'they take the top group away for a weekend on a mountain-top – it never works'. The accusing finger points at the upbringing of top managers. Having risen through operational roles, they lack experience in forming a strategy. Worse, they are hesitant to give up what's made them what they are today – so they interfere in operations, while strategy is often mere reaction.

Learning how to create strategy, and implementing it with the full rigour of Deming's teaching, isn't easy. It's the potential toughness and pain which explain that otherwise inexplicable failure of managements to do what, in their hearts, they know to be right. But buying off pain in the present only accentuates it in the future – if there is a future. Those who truly make it at the top will do so by creating that future. They will find that the new management requires a different kind of toughness – intellectual strength coupled with human responsiveness – but generates far less pain in the process.

You can grasp the full and intimidating extent of the new demands on managers from an anecdote related by Aguayo. He tells of a group of American executives visiting Japanese plants which supply the car industry. After being shown everything in the plants and having every question answered, one of the Americans was curious to know why the Japanese were so ready to reveal all their methods: 'The Japanese executive replied, "We know you won't adopt what you have seen here today, and even if you did, by the time you instituted everything, we will be ten years ahead of where we are now." '

The American competitor who takes that statement as an unalterable fact is little better off than the non-competitor who doesn't even try the new methods of the Deming Age. The American competitor who takes that statement as challenge and bugle call is in there with a chance – and will have behind him the powerful driving force of proving that Japanese wrong.

CHAPTER 11

Hanson: The Big Pay-off

If any successful group encapsulated the spirit of the Thatcher era in Britain, it had to be Hanson Industries. Thatcher expressed her appreciation by ennobling both James Hanson, who masterminded the company from his English base, and Gordon White. The latter lord, starting with $3,000 of capital, built the North American interests to sales of $5.9 billion in 1989, with a return on stockholders' equity of 30.9 per cent – topped by only 39 of *Fortune*'s 500 largest industrial companies.

Not to be outdone, the Hanson parent was the 14th most profitable of Britain's biggest 250 companies, according to *Management Today*, also with a 30.9 per cent return on invested capital and (even more mouth-watering) a 1,608 per cent rise in its share price over the previous decade. This amazing growth and profitability had been almost wholly acquisition-led: in the US, starting with a $32 million fish processor called Seacoast, White cut his teeth on a series of modest buys, from Hygrade frankfurters to McDonough, which was in everything from cement and concrete to Endicott Johnson shoes.

Hanson and White had already developed a taste for selling much of their purchases, partly to finance them, partly to turn a handsome profit. From 1974 to 1978 they spent $139 million, recouped $181 million by sales, and were left with businesses that were valued, in a *Fortune* table of spring 1989, at $1.25 billion. McDonough gave them another taste: for conglomerates. Net of its cement and concrete, the buy cost $132 million to yield a 1989 valuation of $450 million.

Thus inspired, the dynamic duo embarked on an unprecedented splurge: in the period 1984–87 they spent $3.2 billion on four purchases. Three were conglomerates: US Industries, SCM and

Kidde, which owned 163 businesses among them. Even the fourth, Kaiser Cement, mixed Hawaii real estate and a couple of Asian port terminals with the cement.

Disposals brought $1.8 billion back home to leave a net cost of $1.4 billion – less than the value placed in the table on the remnants of US Industries alone. In the UK, what's more, Hanson had been applying the old one–two to equal effect, spending $3.1 billion from 1982–86, reaping $2.6 billion in sell-offs, and being left with $2.5 billion in assets for a net cost of $568 million.

Had the Hanson–White reputation rested only on wheels and deals, their group would be of little interest to serious managers. But many large and important businesses were left in their possession for significant periods. The ability of the pair to wring profits from these assets made them prize examples of what two authors, Michael Goold and Andrew Campbell, call 'financial control companies'. That sets Hanson at the opposite extreme to 'strategic planning companies', in which the centre rules through controlling the strategy of the group.

Somewhere in between lie 'strategic control' companies, which seek to have the best of both worlds: getting involved in the strategy of each and every business, but governing through the expectation and monitoring of financial results. If that sounds a mite woolly, so it is: but that isn't an adjective you can apply to financial controllers like Hanson. They have no formal planning systems, are concerned mainly with financial results, which they control only against annual targets, and they apply strict short-term criteria (two- to four-year paybacks) to investment decisions.

Hanson's managers are bound by a classic system of targets and incentives. To judge by the phenomenal results reported above, there's nothing wrong with the logic or the application in practice. The system for British subsidiaries differs somewhat from the American, but the principle is the same. It works as follows:

1. Basic salary is above average, with bonuses payable only for super-performance, based strictly on the profits under the control of the executive concerned.
2. Each level in the pyramid has its bonus deducted before calculating the bonus for the next level up, which helps ensure that each management level sets demanding targets for the subordinate tier.
3. The bonus target is usually set above both previous years' actuals and current year's budget. For hitting the target, 10 per

cent of salary is generally paid. Bonus rises by a percentage of salary (varying from ½ to 3 per cent) for every 1 per cent by which the target is exceeded. The bonus is capped at from 25 per cent to 100 per cent of salary.

4. A capital employed target also operates. If the target is exceeded, Hanson charges a hefty percentage of the excess over the target. If less capital is employed, Hanson adds the same percentage to the target profit achieved.

To summarise the system, in the words of Hanson's Peter Harper; '(1) Pay on super profits, (2) set targets on personal profit centres, (3) cascade subordinate bonuses, (4) reward achievement and escalate thereafter, (5) set bonus maximums, (6) ratchet up targets, and (7) write to every winner'. It sounds delightfully simple, especially writing to every winner. If that's all there is to successful management, most of the tomes written by the experts down the ages are pretty well worthless, which applies doubly to modern ideas about motivation.

As Goold and Campbell observe in their *Strategies and Styles*, motivation in financial control companies comes down firmly in favour of the stick. 'Their incentive system – the financial carrot – may not differ substantially. . . . But they are quicker to replace managers, fiercer in applying pressure through the monitoring process. . . . They believe that management changes are necessary to raise the quality of managers. . . . Failure is not tolerated in financial control companies. As one business manager put it: "If you succeed, you are rewarded. If you don't, you are out" '.

What the authors find in general appears to fit Hanson in particular: 'Surprisingly, divisional managements are not demoralised by the threat of what might happen if they fail. Instead they try harder, knowing that their achievement will be clearly recognised if they succeed'. Yet there's a strange anomaly. For all the value apparently created so abundantly by wheeling, dealing and financial control at Hanson, the stock market rating as the 1990s began was strictly run-of-the-mill: a fact that proved decisive in aborting Hanson's stab at a possible takeover of ICI. That could be explained by a simple fact: the Hanson method is also strictly run-of-the-mill.

CHAPTER

12

The Reagan–Thatcher Write-off

Western management rests on a number of propositions that seem not only logical but axiomatic, and centre round the hard core of financial results. It's recognised by many critics that financial objectives are not enough. In *Strategic Control: Milestones for Long-Term Performance*, Michael Goold and John J. Quinn make the case for targets that measure strategic progress. But they argue that, when managers have agreed on their strategic targets, they must expect to achieve them and be rewarded for doing so. That is different in emphasis from Hanson's financial control policy, but not in kind. The motivational philosophy is the same:

1. Success is achieved by establishing measurable objectives and reaching or surpassing those aims.
2. That success will be reflected by profit – by the creation of wealth.
3. People respond to financial incentives – and the stronger the incentives, the greater the response.
4. If success is rewarded, people will strive harder to achieve the objectives.

Take these four propositions together and you get the philosophical framework of the typical company. It gears its reward system, to greater or lesser degree, to hitting financial targets. These in turn are geared to annual financial results, and are heavily top-down in application: incentive payments to top management are often many times higher than the total earnings of subordinate managers, let alone still lower employees.

Each year, however, the goalposts get moved. Targets are expressed in terms of improving profit performance or achieving a given return on capital, or both, as at Hanson. It sounds dynamic indeed: but you couldn't have a greater contrast with a Japanese group like Toshiba, which according to Goold and Quinn has 'no direct link between either financial or non-financial targets and personal career promotion or bonuses'.

Even if Hanson were a perfect proof of validity for the conventional Western model, that wouldn't end the argument. What works for a highly acquisitive operator, moving on from takeover to takeover, turnround to turnround, could be completely ineffective for, say, an office equipment company locked in competition with the Japanese. In fact, Hanson has such an interest. Significantly, however, it sold the public half of the business, Smith Corona, the maker of electric portable typewriters, shortly before a sharp nose-dive in profits was reported.

Hanson and the Smith Corona management had already reaped their ripe rewards. That's one general problem with the conventional model: you may be rewarding past performance when the present, and let alone the future, is already showing grave deterioration. To put it another way, how a profit is made may well be more important than how much. A profit earned through reducing costs by more than falling sales, for example, is plainly less worthwhile than gains which come from expanding sales more rapidly than costs.

The first profit means either a declining market share or a declining market; the second implies a powerful surge in either market or marketing strength or both. Of course, taking out cost is a continuous test of good management. But again the 'how' matters, and not only the 'how much'. Are costs coming down because of cutbacks in strategic expenditure on training, quality, brand promotion, research and development, IT, etc.? Or do the cost cuts actually *result* from strategic spending? Negative cost reduction that rules out the positive is a well-trodden road to disaster.

The evidence is now overwhelming that Mrs Thatcher's supposed British economic miracle, with productivity rising faster than that of any major European partner, was the result of cutting back rather than thrusting forward. Her regime (like that of President Reagan in the US) was a mighty experiment in applying the conventional corporate model to the national economy. Massive personal tax cuts were supposed to engender a supply-side revolution as managers at all levels responded to incentives. With top income tax rates halved, the incentive was potent.

Yet the 1990s began, and Mrs Thatcher's reign ended, with the macro-economic statistics as dispiriting as at the start and with an epidemic of micro-economic disasters which afflicted many of the Prime Ministerial favourites. Like Hanson and the other beneficiaries of Smith Corona, most of the fallen pets had already lined their pockets. The British experience, like the American, strongly suggests that enhancing financial rewards at the top by no means enhances performance from top to bottom – and may be counterproductive.

Part of the damage results from the single-year obsession. A calendar or financial year is a purely artificial division. The business doesn't close when the books are closed; like its reputation for quality and service, the business is a continuum. I've long preferred rolling 12-month budgets for control and planning purposes: but quarterly revisions impose a great strain on managers and finance departments. At Toshiba, budgets are prepared for a full year, but only the first six months are approved. The second six months are modified and approved once the first-half figures are known – with the result that managers are always working towards more realistic targets.

John E. Rehfeld, author of a fascinating *Harvard Business Review* article on the experience of working for two Japanese companies, Toshiba and Seiko, observes that, 'If the budget becomes meaningless during the course of the year, the company is like a ship without a rudder'. Taking Toshiba's simple half-year step, he found, greatly improves the quality of planning, control, response and motivation. Interestingly, Compaq Computer (Chapter 2) ran the most successful US manufacturer of the 1980s on a revolving 12-month budget. Plainly, by far the wisest course is to treat the current year as an incident; Japanese companies, whose forecasting of current year results is usually eerily precise, take this attitude.

Japanese companies are also world champions at positive cost-cutting or 'cost-down': witness the extraordinary results achieved in face of the former rise in the yen, which would have crippled less aggressively competent managements. What their powers reflect, above all, is a difference in philosophy. But what's the difference? It lies in four propositions that, while logical, even axiomatic, to the Japanese, are not universally accepted in the West.

1. Success is achieved by establishing general, value-driven objectives and working consistently towards those aims.
2. The success will be reflected in better and better products and in a growing and increasingly powerful market penetration.
3. People respond to a culture of success of this nature, and the stronger the culture, the greater the response.

4. The response is translated into results, not by straining harder, but by working more effectively.

Compare that with the conventional Western model, taken to a fine pitch by Hanson, and the contrasts are glaring. Does the Japanese convention reflect a culture that can't be recreated outside Japan? In the first place, the conventional model by no means accounts for all Western companies. In the second place, truly successful Western firms, even if in other respects they follow the norm, nearly always combine the latter with adherence to the Japanese style of value-driven management (in which quality must loom large).

The best performances in continental Europe have come from companies like Robert Bosch, where the value drive has existed from foundation. Britain has been remarkable for the stable success of two family-founded, long-established retail chains, Marks & Spencer and J. Sainsbury. Newer retail stores stood out among Mrs Thatcher's fallen children, but both these golden oldies have flourished through vigorous use of own brands, involving long-term partnerships with their suppliers and rigorous quality and value-for-money standards.

Value for money doesn't mean cheapest. Competing on price alone has often led to financial disaster in businesses as far apart as airlines, washing machines and personal computers. Pricing must, of course, be 'competitive' – but what does that mean? Simply that the customer wants to buy your product or service, and doesn't find your charge a deterrent; or, better still, regards that price as eminently fair compared to other offers.

That's especially likely to occur when there's literally no comparison, not because of monopoly, but because your offering is seen to stand alone in highly material respects, like the Mercedes-Benz range in its heyday as the executive transport *par excellence*. Even today, when the Mercedes faces aggressive competition from BMW and now the Japanese, perception of its value remains high: the growing issue, though, is whether the value justifies the price that the company likes to charge.

In the classical, Adam Smith model, that's the benefit which competition is supposed to bring: more and more competition generates lower and lower prices. Along with the sovereign power of fiscal incentives, that was the foundation of Reagan-Thatcher economics: deregulation would set the incentivised entrepreneurs free to revitalise whole industries, producing economic gains for the community through higher efficiency and lower prices. The thesis seems to be supported by experience in Japan, where the number of competitors far exceeds those in major industries in the West.

There's a crucial difference, however. The Japanese on home ground don't compete on price, but on internal efficiency and product attributes. The Adam Smith model, in holding that the more is the merrier, specifically expects proliferation to drive down prices with no concomitant losses in quality of service or product, or anything else. Recent experience in the US airline industry, global banking, and American telecommunications, etc. has exposed this highly dangerous fallacy. Clearly, you can have too much competition as well as too little.

The argument is spelt out tellingly in Rafael Aguayo's book on Dr W. Edwards Deming – *The American Who Taught the Japanese About Quality* (Chapter 9). Aguayo's trenchant writing challenges some crucial ideas of the modern management consensus, beginning with the idea that successful competition is about 'winning', in the sense of defeating the opposition, even 'blowing it out of the water'. True competition is about a different kind of winning: gaining the 'delighted' or, in Deming's word, 'loyal', customer.

You achieve that by the excellence of product and/or service. In the process, you may well gain market share from others – but not necessarily at their expense for they, too, are free to explore ways of finding loyal customers of their own, and of serving them with greater value at lower internal cost. Classical price competition says nothing about value: taken too far, competition can destroy value, jobs, and whole businesses.

Nevertheless, that's the weakness of Aguayo's argument. You may be wise enough to compete on value, but price-cutting fools, rushing in where angels fear to tread, can undermine the market and your strategy. In fact, history shows that the fools perish while the truly wise survive and prosper. The competition issue, though, goes deeper still. You can't control the behaviour of external competitors (not legally, that is): but what about internal competition?

Aguayo makes an overwhelming case against both competing with suppliers (who should be on your side, and you on theirs) and competition between your own departments, functions and people. As he points out, collaboration is the only way to achieve effective value-creation within the company and with suppliers. The world's worst purchasers are government departments, often compelled by law to buy on price alone, and to discard any supplier, no matter how long established or excellent, who gets beaten on price.

That's no more intelligent than the practice at one consumer goods company of ranking its salespeople by monthly achievement and summarily dismissing the bottom person. Somebody has to come bottom: the issue, as Deming would explain, is whether the inferior performance results from special causes. If the bottom man's sales fall within statistical control limits (that is, the predictable range of performance of all the salespeople), dismissing him has no value. It won't even encourage the others, whose performance must continue to lie within these limits.

This fallacy is repeated time and again throughout the conventional model. This business or that manager 'under-performed', that business or this manager 'over-performed', so punish the first and reward the second, and overall performance will improve. It won't: the overall result is the sum of all efforts. Aguayo gives the convincing example of Procter & Gamble, which discovered that only 55 per cent of its deliveries were on time, even though every department involved was performing to a highly acceptable 95 per cent standard.

The explanation? The supply chain involves twelve departments: multiply 95 by 95 eleven times, and you end up with 54 per cent. If you want 95 per cent performance from the totality, you must obtain near-total achievement from the components. Given this arithmetical fact, rewards for exceptional performance should relate to the sum, not to the parts. This would partly overcome some familiar difficulties, such as how to reward equally stopping a loss and raising a profit, or how to recognise achievements whose pay-off won't come this year, or even next, but without which the entire future of the business would be in doubt.

Competition and winning are still the names of the game. But the true competition is with oneself, and the real victories are over the inherent tendencies of organisations towards mediocrity or worse. Deming's philosophy of continuous and continual all-round improvement is the only one that makes ultimate sense. It applies not only to the business but to the individuals who conduct the business. They should never forget another cardinal principle of the master: that the effort of individuals doesn't determine performance. The key lies in the effectiveness of the system in which they perform – and which happens to be much the easier to improve.

PART 3
HOW TO TEACH SUCCESS

CHAPTER

13

British Airways: The Flying Business School

The tougher the competition, the greater the part that the intangibles can play. That explains the actions of a company like British Airways. Locked in battle with other airlines flying the same routes with similar planes, and seeking to differentiate itself by better ways of management and service, BA adopted a prime commercial policy that seems at first sight not to be commercial at all. It put its faith in a programme called 'Putting People First' – a title with a double meaning.

As chief executive Sir Colin Marshall explained in 1983, 'We want to persuade our staff that their colleagues are people too, and that the way staff treat each other is just as important as the way they treat the customer'. In other words, to put the customer people first, you must learn how to put your own people first – and 'learn' is truly the operative word. If service is the key to commercial success, training is the key to service. But training has acquired a far wider meaning for companies that honestly are putting people up front.

Chris Lane, who worked on the BA programme with his company, the Danish-owned TMI, has explained that for a start you must train to change attitudes as well as skills. 'When looking at the people aspects of quality customer care . . . a wide range of communication skills are at issue, as well as the technical knowledge relating to the company's products and services'. He makes the important point that 'to improve skills and behaviour, you need to challenge attitudes as well'. It isn't simply a matter of 'how to' training, as Lane says, but much more 'why to'.

That can be taken as a model for management as much as cabin or counter staff. Managers need skills, 'the competencies and capabilities' that the company must have, which can and must be taught, updated and reinforced. But they also need to master the arts of communication, to imbibe the attitudes that, taken together, create the culture of the corporation, and to capitalise on both meanings of 'putting people first'. Management, in short, is an educational process. Everybody learns, both on the job and off it.

Few companies have flown further along this route than BA. It launched an 'open learning' programme, starting with induction (with all newcomers initiated in a way designed to encourage 'learning to learn'); progressed through career planning workshops to 'fundamentals of supervision'; and ended by operating evening classes on-site – leading to an MBA from the University of Bath. Three 'top flight academies' were also opened up: the first level developing future middle managers over two years, and the second (two years followed by a number of job rotations) designed to produce 'a pool of senior managers'.

Both these were in-house programmes: at the third stage, of 'advanced business education and career progression tailored to the needs of specific senior managers', the latter get sent away to international business schools, including Harvard. Wise management education includes mind-broadening studies: chief executive Marshall (who himself went straight from school into the merchant navy) described his ambitious programme as an 'investment in encouraging individual learning and growth' – another piece of putting people first.

Men and women have a right to develop their own careers, and will do so, if given the chance: BA's supervisor programme attracted 700 applicants, no less. The hard idea behind these soft policies is that in growing themselves the individuals will grow the business.

Do they? From 1987, the privatised BA in three years increased its profits 77 per cent on a 54 per cent rise in turnover while major rivals like Pan Am and TWA tumbled towards or into bankruptcy or the nearest alternative, Chapter 11. You can never prove that hard results flow directly from soft causes: the airline industry, BA included, was suffering largely self-induced agonies in 1991, compounding the Gulf War setback by the effects of creating grossly excess capacity. But hard results aren't the only justification.

Any good guru will tell you that companies and their people benefit alike from following the way to the light. That's to the gurus' own benefit, true: even they like money. But what's to be won, save worthless economies, by staying in the dark? What's achieved by managements who do nothing to develop the general and transferable talents that their companies require – as do their people themselves? The circle is vicious: it starts from the narrowness of vision that broader and better education (and reading, something else of which too many managers are shy) would cure.

Peter Drucker refers to managers who are not 'human beings', meaning that they lack the breadth of interests and understanding from which the best leadership stems. The idea is that from individual learning and growth, corporate learning and growth will flow. That's a statement of faith rather than ascertainable fact. But it's a tough, hard fact that, like the airlines, all managements are competing in a tough, hard world where expertise in all areas, from information technology to window-dressing, makes the difference, not just between success and unsuccess, but survival and sinking.

It must be applied expertise, of course. But top managers who aren't developing their own men and women simply aren't applying themselves. The question of whether they should will become literally academic: those companies that don't learn the lessons of learning are liable to disappear. The companies that do learn will be waving them goodbye. In justifying BA's own efforts in training and education, this flying business school quoted Professor Charles Handy: in the matter of education, Britain 'needs to do much more, and to do it more systematically, if she wants her managers to be as good as they can be'. For Britain, read the company – any company. Managers must be taught: which leaves the crucial questions of what and how.

CHAPTER 14

What Managers Need To Learn

In one vital respect the managers of the 1990s differ markedly from any predecessor generation. Typically, they have been educated in their work. If they haven't been to business schools, they have gone on courses in and out of house. Virtually everybody in management has attended a course or seminar at some point. Virtually everybody respects, more or less, the temples of higher management education, from the shrine of the Harvard Business School or one of its prestigious rivals, like the Wharton School, to a European challenger, such as Insead or London.

Some of the loftier-minded managers trained by such institutions think their profession should be just that, a profession akin to those of the law, accountancy and medicine. But Thomas J. Peters and Robert Waterman, Jr. the joint but now separated authors of *In Search of Excellence*, were right to hoot with derision at the very British idea of a Royal Institution, whose members would qualify, just like accountants or vets, for letters after their names.

The idea is no more laughable than the deep uncertainty of some top managers over whether education has any practical value for themselves, their underlings, or their companies; and, if so, what kind of education. Many people, inside and outside business, believe that good managers are certainly born, probably not made, and definitely not trained. The top entrepreneurs always include stars, like the personal computer kings Steve Jobs of Apple and Next and Bill Gates of Microsoft (or their lesser British counterpart, Alan Sugar of Amstrad), who were busily building their millions and billions when other, less inspired fellows had their noses to the academic grindstone at business school.

But the ground noses included those of 214 of the 1,000 top corporate leaders in the US in 1989. Those who have been through

70

the management education mill tend to stay keen supporters, which cynics won't find surprising: Masters of Business Administration aren't likely to bite the hand that educated them, or to pour scorn on their own, hard-earned, precious degrees. But the cynicism cuts both ways. Chief executives who have reached the summit without guides and maps won't be keen to confess that they are badly equipped for their well-paid roles. Their prejudices against management education may be self-defence mechanisms.

It's noticeable, anyway, that many self-made successes totally share the educational faith – like British Airways' Sir Colin Marshall, and Sir David Plastow, who rose to head the Vickers engineering conglomerate after starting working life as a General Motors apprentice. Plastow observed that the Germans and the Japanese (not the Americans, note) 'have the edge in the context of in-depth competence right through their payrolls; they have got better educated people and they spend more time and effort on maintaining that competence'. Today, big business leaders are rarely without a university education and many business educators are rarely without a big business assignment.

The progress from learning and teaching to doing is a crucial element in one of Western society's most practical activities: fighting and winning wars. The victor of El Alamein was not only the country's greatest general of his day: Montgomery was a brilliant chief instructor at the Staff College, a formidable academy. The armed services have always believed in teaching everybody their trade, from commanders to riflemen. It's curious that when the businessmen returned to their desks after the Second World War, all of them didn't practise what the forces preached – and did.

Today the best boardroom successors have come to the same conclusion as the military, partly from clear realisation that in modern business competition is closely akin to war. The winners, as in war, will be the best equipped, the best trained, and the best led. Since Japan is winning or has won so many competitive wars, the description presumably applies to its managers. Yet curiously, as Peter Tasker observes in his *Inside Japan*, 'for a country which takes business in such deadly earnest, Japan lacks a developed system of postgraduate business studies'. The leading companies compete vigorously for the best graduates, and *vice versa*. But the training is mostly in-house.

Tasker says that going on to business school after graduation could easily be counter-productive: 'Holders of postgraduate qualifications in non-scientific fields may well have difficulty finding suitable employment'. The in-house norm removes any necessity to confront some of the questions that bother doubting managers:

Can you teach managers anything except accounting? Are management teachers any good? Are business schools head-in-the-clouds outfits which waste valuable days doing valueless things like sending middle-aged executives to climb mountains? Doesn't the real education of managers take place on the job? Don't many writers on management, like Peter Drucker (and myself), express sceptical views about the temples of management education?

In fact, Drucker is not a witness for the prosecution. He is a great teacher whose long and distinguished academic career has been crowned with his name on a business school in Claremont, California. Of course, there are awful business schools, courses and teachers: but many are very good. The educational sheep and goats are distributed, no doubt, in much the same proportions, in institutions teaching everything from the higher physics to hairdressing. Nobody would argue, though, from the particular of a bad school or professor to the general condemnation of teaching and learning.

Of course, business schools aren't the be-all and end-all of management education, let along management. But they can provide as effective a foundation for real managing as engineering or accountancy or any other fact-based course (the Pritzkers in Chicago use law school to prepare their scions for protecting the family billions). But just as arts graduates need to have their high culture leavened with hard facts, so the factually qualified need to learn to look beyond their ledgers, microcircuits and machine tools. The education isn't a substitute for the indispensable on-the-job learning, but a tool for it.

Every job has special and often crucial requirements. You wouldn't, unless suicidal, entrust an ailing kidney to a general practitioner; your self-preserving assumption would be that special tasks require specialist knowledge. The fault, when executives lack academic equipment for their tasks, lies less with them than their bosses, who deserve to suffer corporate kidney failure – and very possibly do. Managers need topping up, retraining and new training throughout their careers, as some Japanese giants acknowledge by removing all managers from the line at 40 for re-education and reappraisal.

The Japanese management miracle is founded in the fact that 85 per cent of company directors have degrees (mostly in economics and engineering) or professional qualifications. That proportion is the same as in the US (though *three and a half* times the British figure). But in Japan education doesn't stop with the degree. Training helps the uniquely versatile Japanese manager to transfer readily between tasks; so a personnel director, say, can be whipped over to the US to head an all-out American marketing drive.

You need versatility in times of rapid change and fluctuating competition. But that's by no means all the Japanese advantage. Hundreds upon hundreds of thousands of words have been expended on the inimitable culture of Japan, the docility of the workforce, the passion for hard work; but there's nothing inimitable, or peculiarly Japanese, about listening to good advice and taking it – witness that fateful dinner in Tokyo in 1950 which made W.Edwards Deming a national hero in Japan (see Chapter 9). The key wasn't just that for a solid hour he advised a score of the leaders of Japanese industry, then flat on its back and a byword for bad goods, on why they should obey his commandments. Most important by far, they obeyed him.

By contrast, as noted, it wasn't until 1980, when an NBC documentary on Japanese industrial superiority picked up the Deming contribution, that at last the prophet (by then an octogenarian) had honour in his own country. In the West, chairmen and chief executives may occasionally sit at the feet of management gurus. But even the sitters are unlikely, supposing that they have heard, marked and inwardly digested, to remake the organisation according to the new gospel – for example, the participative, responsive, quality-driven, humanistic, customer-dominated, innovative pattern favoured by the above-mentioned Tom Peters.

Peters has broken away, not only from his literary partner for *In Search of Excellence*, Robert H. Waterman, Jr, but from his former idol – the large American business. His anti-bigness teaching is marked by a messianic, haranguing fervour: he prowls about his audience like a hungry predator, almost shouting his scorn for the methods of large managements and his enthusiasm for the iconoclasm and energy of the middle-sized superstars like Milliken, the family-owned textile company, or Nucor, the maverick steel producer. But the lessons aren't peculiar to Peters: nor is the message especially new.

Throughout most of the postwar period, management philosophy has advanced along three axes. First, so-called 'scientific management', whose god was the stopwatch, has progressively given way to humanistic management. Heavily influenced by behavioural psychology, the gurus have moved thinking bodily forward from the stick to the carrot. Instead of forcing management and men to work as authority demands (Theory X, in Douglas McGregor's brilliant formulation), the new school seeks to harness people's own motivation to that of the organisation on the argument (Theory Y) that work is as natural as play.

Second, hierarchy (at least in theory) has receded in favour of looser organisational forms. Closely allied to the humanistic school, this mode of thought seeks to adapt the organisation to its purpose, not *vice versa*. But what is its purpose?

Enter the third school of thought, which holds that the only object of business is to compete with others for the favours of the customer king or queen – he or she who must be obeyed and satisfied. The company seeks to win by obtaining 'competitive advantage' (the formulation of the influential Harvard guru, Michael E. Porter) through concentrating on building an invincible, innovation-led business system in the selected markets where it competes.

These three powerful strands didn't spring from the ether. They are the consequence of developments in society and the world economy. Authoritarian methods and hierarchical control have been breaking down for years, all the way from the family to (the latest manifestation) the unmourned Communist monoliths. As the centre of gravity in business has shifted from manufacture to service, from brawn to brain, the brain-workers have required an organisational climate better suited to mind than to muscle. All this has happened against the background of a rapidly changing market environment.

Markets, too, have shifted away from producer control as new technologies, deregulation and liberalisation, disappearing frontiers between nations and industries, and general abundance of both supply and money have destroyed the old monopolies and quasi-monopolies. All these developments, and their impact on management, have been foreseen and brilliantly articulated by Drucker, the end-century's pre-eminent guru.

Drucker's vision of the changed order, expressed pithily in *The New Realities*, describes management as being 'about human beings'. It 'deals with the integration of people in a common venture' and is therefore 'deeply embedded in culture'. The enterprise requires 'commitment to common goals and shared values'. Every enterprise, too, 'is a learning and teaching institution' that 'must be built on communication and on individual responsibility'. Then, neither 'the quantity of output nor the "bottom line" is by itself an adequate measure of the performance of management and enterprise. Market standing, innovation, productivity, development of people, quality, financial results – all are crucial to an organisation's performance and to its survival'.

Finally, 'results exist only on the outside. The result of a business is a satisfied customer'. As these quotes show, most other gurus are simply repeating the lessons of the old master (Drucker was born in 1909) in their own manner. But are management gurus condemned to be Cassandras – heard, but not heeded? Part of the trouble is that wisdom can become obsolete. Theodore Levitt became famous for his marketing myopia thesis, which warned against inadequate technological foresight and weak definitions of the business in which you're engaged. Myopia's moment passed, though Levitt has hit the headlines again by anticipating and elucidating the trend to global marketing.

Management by objectives, which sprang from a Drucker insight, had its moment of glory, and its time of decay – and so on. But teachings like Deming's and Drucker's don't truly date. Western managers who have become increasingly avid customers for the wisdom of the East (even seeking strategic lessons from an ancient guide to samurai swordsmanship) would do well to concentrate on the wisdom of the West, while bringing to bear one priceless Eastern power. That is the ability to listen, learn, adopt, adapt and continually improve. They're the most important talents that anybody can teach, the easiest aptitudes for the willing to win – and the best tools with which to win.

CHAPTER

15

Nintendo: The System Game

The Age of Competition has seen some of the most startling marketing successes of all time, and none greater than those of Japanese companies whose reflexes are sharpened by incessant, furious competition at home. In that ferocious market, competing on price has always been discouraged. That has developed remarkable powers of competing along other dimensions of which Western rivals are only too well aware, and which they now have to master themselves.

As Professor Xavier Gilbert of IMD in Lausanne explains it, the first reaction to competition from the East was to raise quality. Once the quality edge gets blunted, though, firms turn to cutting costs, followed by prices, to keep down competition. As others take the same path, all contestants head into a commodity market, in which profit margins are enforced, not made. That's no fun for anybody. As a demonstration of how to gain and keep a competitive edge in the 1990s, Gilbert cites Nintendo, the computer games company, which competes not just with a product or products, but a whole business system.

Nintendo's company name means 'leave it to heaven', but little was left to chance during a growth phase that multiplied sales by ten times in ten years to $2.5 billion. Under its multi-billionaire president, Hiroshi Yamauchi, the company had applied more and more sales appeal to its products and fastened a tighter and tighter grip on its market. The grip springs from total control over supply of hardware and software and distribution, covering a barely believable 80 per cent of the world market in video games. That control, however, is achieved by systematic management at its most developed.

HOW TO TEACH SUCCESS

When it introduced its Famicon hardware, Nintendo selected a price point and quality standard and then created an entire network – design, production, software, retail and after-sales service – so hugely comprehensive (the initial order for circuit boards was no less than 3 million) that competition was all but barred. The business system and thus the product were smash hits. Gilbert observes that 'from the beginning, activities operated in network, not in sequence' as Nintendo selected its target, oriented its product, and rationalised the system.

Getting production, marketing, distribution and the mass market aligned is what also saved the Swiss watch industry with the invention of Swatch. The first reaction to the Japanese *blitzkrieg* concentrated on cutting manufacturing costs, ignoring the realities of the business system. The factory accounted for only 22 per cent of the cost to the customer. Given the extent of Japanese undercutting, bringing the cost of manufacture down to zero wouldn't have made enough difference, for 70 per cent of the delivered cost occurred between the manufacturer and the point of sale.

When Swatch examined the system and shifted the point of attack (using a vastly improved and much more efficiently made product), it more than halved the cost of retail and wholesale distribution by moving to new channels – and brought down the cost to the customer by an eventual 55 per cent. Nintendo's Yamauchi, who led the old family business from old-fashioned *hanafuda* playing cards into the new age, once told *Fortune* that 'I don't really like videogames': but he does like the Swatch game of combining low prices with high margins – and that tight control.

The magazine notes that, 'To earn a licence, a software supplier must develop a game on spec, win Nintendo's approval, pay Nintendo to manufacture the cartridges, bear the cost of marketing – and agree not to supply the game for other makes of machine'. What Yamauchi can't control, however, is the market reaction. The success of Swatch in the final analysis depended on the appeal of switching watches from timekeeping to fashion accessory. In an even more fashion-conscious industry, Nintendo is at unavoidable risk of going out of fashion.

The main visible dangers here are that its hold might be rocked by rival products that suddenly steal the market's fancy; or the whole fashion might fold. But any rivals will still have to buck that system. Early in the 1990s, Yamauchi had started extending into the adult market, into second-generation Super Famicon hardware, into information networks, into Europe and possibly into education. The true measure of the intensity of modern business pressures, though, isn't Nintendo's strength, nor those new opportunities just listed, but the way in which the weaknesses and threats, for all its systematic disciplines, came to the fore.

The share price halved from the August 1990 peak, double the fall of the Tokyo index, not because of bad news, but because of fears of future ill tidings. Would Super Famicon pick up the torch from a faltering Famicon? Was Super Mario, Nintendo's video hero plumber, losing his mass market appeal? In an earlier era, the questions would have ended right there. A company like Atari, zapped by the collapse of a previous video hit, had nothing on which to fall back. It was awfully managed: Nintendo is the opposite.

Nintendo's risk exposure, despite leaving nothing to chance, is the result of endemic change. Where previous winners, many of them still today's great brand names, could expect long and unbroken runs, latter-day champions climb mountains from which it is easy to fall. Another Japanese president, Hirotaro Higuchi of Asahi Breweries, faced exactly the same situation as Yamauchi after a classic display of underdog marketing. Following four decades of steadily falling market share, Asahi worked an impossible transformation: from a trailing third place of the Japanese market with 9.6 per cent to a second place share of nearly a quarter.

The key was Super Dry, Japan's first dry beer, which sold a world-record 13.5 million cases in its launch year. *Business Week* reported early in 1991 that, after investing $2 billion to treble capacity, Asahi needed to move 30 million cases in first-year sales of its new beer named Z, it would, according to an executive, 'decide the fate of our company'. Like Nintendo, Asahi has been effectively a one-product business: 95 per cent of 1990 sales came from Super Dry.

When such recently successful companies face such threatening challenges, the ante has plainly been raised right across the board of world commerce. The business system which Nintendo mastered leads through inbound logistics, operations, outbound logistics, marketing and sales, and ultimately service – supported by the corporate infrastructure, people management, technology and procurement. Get any of them wrong, and the whole system may come apart. Which means that, more than ever before in the history of management, success depends on how much managers actually know – at every point along the chain.

CHAPTER

16

What Managers Need to Know

Management is notoriously a 'soft' science, if a science at all. Practitioners of 'hard' disciplines, like engineering and chemistry, have been able to turn up their noses, not only at practising managers, but at management academics, whose 'research' often has no use, save for their professional credits. But maybe the scoffing has to stop: for the preaching and practice are hardening up decisively.

Take three tough and technical management approaches that are yielding rich commercial results: total quality, management by time and, Nintendo-style, mastering the 'business system'. The trio are closely related. Total quality management seeks measures by which every function of the business can be consistently improved. The managerial timelord concentrates on the time every operation takes, from the first response to a customer to the development of new products. A business system such as Nintendo's likewise runs from the very start of the process to delivery to the customer and on into after-sales service – and more.

All three disciplines rest on detailed study, which establishes how to improve quality by improving the process, which also saves time; how to select the process elements that can be compressed or eliminated to save still more time, which is always money; how to understand the business system so as to reconstruct it in the most effective and powerful way possible – for the stronger the system, the greater the competitive advantage.

One classic system was Gillette's. In its heyday, by virtue of supplying the razor, it could easily monopolise blade sales, and thus maintain a stranglehold on both the consumer and the distribution system. Xerox once had a similar position in copying, as did Eastman Kodak in film. The fact that all three business systems weakened, laying the companies open to fateful competition, was the result of neglecting key components of the system – for, like quality and time-based management, systems need constant renewal and reinforcement.

Gillette's error was to suppress stainless steel technology, thus letting in a rival with a superior product. Xerox neglected the lower end of the market, opening the gate through which the Japanese poured. Kodak allowed itself to decline as a supplier of cameras, the vehicles in which the film was carried and used. These could all be categorised as strategic errors – and strategy, though it should be based on the hardest of analysis, is a 'soft' discipline; that is, there are no hard and fast answers. You always run the risk of being wrong, or wrong-footed.

But had the Gillette, Kodak and Xerox strategists thought literally hard, applying sufficient rigour to their business systems, probing for weak spots and searching for added strongpoints, their systems would certainly have proved much more difficult to crack. The concept can be expressed another way: instead of 'competition', the leader engages in what the highly original thinker Edward de Bono calls 'sur-petition', forcing the opposition to compete on your own terms and seeking to create your very own 'value monopoly'.

Rivals thus have to buck, not just the product or service, but the whole system, and the systematic manager today has many hard tools available to reinforce his defences (which, in the best military tradition, are also a means of attack). For example, for 'distribution' read 'channels'. The Index Alliance consultancy has identified no fewer than seven winning strategies in what it describes as 'channel warfare':

1. *Making it easier to do business.* ICI strengthened its engineering plastics business by in effect devising 'what is essentially a bidding package' for injection moulding shops, enabling them to determine the mix, the moulding process and the costs.
2. *Broadening the line.* Brewer Stella Artois used the French national videotext system to make itself appear to be the total food and beverage provider to institutional cafeterias, with an on-line menu-planning and ordering service that forced other suppliers into its system.
3. *Controlling intermediaries.* A greetings card company used its database to ship retailers what were shown to be the best-selling cards, thus greatly strengthening its hold.
4. *Information disintermediation.* With the old delivery by sales-ladies ceasing to be effective, Tupperware arranged for the

sellers to phone orders straight to the warehouse, bypassing the regional sales office.
5. *Creating new channels.* Otis Elevator installed microprocessors that automatically signal failure or incipient failure back to a central service dispatcher.
6. *Resolving information-related customer problems.* A car coatings company got into body shops and now 'owns the market' (i.e. has a value monopoly) by installing systems that estimated repair costs and matched the damaged car's colour.
7. *Information brokering.* A Swiss-based entrepreneur used IBM's Information Network to act as broker for freight containers available all over Europe.

The common factor in all the above examples is the customer. In every case, the successful use of channels increased value for the customer. That is also the object of time-based management (offering much faster delivery at lower cost), of business system planning (offering both the latter benefits and those of channel strategy, etc.), and (naturally) of the Total Quality Management (TQM) discussed in Chapter 38.

Total quality, managing by time and business system analysis are not either-ors, mutually incompatible alternatives. They all fit together, and they all have the same wondrous characteristic: it is exemplified by the new approach to the pivotal issue of process time. It's notorious that actual manufacture occupies only a fraction of a product's passage from A (the factory entrance, as raw materials and components) to B (the exit, as finished goods). As every management consultant has long known, said and proved, reduce the time and you cut the costs – often dramatically. And that's the highest common characteristic of much valuable new management lore.

You can see its worth from a casual glance at a few figures. The Japanese brought down the development time for a car to 30 months or less at a time when the record for Ford in Michigan was 11 months longer. The cost of bringing a new car to market after the usual three to four years of American gestation ranged from $3.2 billion to $4 billion. This compared with a figure in Japan, with a cycle not much over a couple of years, of $1 billion to $1.5 billion. Plainly, the consequent Japanese cost advantage is huge; but cost is only half the story.

Time isn't only money. It's competitive advantage. The faster you can react to the market, the quicker you can meet its changing needs. The lower the development time and therefore cost, the shorter the model runs required to amortise the capital investment – and the greater the variety of products you can afford to market. Yet many major companies in the West (and not only in manufacturing) have been locked into long cycles that were apparently as immutable as the four years taken over a new car: a lag that has always seemed very odd, given that the longest lead-time involved isn't anything like 48 months.

The conservatism and mistaken concepts responsible have been systematically exposed and destroyed by the work of the Boston Consulting Group. As the preface to *Competing Against Time* by George Stalk, Jr, and Thomas M. Hout explains, the consultants were alerted by the performance of a client's Japanese subsidiary. It outperformed the parent group's Western companies, even though the latter had the much higher volumes and lower variety which conventionally spell economic advantage. The BCG's leader, Bruce Henderson, observed then and there that 'Until the causes of these differences can be explained, much of the conceptual underpinnings of corporate strategy are suspect'. Several years' work came up with the missing explanation: time.

The work also stood many received ideas on their head. Costs go down, not up, as the length of production runs falls. The greater the quality, the lower the cost. Cost also comes down as variety increases – and as the response time shortens. Also, the principle applies to services as much as manufacturing. In both, the impact of enlarged choice and swifter response isn't a marginal increase in sales, but a sharp advance to highly profitable market leadership.

In a prize-winning *Harvard Business Review* article, one of the authors, George Stalk, Jr, cited an industrial door manufacturer, Atlas Door. Its response rate is two thirds faster than the competition, its growth three times as high, its return on sales five times. But how do you get to the promised land – or time? Stalk and co-author Hout state emphatically that you have to redesign the organisation. That sounds intimidating, although the key questions are very simple:

1. What deliverables do my customers want?
2. What organisation and work processes inside my company will most directly provide these deliverables?

These questions are far from new. They have always been fundamental to organisation studies. But you still find many, many companies where, to take a Stalk/Hout example, 35 people doing seven days of value-added work will need '16 cross-functional handoffs, 25 signoffs, 11 transfers between locations, and 91 days to get it out of the door'.

To escape from these costly and time-consuming man-traps, companies have to shift to the time-based mode. That means focusing on the entire business system and its main sequence – not, as in the traditional company, seeking improvement function by function. It means generating a continuous flow of work, rather than working by department or in batches. Where the traditional company tries to remove bottlenecks to speed the work flow, time-based managers change what happens upstream to reduce the pressure back down the sequence, and they invest, not to reduce cost, but to cut the expenditure of time.

Since the object of the exercise is to satisfy customers better and faster, customer information is a basic tool – along with information in general. You don't, as in the traditional mould, rely on specialists to generate information which is passed to users: instead, people working in teams both create and use the information. You don't rely on managers in different areas giving information to each other. Those same multifunctional teams assemble the information they need to function day to day. Central data processing with its slow feedback is out; local processing and fast feedback are in.

The authors have a splendid analogy for this approach, which is the essence of the revolutionary information technology now available for any desktop. Their metaphor is the 'OODA Loop', which derives from the method of victorious fighter pilots: the letters stand for Observation, Orientation, Decision and Action. The faster that the pilot, or the firm, travels round the continuous loop, the more likely the victory or, to put it another way, the better the performance. Here Stalk and Hout have another very valuable contribution to make to a long-vexed question: measurement.

The time-based competitor measures performance by time rather than cost, physical rather than financial results, throughput rather than utilisation, teams rather than individuals or departments. A whole new set of yardsticks assume importance – or rather are accorded the importance they have always possessed, like the time lost waiting for decisions, the time taken from idea to market, the time from a customer wanting the product or service to its actual delivery. The BCG work is wholly convincing on these specific points, as in its overall thesis that 'the future belongs to the time-based competitor'.

When, as the authors note, 'mass markets for goods and services are disappearing' thanks to the fragmentation of demand, the 'leading edge of competition' has to be 'the combination of fast response and increasing variety'. The 1990s are no world for the fat, flabby and slow. The new hard bodies of knowledge about quality, time, systems and much else, like all irresistible concepts, are in tune with the times – for the banes of business, from too much bureaucracy to too little creativity, must melt away before the organised effort of those who are lean, fit and very fast.

CHAPTER

17

General Foods: The Jump In Jell-O

A truism of the management times is that information may be the decisive force in the battle for markets. As with most truisms, the meaning isn't spelt out. But one clear example of applied information is the analysis of which businesses are, and are not, worth backing. If the received and interpreted information leads to a business being cut out, cut down or cut off from nourishment, there goes the market: by definition, the business can't grow and prosper.

Very often these no-go areas are being looked at through the wrong end of the information telescope. By looking through the correct end, managers can find true gold. Which end of the telescope does the famous Boston Consulting Group matrix employ? It encourages managers to classify their businesses as stars, wildcats (which might become stars), cash cows, and dogs. That's an ideal set-up for a far from ideal result: the self-fulfilling prophecy. The results run against a sermon that I've been preaching for many years: that the product life-cycle is not immutable.

Managers turn life-cycle into death-cycle by neglecting the potential, not of new ventures (with their high proportion of failures), but of old products which will generate new profits at minimal risk. A new text for this sermon comes from *Fortune*, which looked first at Richard Mayer, who had recently been made president of General Foods (the giant subsidiary of Philip Morris, which merged GF with its mammoth $12.9 billion Kraft purchase in 1989). Gazing afresh at the portfolio, he thought 'why not leverage some of the best-known brands in the world, Jell-O, Maxwell House, Kool-Aid – monster brands, monster equities that were capable of growth?'.

Under the previous management, Jell-O (the market leader) had been cursed as a cash cow. Shorn of investment, the cow lost sales by some 2 per cent a year. On simple arithmetic, Jell-O would have halved after three decades; by simple management, it would have died well before as the cow was reclassified as a dog. Mayer, though, invested most of a $50 million marketing budget in something called Jigglers – a jelly snack.

He threw in point-of-sale displays, premium offers and TV advertising (complete with an expensive star turn by Bill Cosby) of a kind the brand hadn't seen for years. Sales started to run 40 per cent above the previous year, and the Jell-O profits began to improve. Obviously, they couldn't continue to rise without continued enriching injections of marketing money.

Clark Equipment is a second such case. Its forklift business, losing money heavily, was regarded by some managers as a dog fit for destroying. But Leo McKernan needed more information. He broke the business down into its component parts (which is this top manager's good habit) to assess their strengths. He found three plus points: a strong brand, a good distribution system and high quality. The minus was high pricing. After $100 million in capital expenditure, in a year when Clark lost $60 million, McKernan brought down costs and hence prices. In consequence, earnings grew threefold.

McKernan's approach is unarguably right. The Boston matrix basically rests on analysis of market share and growth. The result of the analysis determines how you regard, value and ultimately feed (or starve) the business. But strict analytical parameters are nothing like enough. You need a far broader survey so that any business can be measured against the one yardstick which counts above all: if my entire livelihood depended on this business, what would I do? Liquidate, or devote body and soul to its nurture?

A family brewery in the Netherlands illustrates by far the more likely answer. Its non-alcohol beer was lagging hopelessly in the market. A family conference considered the options, and chose one that had never been tried before – by themselves or anybody else. They loaded trucks with cases of the brew and, over the weekend, visited every retail beer outlet in their small country. At every stop, they offloaded a case; whether or not the case was sold, the seller got a large discount. On the Monday, four fifths of the outlets reordered and the beer was on its way to a 50 per cent market share, obtained entirely without advertising.

Super-performance like that stems from devotion to the business, from refusing to accept given information as final. Underperformance stems from unthinking policies like giving a dog (or a cow) a bad name. Sometimes a dog is really doggy: McKernan abandoned Clark's crane business because the pluses were far outweighed by such heavy minus points – manufacturing, distribution and products were all deficient – that resurrection was uneconomic. But any business with a significant market share and established brand or trade reputation is innocent until proved guilty. Very possibly, the reason for the threat of cash cow status, or worse, isn't shortage of potential, but lack of informed ideas.

Much of the information on which the ideas can be based lies within the company – as in the GF and Clark cases listed above. Other data may lie outside the firm. The need isn't simply to gather the information, however, but to process and share what you have learnt, and to test and analyse the results. In the past that meant innumerable heavy reports, based on staffwork and passed by the staffers to line management. Small wonder that short cuts like the Boston Matrix became so popular. They saved a deal of wading through muddy waters. Today, thanks to the miracles of information technology, the company can become transparent – but only for managers who truly want to see.

CHAPTER 18

The Genie of the IT Lamp

Imagine the chief executive of a thriving, thrusting international company, sitting at his imposing desk, admiring the bronze pot purchased on a recent business trip to the East. He rubs the pot to enhance the sheen – and out pops an enormous genie. 'O, Master,' says the genie, bowing and scraping in the manner to which chief executives like to be accustomed, 'I bring you wonders beyond measure' – and then spells out the following benefits.

The Master can in minutes find any financial or other information he wants about the business of the company and its markets in any of its operations round the world. He can check on the whereabouts of any of his key people. He can communicate with them instantly anywhere in the world, and his memos and their replies will be instantly filed. He can monitor the progress of any project by calling up the relevant files, including files kept by other executives.

He can use all these powers to work on the strategic issues that concern him above all (literally) other executives. He can check his assumptions by running 'what if?' tests instantly. In doing this work, he can call easily on vast banks of information held outside the company, including rapid screening of possible acquisitions that might help the strategy along. All his mental doodles, memos to himself, notes of conversations – these, too, will be immediately filed for safe keeping and instant recall.

The Master glares at the genie, orders him back into the pot, puts on the lid and throws pot and genie out of his 23rd storey window. This is no fable, either. Many of today's senior managers are rejecting the genie. His name is the networked personal computer, and this isn't the dream of the future, or even the state of the art, but a tool as practical and available as the telephone. Without question, it will be as ubiquitous as the latter, which is another strange aspect of the mystery.

With something like 30 per cent of all PCs connected to others via a network by 1992, even if the rate of progress *halves*, every appropriate PC will be networked by the time the new century starts. Unless the galloping pace of information technology generates some new and unforeseen wonder, this will be the major mode of management activity; 'paperwork' will have become 'computer-work'. Senior executives now passing by on the other side are the spiritual descendants of the many managers who initially shunned the phone.

Once forced to swallow their aversion, those earlier technophobes found comfort in the illusion that this new-fangled communications device would enhance their control over subordinates. It didn't work out like that. Underlings found it easier to answer back when the boss was disembodied, and two-way management interchange was hesitantly born.

The networked PC truly does offer greater control. More, it provides the only visible solution to a besetting dilemma of modern management. That is the necessity to devolve power and responsibility while remaining both powerful and responsible. The chief executive must delegate authority all the way down the line: not only to the manager running an autonomous operation, but to the employee at a machine or a counter. The boss must know what is happening, and wants assurance that the results are desired and desirable. The genie, by providing information accurately, fast and in depth, allows senior management to supervise without sapping people's independence or hampering their effectiveness.

True autonomy demands the ability to take decisions without waiting for word from on high. This isn't a matter of management principle alone. Sluggish decision-making and needless second-guessing are major sources of competitive failure and excess cost. Work by the Boston Consulting Group (Chapter 16) has shown that the 'value-delivery system' is grotesquely inefficient. That is, from receiving an order to satisfying the customer, only 0.05 per cent to 5 per cent of the time expended involves activity of any kind; 95 per cent to 99.95 per cent of that period is spent just waiting around – and roughly a third of that barely credible wastage is spent waiting for management to make up its mind and to turn that decision into execution.

Without question, the delay factor applies as strongly in that 23rd floor executive suite as in the production director's office at the plant. Take typical chief executives. Will they, having read the last paragraph, immediately launch an investigation to check on the time taken by their 'value-delivery systems' and to instigate early action to compress the period, saving both time and money in the process?

First, the typical chief executive probably won't: the disease of executive inertia will take over. Second, if he is stirred to investigate, the absence of a PC network will make the process, and its monitoring, laborious and lengthy. Executive inertia thus feeds on itself – for that is the main reason why the genie is kept firmly in the pot. It's not that senior managers are lazy. They are mostly not only very busy, but too busy, partly through lack of these electronic aids, or aides.

The wordplay is significant. Much of the genie's offering can be supplied by aides: secretaries, personal assistants, researchers, corporate planners and the like. Why should the top manager bother to acquire what is already supplied? After all, nobody expects him to type his own letters or place his own phone calls (though one of Detroit's top managers reportedly did busy himself with the wines, salted nuts and music supplied on the company plane). What's the difference?

In the first place, working through all these acolytes consumes time itself. At accountants Touche Ross, senior people began using their PCs to produce finished documents and found themselves spending *less* time in total as the keyboard replaced handwritten draft, dictation and correction. Part of the difficulty is right there: the chief executive can get everything faster, and work more productively himself, but only if he uses the keyboard, and many of today's 50- and 60-year olds reject that out of hand.

That's not too far removed from refusing to use the phone because you don't like dialling. True, even a dab and willing pair of hands at typing doesn't let the computer genie out of the bottle. PCs have rightly been condemned as awkward and difficult to use, with tortuous manuals composed by sadistic engineers, and programs that require knowledge of codes devised by refugees from MI5. That era, though, is in the past. PCs are rapidly nearing the point of total ease of operation, responding not only to typed ordinary language, but to speech – and replying in the same normal lingo. The wizardry from now on will lie in the works, not the use.

The past inadequacies of computer suppliers, with their user-hostile products, have unquestionably left a hangover. Senior managers, too, have had miserable experience of costly data processing 'systems' which took years to complete, and then were pronounced obsolete as soon as they came on stream. Networked PCs are not a system in the same sense: the network is a carrier of many systems, and is itself composed of proprietary products, bought off the shelf, that are amazingly reliable.

The only problem with the products, in fact, is that galloping and mushrooming technology. The power of PCs has multiplied more than fifty times since IBM entered the market in 1981, while costs have headed smartly in the opposite direction; and the number of major suppliers (never mind the minors) makes for an embarrassing choice. Doubts over what to buy and when, bad past experiences, and keyboard phobia are all fodder for executive inertia – the disease which makes managements prefer the *status quo*, no matter how great its drawbacks, to any new order.

The ailment has many components. Change demands choice, and that involves risk – the risk of being wrong. Worse, as I wrote earlier in this book, changing to a new *modus operandi* means admitting that you *are* wrong. Dashing out to check the time consumed by your value delivery system involves accepting, as a premise, that for years your factory may have been needlessly devouring shareholders' funds. Even if the shareholders are you and your nearest and dearest, that isn't a comfortable or comforting thought. Bizarrely enough, it's more comforting to continue with the waste and the excess cost – up to a point.

That point occurs when the money, instead of running out of the factory, just runs out. Crisis is a wonderful cure for executive inertia. The absence of a PC network doesn't represent a critical threat; or rather, there is an insidious crisis which is all too easily ignored. The company which seizes the potential offered by information technology not only reduces costs but increases effectiveness. In marketing alone, one US company, for instance, slashed $3 million off its budget while gaining 10–20 per cent in sales force productivity. Another now takes two days instead of two weeks to roll out a pricing and promotional programme.

Such gains add up to the magic Michael E. Porter phrase 'competitive advantage'. By the same token, those who stay off the bandwagon – and remember that the networking of PCs is spreading fast – will encounter competitive disadvantage. Gains like those just quoted can be obtained without PCs, true. Moreover, they are functional, confined to departments far below the senior management eyries, physically as well as hierarchically. Staying aloof from such systems is feasible and only foolish to the extent that, unwatched, they may be under-provided.

But the networked PC is a management tool that achieves full effectiveness only when extended right to the top. And there resistance can be so entrenched that managers won't even sample the goods. One British multinational, for instance, was headed as the 1990s began by four able executives: only one, the finance director, had ever sat in front of a PC, and that was several years back, in a four-hour indoctrination course which failed abysmally. Very typically, a tide of PCs (unconnected and thus unable to communicate) had risen in the building without even lapping at the feet of the top floor inhabitants.

In another giant company, the name of a rudimentary management information network is very close to that of a popular brand of booze: the chief executive asked his secretary for the latter, and was amazed to find the former on his desk in the morning. Since the machine was sitting there, he tried it for a while, but back downstairs it went. The hang-ups are heavy and deeply rooted. That's why I called my book on this office revolution *Culture Shock*; and the reactions of the shocked are highly defensive.

Managers will protest, for instance, that computers can't manage, that the human mind must rule, missing the point that working through a PC is no different in principle from using pen and paper. The difference lies in the fact that the computer is faster, stores as it works, calculates brilliantly, provides information, sends messages, and so on – and, moreover, will do so wherever there's a telephone line.

One manager, hired by ICI after working for a computer company in North America, with a computer population of 1.3 per person, described it as going back to the Stone Age. No longer could he work from his home or his hotel room with all the facilities he had in the office. That's another crucial advantage. Very few managers are in the tycoon class, able to transport a phalanx of human aides in their globe-trotting footsteps. The genie enfolds all the aides in laptops that fit into briefcases, whose rise in power and speed is matching the sensational surge of desktop PCs before them.

Executives at all levels have succumbed to the mobile phone, because they know how to dial: more and more are succumbing to the mobile PC – which means they know how to use it. For up-and-coming generations, that is no problem. They have learnt computing as their fathers learnt to spell. The common complaint of their seniors, and a source of many corporate ills, is that they don't have enough time to think. The genie gives them not only more thinking time, but more thinking power. By holding back themselves, victims of culture shock hold back the company, and to no good end. Nothing can stop the revolution.

PART 4
HOW TO MAKE TOP MANAGEMENT RIGHT

CHAPTER

19

Campbell: Deep in the Soup

The best Japanese companies, no matter how great their success, have continued to seek enlightenment and improvement with indefatigable zeal. But Western management can be equally zealous for new lore. At Campbell Soup in Camden, New Jersey, for instance, the company took to heart W. Edwards Deming's powerful teaching on quality (Chapter 9). The company had soon sent 210 senior people to the Deming seminar, which lasts four days; it despatched 55 more people to university training in the necessary statistics; and gave 2,000 hourly workers a four-hour quality introduction.

Author Mary Walton (*The Deming Management Method*) doesn't report what this four-year programme did for Campbell's costs or quality, but it didn't save the company from deep trouble. In its 1989 financial year, profits were only $13.1 million on sales of $5.7 billion; dissident members of the Dorrance family wanted to sell; and the last patriarch's successor was abruptly changed. The ousted chief executive, R. Gordon McGovern, had brought avid enthusiasm for new management thinking to bear, but to no personal avail.

Not only did Campbell embrace the Deming method under his aegis; McGovern was also inspired by the 'intrapreneur' creed whose best-known advocate is author Gifford Pinchot III. Fifty general managers were told to run 50 business units independently and entrepreneurially in the spirit of yet another book, *In Search of Excellence*. That all sparked a new product splurge: 334 in five years. Yet in January 1990, *Business Week* reported that, while the 'mainstay condensed-soup line has been losing market share for years... new recipes haven't come along fast enough to keep earnings hot'.

The best you can say for the results of all that management lore, then, is that without it Campbell might have been even deeper in the soup. That's a very downbeat conclusion for such an upbeat philosophy. What went wrong?

For the answer, turn to another guru, Igor Ansoff, the father of modern strategic planning. As reported in Chapter 6, research has left him convinced that the key to survival, success and high profits in any business is the closeness of fit between that business and its environment. The degree of 'turbulence' in the environment determines how rapidly and continuously the company has to adapt its strategies. Today, turbulence is very difficult to escape: get out of step with the environment and you suffer rapidly in consequence.

Campbell's new product programme can't have been properly focused on the turbulent marketplace; rather, such a plethora of new products must have created internal turbulence of a massive nature. And that sagging share in condensed soups quite plainly indicates strategic mismatch. Hearing the right message will merely palliate the damage if you're doing the wrong things in the right way; do the right things the right way and the ideas of the gurus will return your investment a thousand-fold.

The role of the chief executive, though, isn't to act as conduit for the thinking of others: it's to be a thinker himself, and to stimulate thought throughout the company. The tragedy of Campbell's is that the business is fundamentally sound, both in its product line and in its tradition as a family firm. The dissension of the Dorrance clan, and its alienation from the executive management, robbed the company of that powerful motivation, carrying right through to multinational scale, which family ownership and personal identification can uniquely provide.

Families also have disadvantages. Campbell's seems to have fallen prey to some of the drawbacks: they notoriously include autocracy (and its aftermath), inbreeding, nepotism, difficulty in recruiting able outsiders, and (all too often) diminishing commercial drive over the years. According to a study by accountants Stoy Hayward and the London Business School, the No's have it: the average life of a family business is only 24 years, and only a fifth last beyond the second generation. Yet many of today's giants, with or without the founding family on the premises, haven't lost the founding drive.

In Campbell's own industry, close rival H. J. Heinz earned 32 times the former's 1989 net income on sales only slightly higher. Under Tony O'Reilly, as hard-driving an exponent of incentive-led management as he was an international rugby wing, Heinz raised its earnings per share by 15 per cent annually between 1979 and 1989. Campbell's earnings *fell* by an average of 21 per cent. Even before the latter's calamitous 1989, Heinz was earning twice as much on shareholders' equity. The Heinzes showed more wisdom than the Dorrances in choosing the executives to whom they entrusted their wealth.

In 1989 O'Reilly was fourth on food's key statistical test, net sales margin. The three firms ahead of him have an interesting link with each other and with Heinz. They were led by McCormick's under chief executive Charles P. McCormick, Jr ('Spice scion is cooking up bigger market share, higher profits', according to *Business Week*); Wrigley, led by William Wrigley ('Continues to chew up competition with inventive marketing, clever pricing and new products'); and Kellogg under a 39-year veteran, William Edward LaMothe ('Nutritious recipe: High margins pay for spending on new products, efficient plants, snappy marketing').

All four are family foundations, two led that year by family members, two not. The entrepreneur's great task, after maintaining the enterprising breakthrough, is to establish an organisation that will not only serve all immediate purposes, but outlive the entrepreneur, and grow and develop as it does so. In that last sentence, substitute chief executive for entrepreneur, and you have the essence of the chief executive's true role for the 1990s and beyond.

CHAPTER 20

The Once and Future Chief Executive

Is there any point in writing about the chairman as distinct from the chief executive, or asking whether they should be one and the same? In the interests of pure research, I was once going to tabulate how many of America's top chief executive officers, as listed in the *Business Week* executive compensation scoreboard, were also chairmen. Statistical effort proved unnecessary. Page after page was filled, not only by the legend 'chmn & CE', but in many cases (just to rub it in) by 'chmn., pres. & CEO'. It might be better to plump for the title 'supreme commander' and have done with it.

The title 'chief executive' has gathered currency remarkably thick and fast; in the US, not that long ago, the shots were mostly called by the company's 'pres.' or 'president'. Then, presumably through the endeavours of the management consultants from whom most newspeak flows, 'chief executive officer' or CEO began its surge. The process worked in parallel with the growing conviction that the supreme executive role is primarily strategic. Tactics, or operations, were a lower-order activity that could and should be left to the next rung down.

That strategic emphasis, in theory, removed the necessity to have a separate chairman who controlled neither strategy nor tactics. Today's theory, anyway, holds the board responsible for strategic direction, which makes the chief strategist the obvious, if not the only, logical choice to take the chair. Yet Western management is supposed to be moving away from the traditional mode of one-man dictatorship, which is benevolent only if the company is lucky, and towards collegiate styles.

The supreme commander motif, in reality, is substance, not mere form. After all, Tony Berry, the former overlord of one company, Blue Arrow, seems, on his own initiative, to have authorised a £25 million loan for remote purposes at a time when the group had plunged deep into trading troubles and controversy arising from its over-ambitious purchase of Manpower, Inc. You can get even more substantial than that. In the US, F. Ross Johnson not only single-handedly put his company, RJR Nabisco, in play for an eventual tally of $25 billion: according to *Fortune*, he pocketed, without the shareholders' knowledge, 'restricted shares' which on that takeover must have been worth $20 million. Was Johnson wholly ignorant of the concealment of his riches?

Whether it's a matter of accountancy or forcing through decisions, the truly chief executive has tremendous clout. For instance, under Roger B. Smith General Motors launched the $5 billion Saturn car project, designed to show that Detroit could out-Toyota Toyota. The signs, as of the Saturn's debut in 1990, were that it would actually achieve nothing of the sort. A couple of years back, expectation of that tough truth prompted a former GM senior executive to say this: 'If Roger Smith died tomorrow, the headline would read GM CHAIRMAN DEAD. The following day the headline would be, GM CANCELS SATURN PROJECT'.

Smith didn't die and the project, for good or ill, wasn't cancelled. But if that was true of a group employing 766,000 souls, how much effective power do the undisputed bosses wield on smaller stages? They are plainly a race apart, and see themselves as such, to judge by some research reported in the *Financial Times*. David Norburn, director of the Imperial College Management School, found significant differences between 108 chief executives who replied to his questionnaire and the three-apiece nominated members of their 'top management team'.

The chieftains had worked for the company for more years (by almost a quarter) and had job-hopped less (2.5 employers against 3.2). They thought themselves more authoritarian, and were more satisfied with their careers. They had worked in more functions within their businesses, and in more countries. This all suggests that they were more successful corporate careerists. You can understand the relative dissatisfaction of their immediate underlings, outraced to the top rung. Their less authoritarian style would follow equally logically from the fact that they have less authority to exert.

Has the resurgence of executive summitry been a response to managerial necessity – to the blunt truth, perhaps, that more open-plan management doesn't work? Or to competitive pressures that have forced a concentration of power where it is most effective, at the very top? In truth, as McKinsey's Ennius E. Bergsma has acutely pointed out, the big companies' inertia and complexity are drawbacks as heavy as their central bureaucracies. The latters' cost, he reckons, equates to almost a fifth of the total market value of debt and equity for America's 25 largest companies.

This analysis suggests that giants should indeed be striving to find simpler, more energetic, less centrally dominated life-forms, and certainly not investing more power in a chief executive surrounded by a costly corporate centre. The over-concentration of personal powers which are far better diffused could be the reason why the formidable human and physical resources of large companies too often run to waste.

The centrifugal tendency of executive power reflects not only organisational structure but human characteristics, shared by men (not women, note) brought up and even selected in the same mould, in the spirit of a great *New Yorker* cartoon. Two identical men are facing each other across a desk, shaking hands. One has just been given a job by his *doppelgänger* because 'I like the cut of your jib'. On the findings of a *Business Week* 1989 survey of The Corporate Elite, the would-be CEO should cut his jib by being born in New York State, attending an Ivy League college, going to Harvard Business School, and working his way up the finance and financial-control ladder (264 of the 1,000 CEOs). Merchandising/marketing (217) was a strong runner-up, easily outnumbering production/manufacturing (110) and law (73) combined. As a footnote, corporate development/planning (a mere 0.7 per cent) isn't a bright choice, while personnel (a single boss – Ronald Allen of Delta Airlines) is best forgotten altogether. Whatever the path, expect it to be a long one. The average age of the 1,000 was 56, and the average tenure under nine years: *ergo*, the typical American CEO of this vintage was 47 on taking office.

That may also be true in Britain, where the top executive profile, according to the 1990 survey by Korn Ferry, is broadly similar. It showed 70 per cent aged between 45 and 59, with 74 per cent having been in the job for under nine years. But 59 per cent had been with the company for 15 years or more. Half had degrees, but very few (9 per cent) had MBAs; 40 per cent were professionally qualified, over half of them as accountants.

The American figures must, however, exaggerate the corpocratic youth: no fewer than 133 of the CEOs got there by founding the company, which is most unlikely to have happened as late as 47 years of age. The question is whether the picture still holds in the frame. This is the class of 1933 by birth. The CEO taking office in the year 2000 will belong to the class of 1953, using the existing average age.

It's hard to believe that a gulf of twenty years, divided by the great watershed of the Second World War, won't produce some crucial differences. Indeed, who's to say that the average age of chief executive stardom won't be much younger, or the degree of stardom less starry?

In 1989, the executive search company Korn/Ferry International published a study whose very title, *Reinventing the CEO*, strongly indicated that radical change was afoot. Across the world, the respondents expected strategy formulation and human resource management to gain notably in importance, and marketing/sales and negotiation/conflict resolution to decline.

The 'biggest changes expected in management style' present a piquant contrast. The Americans expected a big jump in the importance of frequently communicating with customers, and with employees, and in 'readily reassigns/terminates unsatisfactory employees'. That isn't exactly what is usually meant by 'human resource management'; nor is it an attribute, given the mass sackings of middle managers and production line workers, which American CEOs seem to have lacked in recent years (except where they themselves are concerned). And the need to talk to customers is surely a crucial factor in the marketing/sales function which is, apparently, to diminish in importance by the year 2000.

The survey doesn't portray the CEO of the year 2000 with any great clarity – for one obvious reason. No part of a long questionnaire related to the crucial issue of corporate structure and the role of the CEO within that power system. The drift in all the answers concerning management style (on communications, sharing decision-making, personal appearances) was strongly towards more open management. But the nearest the questions came to substance as opposed to style was delegation: the US result, with an increase from 67.5 to 77.5 in importance (50 equalling 'moderate) between 1988 and 2000, was close to the global average.

The West Europeans were broadly in line with America on some matters. But they were notably less keen on frequent communication with customers, expected to use outside consultants much more, had less commitment to community and public affairs, looked far more to the world market, were less preoccupied with staff numbers, and, most surprisingly, attached less importance than the Americans to ethics. On delegation, though, there had been a great leap forward – from 60 to 85 per cent.

Both America and Europe also showed big jumps (76.3 to 92.8 per cent in the US, 74 to 97 per cent in Europe) in 'conveys strong vision of the future'. It's logical: the chief executive is the manager who should exert most influence over the corporate future. But how is the CEO to give shape to that future? Can the person who leads the upper executive echelons at one and the same time master the details of its present and bring its future into potential existence? This Superchief, whose concentration, at least some of the time, must be on that distant horizon, often has the least time – maybe the least ability – to focus on anything much further away than his nose.

Yet even the busiest chief executives sense, like the respondents to the Korn/Ferry survey, that conditions are shifting beneath their feet. In the 1960s, the emphasis was on aggression. Companies sought bosses, possibly victors in the marketing wars, who could lead the troops to bigger and better victories. In the 1970s, chief executives pondered over whether, in troublesome times, the defensive attributes had become central.

In the 1980s, the feeling of change appeared to swell. Gradually, as the technology and the capability of the business itself evolved, the computer-based office revolution laid down some of the lines of probability. As the 1990s began, the information technology breakthrough was at hand: the chief executive no longer faces the danger of being trapped in a welter of information that he can neither control nor absorb; instead, he has the opportunity of using much refined and far faster information to gain much more responsive command and control.

If you can't take that opportunity, the future holds the intimidating prospect of increasingly complex means of playing a game with more and more complicated rules. Already a waking nightmare exists: that the freedom of the chief executive to create has been restricted by the steady increase in day-to-day pressures. Every day, to these men, looms ahead with an agenda they haven't chosen. Their style is that of worried individuals, obsessed by the necessity to ensure that the group operations work smoothly – but who are themselves on a jagged run all the time.

The aircraft seat has become as familiar to many chief executives as the chair behind their desks, the place where they are supposed to sit and think about present and future alike. Chief executives have been complaining for years that they no longer plan but spend all their working hours controlling, ostensibly with a high degree of delegation; yet they even lack enough time to give delegation the supervision without which it collapses. So anxiety about possible failures of control gets added to the anxiety about pressures from above, although here the pressure is often self-inflicted.

The great bulk of the pressure (80 per cent on one informed estimate) comes from themselves. Part of that pressure is the chief executive's conviction that people above are leaning on him, or will lean unless his performance reaches an impossible perfection. This mild paranoia became intense when the predators began their prowl: in the US the reaction (the golden parachutes, poison pills, and so on) has increased the personal security of the directors – though often at the expense of the corporation's long-term interests.

The harassed and time-pressured chief executive is boxed into a situation where he can't perform satisfactorily either as overlord of the present or creator of the future. He is the bureaucratic descendant of the entrepreneurial boss, with none of the personal charisma and with far more detailed responsibility. But the ultimate truth about the globe-trotting, fire-quenching chief executive is that he is superfluous.

Paradoxically, the less the chief executive does in this sense, the more important the role becomes. The open secret is that a change in management style from the 'executive' to the 'chief' – a concept that is exemplified by the accounts of Akio Morita and Yutaka Kume in the following chapter – is essential, potentially effective and readily achieved. That way lies the true destination: the Once *and* Future Chief Executive.

CHAPTER 21

Sony:
The Magic of Morita

Strategy is what generals (or chief executives) get paid for; tactics are left to their subordinates – or should be. They are by one particular industrial leader, whose credo is exemplary:

1. Spend your time correctly judging future trends.
2. Leave details of daily operations to the responsible personnel.
3. Insist that they make consensus decisions.
4. Always approve what they ask to be done for short-term tasks.

The leader, not surprisingly, is a Japanese, Akio Morita, the chairman of Sony – and he practised what he preached, according to an account of the birth of Sony's Walkman. To an exceptional degree, this was the baby of the chairman. To quote Yasuo Kuroki, the director of Consumer Product Design, 'Mr Morita, as he claimed, was the project manager. That's the way he liked to think of himself. But what do you think? On something like this, *do you really think the chairman of the board would be able to serve as the project boss?*'.

The italics are mine, and the answer is obvious. Morita left 'details of daily operations to the responsible personnel': his major role was to sustain the project against the 'marked lack of enthusiasm' for the Walkman reported in a fascinating study in *Breakthroughs!* by P. R. Nayak and J. M. Ketteringham. Morita's method included a very rare meeting in his office with the unenthusiastic 'young engineers' on the project. This meeting had three significant aspects:

1. Kuroki told his people 'if you disagree with Mr Morita, feel free to say 'No'; unfortunately, they said nothing but 'No', and the meeting failed.

HOW TO MAKE TOP MANAGEMENT RIGHT

2. The key issue was the price, which Morita wanted to be low (35,000 yen) to attract teenagers. His ostensible subordinates, who needed 49,800 yen to break even, were insubordinate on the point because *'The division has a right to refuse'* (my italics).
3. Kuroki had to resolve the problem at a subsequent meeting with Morita and the staff. They agreed to cut their price by a fifth to 40,000 yen. Said Kuroki, 'It was not because the chairman instructed us. It was not a command, an order. We were very aware of the enthusiasm, the emotion in Mr Morita. We responded emotionally. We sympathised.'
4. Given an inch by this 'sympathetic' decision, Morita took a mile. He declared that the price would be another 7,000 yen less, which was 2,000 yen below the figure the division had originally refused, and he also set an 'impossible' four-month deadline for the product launch.

The cynic might well conclude that, for all the argument to and fro, the boss got his way in the end. But the division *did* have rights; the young engineers *could* argue their case and be heard; Morita *had* to win their consent before he could do as he wanted. In less highly charged circumstances, it's conceivable that the argument and the outcome could have gone the other way. That is never the case in traditional Western hierarchical management, where the power of decision resides firmly at the top, the divisions have no rights, and consent is no part of the deal.

Incidentally, Morita was wrong about the price. The Walkman sold, and in a sudden surge of demand, not to teenagers, but to the yuppy market, which would have swallowed the division's breakeven price without a qualm. Both Morita and the young engineers were acting on inadequate information about the market potential. Walkman's success simply proves that you can't keep a good product down – and in sensing that the product was good, Sony's chairman fulfilled his vital role of 'correctly judging future trends'.

It has to be said that other versions of the Walkman story exist, and that Morita's own account, in his book *Made in Japan*, projects his role in more masterly and masterful manner. But the *Breakthroughs!* version has the ring of truth, both in particular and in general. The Japanese chief executive possesses enormous powers in theory, but he exercises them in a context of consensus – if, that is, he exercises them at all.

In his book *Inside Japan* Peter Tasker argues that 'Generally, company presidents have nothing like the influence of their Western equivalents.... In extreme cases the president is little more than a corporate diplomat, of greatest use to his company when on the golf course with other presidents, clinching deals that were planned at lower levels'. Tasker notes that attached to the position is 'a degree of formal subservience unthinkable in a Western company'. The 'unthinkable' may be thought far more in the West than Tasker believes: equally, the influence of the president may be all the greater for being applied with circumspection and respect for other and humbler corporate citizens.

Nobody can miss the loud echoes of the Walkman story in the saga of Nissan's Maxima model, a smash hit launched after only 30 months of development time (eleven months less, as noted elsewhere, than the American record established by Ford). The project head told the *Los Angeles Times* about the role adopted by his president, Yutaka Kume. The latter 'made it so that he stayed out of design and he ordered all other managers to do the same. The president is not familiar with the product, so he doesn't make decisions about it'.

You can't say fairer, or truer, than that. There's magic in the unmagical formula. But detailed accounts of the way in which Japanese companies operate reveal a very different world from that of the typical Western company revealed by studies at the London Business School. The studies portrayed subsidiary managers, one after the other, coming to head office for dissection of their plans – which were often remade by unsupported decisions of the boss. Whose chief executive magic makes more sense: the creative magic of Morita or the black magic of those Western chief executives?

CHAPTER 22

The Nine-Yes Chief

Just as failure often points the way to success, so incompetence can define competence. Sir John Harvey-Jones, the saviour of ICI, which he raised from loss to Britain's first billion-pound manufacturing profit, toured a bunch of companies, several family-owned, for a television series entitled *The Trouble-Shooter*. He found trouble indeed: turned inside out, his findings are a résumé of what's wrong with top management stuck in the past and a recipe for what will be required for and from top management in the future.

With the greatest good humour, the trouble-shooter relentlessly exposed muddled minds, wishful thinking, basic incompetence, inadequate delegation, hopeless misinformation and management which is neither production nor marketing-led, but floundering in some morass in between. Many of his studies, what's more, seemed equipped by neither nature, nurture nor experience for their posts – middle or major. This recipe-in-reverse for the business leader of the future is a chief executive's questionnaire. It reads:

1. Do you have a clear strategy for your business?
2. Does that strategy include clear objectives, clear understanding of the market forces, clear grasp of the key factors governing success, and a clear programme of action?
3. Are all the above founded on a totally realistic assessment of strengths, weaknesses, current performance and future potential?
4. Are the professional standards of every function (including your own), and of every service rendered to the company, the highest possible?
5. Do all managers have full authority, freedom and resources to perform their own jobs superbly – and to contribute beyond the formal limits of those jobs?

6. Do the information systems tell you and everybody else accurately what they need to know, when they need to know it, and in a way that enables people to share the information freely and fully?
7. Do production, marketing, development, design and all other functions form a planned, collaborative whole?
8. Is that whole directed towards supplying customers in ways that enhance satisfaction, reputation, market share and profitability alike?
9. Do you employ only good people – and continuously improve and broaden everybody (this includes you) by education and training and, above all, by the working culture of the company and the content of their jobs?

The essence of the Nine-Yes Answer is timeless, which explains why it would make perfect sense to a good manager from between the wars. The difference, though, lies in immensely important changes. First, the urgency of the nine yeses has been intensified by the pressures of competition and the speed of technological and market change. Second, the ever-increasing complexity of modern business demands a degree of all-round expertise, constant monitoring and rapid deployment whose best analogy is with modern warfare. Third, as in warfare, business has quite recently acquired many conceptual and technological weapons that make difficult, near-impossible tasks much easier.

This introduces a fourth factor: the bounds of impossibility have been pushed right back. You can even, for example, manage under a monthly inflation rate of 90 per cent. The Brazilians, perforce, became rather adept at that hazardous game. Far from destroying growth, the inflation kept Brazil bounding along at a remarkable rate that, averaging 5.25 per cent per annum since 1900, almost untouched by all recessions and depressions, actually outgrew Japan and West Germany.

The Brazilians may be better managers, relatively speaking, than they know. To survive at all in an environment of inflation, they have had 'to plan, to control financial costs, to manage all the variables that may interfere in the functioning of the business, to spot new trends'. Again, that's a very fair recipe for the future chief executive. The words, however, are from an article in the business magazine *Exame*, whose main theme was that Brazil's small and middle-sized firms fall short on meeting the above prescription.

The case histories, though, show much managerial agility, like the gymnastics of one firm, making microcomputer safety equipment and peripherals, that achieved zero defects during the six-month period of its product guarantees – hence, no warranty costs. Nor did it give discounts, while demanding them for buying its components cash on the nail. Its rich reward was a net of 30–35 per cent on billings. The tactics of such sturdy survivors – including a storeowner who updated his prices every time suppliers changed theirs and bumped interest costs into all credit card sales – carry a lesson: they would also be mightily effective in a time of normal inflation.

Like hyper-inflation, crisis forces managers to manage in ways that, had they seen the light earlier, would have forestalled crisis in the first place. It forces companies to make the ripest use of the managerial talent which would have had exactly that forestalling effect. The pivotal defect which sacrifices talent and with it corporate prosperity is actually in the boss's hands – excessive operational responsibility at the summit. When Harvey-Jones was quizzing one boss about his dominance over all decisions, the man argued that his computer company's destiny depended so heavily on each and every one that, as its head, he absolutely had to shoulder the burden.

The trouble-shooter rightly didn't think much of this line, and nor would the Japanese (who in fact took that boss's manufacturing side off his hands when its losses became insupportable). The Japanese president is a non-playing captain or coach – not, like that chief executive, coach, centre forward, full back, centre half, goalkeeper, and every other position rolled into one. The Japanese recipe has an interesting reflection in Brazil, where Ricardo Semler, the young manager of a family engineering business, became a national and US celebrity through his turnround efforts and his book on the saga, *Turning the Tables*.

Semler operated on a blend of humanism and profit motive. The two are by no means incompatible. For example, he gave all employees a monthly balance sheet and profit and loss statement for both their units and the company. The message communicated by this reform is humanistic, but the knowledge and involvement conveyed enhance the business, whose turnover rose from $4 million to $50 million in a decade. As for delegation, Semler made a point 'of leaving sometimes. It's a good exercise, because during my absence everybody forgets who started all this'.

That's another test for the future chief executive. Can you walk away from the company in total confidence that it will be managed as well, if not better, in your absence? Progressive managers have gone away on sabbaticals in recent years. John Sculley did at Apple Corp., but this may not have been a success: some of Apple's later troubles have been blamed on the sabbatical. This, however, had less to do with Sculley's absence than with his brainwaves during the months away. The sharing of powers isn't the right management in itself. It's a means to that end.

Nor does the right management obviate the right and power to take decisions, including unpleasant ones. Semler's rise began with the sacking of one third of the workforce. Not 'democracy' but 'neo-democracy' will be the correct description for the company of the future, in which team production on the shop floor is matched by team management in the executive suite, and by specialists in between taking the key decisions. But even neo-democracy will without doubt qualify the chief executive's supremacy. The corporation may no longer wish to be seen to be led, to have at its summit a single person with the final authority to take the decisions – never mind how democratically they have been discussed.

Here, too, there's no real incompatibility. Intelligent self-denial like Semler's holds the key. The essence (as opposed to the charisma) of the chief executive is probably irreplaceable. In any grouping of human beings, activity tends to coalesce round a leader, otherwise the group loses focus. The chief executive will always be there: even if it's a secret one, hiding behind or concealed by a collective leadership. One-man bands love to boast of non-existent teams, but the growing complexity of business must turn the empty boast into a reality, and the chief executive into a team-leader.

The boss is consequently becoming less hierarchical, more the skilled orchestrator of disparate talents serving a common purpose. Curiously, that's not among the ten top areas of top man expertise ranked by Korn/Ferry (in the survey reported in Chapter 20) for either 1988 or 2000, unless it comes under 'human resource management' and/or 'negotiation/conflict resolution'. If the latter, that misses the whole point of collaborative, collegiate management, which is to move ahead by consensus rather than conflict.

The trouble is that in a society conditioned to simple hierarchies (the family, the school, the army, the university, the government) authority is expected to flow to the top, which presupposes that a top exists. But this isn't some immutable fact of human nature or of business organisation. Partnerships, especially in their early stages, are classic illustrations of collective management; and many corporations, effectively partnerships in their formative years, have kept the traditions of partnership alive without losing effectiveness.

HOW TO MAKE TOP MANAGEMENT RIGHT

In modern conditions, the flatter the organisation structure, the more effective the management is likely to be. The trend toward flattening out could be observed long before gurus like Thomas J. Peters, who has been preaching the gospel of 'beyond hierarchy', sang the praises of flatness. Its development, moreover, suits the appearance in management of a more democratic, less prestige-conscious breed of chief executive – and a younger breed, at that.

The general belief that chief executives are getting appreciably younger may (as the *Business Week* collective portrait in Chapter 20 shows) be misleading, a matter of appearance rather than reality. True, a rising proportion of chief executives tend to have dark hair (sometimes even real) and to play tennis or other vigorous sports, but this reflects trends in expectations. The top manager has had to live up to a younger image. Just as the female body seems able to adapt well to severe changes of fashion, so managers can mould their appearances. Some matching reduction in age has come about: but given the high average remaining, it can't be that great a fall.

In the debate between youth and experience, however, the truth has to be faced. If vision and creativity are the essence of management 2000, they are more likely to be found in the young. But, of course, young people grow old. That may partly explain the tendency of corporate performance to deteriorate as the chief executive's tenure lengthens. How do top people react once they have held four-star general's rank for a long time? Over-lavish pay and benefits put many executives in financial clover long before the standard retirement age, and will do so even if the latter comes down from sixty-five to sixty.

How is their motivation to be maintained? What will keep them off the prestigious committee, the lucrative lecture circuit, the unnecessary foreign junket, or the golf-course? Rafael Aguayo tells of the homily one guru delivered to an American trade association: 'While you are out on the golf course this afternoon, waiting for your partner to tee up, I want you to think about something. Last month I was in Tokyo, where I visited your trade association counterpart. It represents the roughly two hundred Japanese companies who are your direct competitors. They are now holding meetings from eight each morning until nine each night, five days a week, for three months straight' – with the aim of achieving a particular technological breakthrough.

For such Japanese managers, business itself, not its perquisites, is the seduction. The future chief executive will be the champion who can make the most successful use of resources, but with an added dimension: he must also be capable of doing so in face of that kind of unrelenting competition. The whole point of the arsenal of drive, tact, diplomacy, skill and negotiating ability which future chief executives are supposed to deploy is to enable the corporation to succeed in its business. That is mandatory. No company is well served by someone who creates all-round happiness but can't deliver the short to long-term results which are the lifeblood of the corporation.

The job, above all, is to set the style. But as hierarchies change, flat structures replace pyramids, and group management beats out the superior-to-subordinate mode, the concept and style of chief executives will change, too. They have always had the most demanding jobs in the company – nothing else justifies the high pay – and that isn't going to change. As Harvey-Jones found, a massive rise in professionalism and all-round competence is needed, but so is something else: the ability to achieve the Nine-Yes Answer through management that is permissive, democratic, participative, collegiate.

The essence of a Nine-Yes chief executive has to be not only even more numerate and technically and financially aware, but more decisive, objective, analytical and, above all, humane. The time has long passed when companies could be well led by top people who lacked those qualities; the time is coming fast when, without such qualities, they can't be led at all. The qualities needed exist in managers who are already alive, well and at work. If allowed to, those aptitudes and attributes will produce miracles.

CHAPTER 23

Chrysler:
The Cult of Iacocca

The changing nature of capitalism has altered the nature of the Superchief. Until after the Second World War, the manufacturing giants mostly made their fortunes by exploiting the economies of scale. With huge markets sewn up, vast installations operating at lower and lower costs, and prices whatever they cared to charge, the chieftains of Detroit, Birmingham, Stuttgart and the other smoke-stack zones of the West had no need, and generally little use, for a cult of personality.

Not so Lee Iacocca. When he was ejected into Chrysler by the grandson of Henry Ford, Iacocca found himself running a company that had no money and no models – at least, none of enough appeal to achieve recovery. The hastily created K-cars were adequate, but no more. The winning difference was created partly by Iacocca's own cult of personality. The chairman himself was the Unique Selling Proposition, the reason for buying a Chrysler rather than a Ford or Chevrolet. Appearing incessantly in Chrysler commercials, Iacocca became a mega-star: there was serious talk of running him for President. And Chrysler was saved, making the boss indecently rich in the process.

Iacocca's example hasn't encouraged many other corporate chieftains to go on television – perhaps fortunately, since the pundits query whether this aspect of cultism is a boon to the company, never mind the personality. But Mike Harper, head of the food conglomerate ConAgra, puffed special-diet frozen meals on the strength of his own recovery from a heart attack. Martin Shugrue embarked on the long and lonely task of persuading all concerned that the bankrupt Eastern Airlines was good for passengers and employees alike.

Everybody knows Victor Kiam, and the Remington razor that was so good he bought the whole company. Few know that Kiam was given a 'badvertising' award by the trade magazine *Adweek* in 1985. It didn't put him off. The longest runner in the US is probably its equivalent of Britain's turkey-touting Bernard Matthews, Frank Perdue, who started selling chickens on television in 1971. But one aspect of paid-for television stardom should start alarm bells ringing. A well-established stock market principle lays down that the larger the chairman's personality looms in the publicity, the stronger the sell signal for the shares. The theory behind the principle is simple: the man may be placing his ego before the corporate good.

An accompanying rule advises selling whenever the company concerned moves to a splendiferous new building. The two rules are related, since it's often the chairman with an inflated ego who orders the new premises. Conversely, when Sir John Harvey-Jones prematurely announced to the world that ICI was down-sizing its headquarters and moving out of London's Millbank (it didn't actually have anywhere else to go, and didn't), that's a strong signal to buy – as it proved in ICI's case.

At Smith Kline & French (later to become SmithKline Beckman) the opposite move, to shining new offices in Philadelphia, expressed the hubris created by the runaway success of Tagamet – the first effective anti-ulcer drug, and the first drug of any kind to hit a billion dollars in annual sales. The sell signal was absolutely right. The move was of a piece with the company's addle-pated diversification into scientific instruments (hence the Beckman) and its inept mishandling of the challenge from Glaxo's Zantac.

The errors explain why the Americans eventually sought refuge in the arms of Britain's Beecham Group. That firm's growth to stardom is instructive. Its rise in fast-moving consumer goods and pharmaceuticals was conducted throughout by Leslie Lazell, an ex-accountant who never sought publicity, never received adulation, was rarely (if ever) profiled, and never got knighted – let alone ennobled, like many far less worthy magnates. Iacocca, however, went on getting more and more conspicuous – and after a point, the more conspicuous he became the worse the company performed.

It took Chrysler from September 1979 to June 1981 to return to profit, but in 1982 dramatic re-rating followed: the shares rose in consequence by 419 per cent. By 1984, profits were rolling in at $2.38 billion, meaning that Iacocca's profits over three years had not quite equalled the losses of the previous three. In five years thereafter profits fell steadily to half the level of 1983; the share price in 1990

HOW TO MAKE TOP MANAGEMENT RIGHT

duly dropped to a level little above the stopping point in that wild upward ride of 1982 – and for good reason.

According to *Business Week*, the hero told his senior management in December 1990 that 'If you're not scared, you're too stupid to work here'. The scary financial facts were that, with a life-or-death, five-year $15 billion product programme coming up, the debt-laden company had been losing cash at $2 billion a year, and had $3.6 billion in underfunded pension liabilities hanging over its head. In the first two months after that scary meeting, sales dropped by 24 per cent, following an 11 per cent drop in 1990 market share. Underinvestment in new products when the good times rolled was plainly and painfully coming home to roost.

The blame for this reverse turnround lies, in theory, not with Iacocca alone, but with the board of directors. The blame, however, is built into a system which subjugates the board to the boss. That's nowhere more obvious than in the matter of top executive pay and perks, where the board in general and the non-executives in particular are supposed to have the final word. It's usually a word of assent, no matter how outrageous the amounts involved – like the $7.2 million the boss of Ford earned one fine year, inspiring a critic to say, 'You reach a point of asking "How high is up? How high is tolerable for a public corporation?" '.

Much higher, evidently. The critic was Iacocca. A year later he pocketed $11.4 million and the next year, not to be outdone by himself, made it $20.5 million. In 1990, for the third year running, Iacocca headed the *Business Week* list of executives who gave shareholders the least for their pay; in 1986–88 he collected $41.9 million during three years when shareholders received only a 38 per cent return; in 1987–89, the score was $25.2 million for a minus return to investors of 10 per cent.

No doubt, Iacocca collected his reward without a murmur of boardroom dissent. The suspicion must be that companies would be better run if more dissent were possible, if the board ran the boss somewhat more and, most important of all, if the boss ran the board a great deal less.

CHAPTER 24

The Boss and The Board

The dominant boss's final opportunity to dominate his board is terminal: when a successor must be appointed. Henry Ford II spent much time and thought on the succession. After ousting Lee Iacocca, the eventual decision to step down in favour of Philip Caldwell was one of Ford's best. The family's stake is only a shadow of Henry I's total ownership; although the aura and the memory linger on (as does the presence, in the shape of younger and by no means quiescent Fords), that succession was possibly the last assertion of the dynastic rights of the Fords.

After all, Henry II's name, as he liked to point out, was over the door – for in the beginning was the Founder. Most of the world's great businesses (and, for that matter, most of the small and middling) trace back to a dominant figure or double-act, and much of the power and deference accorded to the boardroom boss has flowed down the generations from those creators of commercial genius. Often, they towered above contemporaries at a height barely imaginable today. Late twentieth-century commerce abounds with monumental egos; yet, compared to J.P. Morgan, John D. Rockefeller and Ford today's giants, if not pygmies, are decidedly undersized.

The modern chief executive doesn't need to fit that oversized mould. Great companies have great founders because it takes a driving genius, a prime mover, to animate an organisation and move it bodily forward, to set the style and generate the ethos. The self-made entrepreneur in the classic style, a demon for work, highly paternal, immensely innovative and deeply thrifty, can still create economic miracles; Japan has thrown up many such models. With luck and judgment, the prime mover finds a professional successor to move the business mightily on – like Ryuzaburo Kaku, who took

Canon, the entrepreneurial creation of a medical man, from modest status to sales of $10 billion.

The Canon founder continued to preside as chairman of the board, just as Robert W. Galvin, a preternaturally successful heir at another $10 billion company, Motorola, wielded his very active influence as chairman of the executive committee, with a professional chief executive (George Fisher) running the show. Those circumstances get nearest to the ideal relationship between boss and board. Cases like that of RJR Nabisco get furthest from it: when an exploitative top management includes the board among the exploited.

Exchanging ill-use for ideal isn't easy when the chief executive, wrapped in the full panoply of an imitation founder, is chairman as well. Even then, if properly used, the board can be a powerful tool at the disposal of the chief executive for better purposes: Sir John Harvey-Jones, as part of his brilliant rejuvenation of the chemical giant, ICI, slashed the board numbers and used the reduced team ably and deliberately. As he points out, though, only one person, the boss of bosses, 'can develop the board as a collective organisation, handle, select and motivate its members, and manage its work'.

That quotation from his book, *Making It Happen*, makes the real point: all is at the chief executive's option. If he so chooses, the board can become 'purely ritual dancing', or at the other extreme, a place for 'seemingly endless, fruitless debate'. Plainly, any institution which is wholly at the mercy of one individual has no institutional power at all. Anyway, isn't the board supposed to monitor and to that extent control the actions of the chief executive? How can that be accomplished when in reality it's the chief executive who controls the board?

The views of powerful business leaders on the role of the board are as diametrically opposed as those last two questions imply. Take these two quotes: 'I think the owners of the company should be represented by the directors. That has ceased to happen at a lot of companies where management dominates the board.' So spoke Benjamin Rosen, the prolific venture capitalist who is a non-executive chairman of Compaq Computer, whose board in 1991 duly ousted the founding chief executive.

Another *Fortune* interviewee thought quite otherwise: 'The role of the board is not to be a contender against management. The role is to help management.' The speaker here was Harold S. Geneen, who came to great fame as chief executive of ITT, where nobody on the board, you may safely bet, said 'boo' to the boss. On the other hand, the retired, non-executive Geneen was instrumental in booting out his own chosen heir, which the latter may not have construed as help.

Oustings are relatively uncommon; at major US corporations, the topmost executive ranks have remained largely intact throughout the eras of scandal, predatory prowling and absolute or relative failure. The main exceptions are the several chief executives (like those of RJR Nabisco and Revlon) whose golden parachutes opened so lucratively on takeover. One American academic regards the latter phenomenon as a gain for stockholders, rather than the boss, because they positively encourage the management to drive the company into the arms of a purchaser, for a price which always exceeds the current stock market value.

This theory has somewhat strange connotations. Could a chief executive deliberately run a company into the swamp, vote himself and other top executives inordinately golden 'chutes, provoke a predatory bid and then gleefully depart? Many recent US events appear to follow exactly that scenario. It may be mere coincidence that RJR Nabisco's F. Ross Johnson, in proposing his group's buy-out and break-up, followed a very similar line of reasoning. Nothing but a leveraged bid, he argued, could create a satisfactory rise in the share price.

Johnson's bold move ended in failure, from which he achieved financial gains totalling $53 million. But the plan was at first rubber-stamped by his board. The directors were then driven towards a full and final reassertion of the independent powers of the board against the boss. But that bizarre story of true greed gives a vivid picture of how concentration of powers in one forceful man can emasculate an entire board. There is a line drawn somewhere; but only when the chief executive oversteps that line does his position weaken and the board regain its full legal powers.

On this reading, the board in normal circumstances is only fully itself when tackling the top succession. The worst of these times comes when the best of leaders has to be replaced. The first problem is that finding one towering genius after another is no likelier than drawing two straight flushes in succession. The second, less obvious, but equally severe difficulty is that the higher the departing geniuses tower, the more likely they are (like Henry Ford) to exercise a decisive voice over their successors.

Their sentiments may genuinely echo these: 'I built the damn thing. I really would like to have somebody who I really could say with pride, "He can run it" '. The ungrammatical speaker, Harry J. Gray, is quoted by Harvard Business School professor Jeffrey Sonnenfeld in his study of chief executive departures, *The Hero's Farewell*. Gray began by saying that 'boards have a tendency to create mediocrity', a bitter observation on his own ousting from United Technologies at 66. But Gray had previously pulled the rug from under his heir-apparent in so outrageous a manner that his own upsetting became inevitable.

For all his protestations about wanting an excellent successor, Gray was typical of chief executive heroes (and bums, for that matter) in trying, no doubt subconsciously, to ensure the opposite: that nobody would ever outshine their own departed glory, if any. The usual consequence is that, although their own glory may survive, their creation dims – as at Pan Am, whose creator, Juan Trippe, made doubly sure by picking a terminally ill successor.

Sonnenfeld breaks down his chief executive departures into four types: monarchs, generals, ambassadors and governors. Rupert Murdoch, the creator of the News International media empire, is plainly a monarch; he belongs among the types who, if they follow the author's prognosis by staging monarchical departures, will keep right on to the end of the road. Monarchic successions are often the messiest, especially if the ruler (usually alone in the belief) thinks his son can succeed, in both senses of the verb.

The Lords Hanson and White, typically enough, in 1991 declared their intention to stay on at Hanson Industries into their 70s, an announcement that produced some indignation, but not sufficient. White's *modus operandi* at Hanson, though, sounds less like a monarch's than a general's, given that, despite his decisively shaping hand and unchallenged rule in the US, he stayed far from the front line. White never visited any of the many companies he bought (and sold); didn't even know some of the men who made his money; and never visited his own head office in New Jersey.

That style couldn't be much further from the compulsive interference of Geneen, nominated by Sonnenfeld as a general. The distinction between Geneen-type generals and monarchs isn't very convincing. 'Ambassadors', in contrast, seem to behave more like constitutional monarchs, to judge by the good example of IBM's Tom Watson, Jr. He took immense pains throughout his reign to surround himself with able satraps and a strong, continuous culture, and abdicated accordingly.

The difference between these ambassadors and 'governors' such as Textron's Royal D. Little, who walked cheerfully away from his self-made empire, is that people like Watson retain a close interest in their businesses and their successors. But governors, according to

Sonnenfeld's research, have the largest rise in profits over their last two years: their average is 89 per cent. The monarchical hangers-on tend to preside over declining profits, not least because of their own failing powers and fawning courtiers.

The remedy is clear technically, but difficult to apply psychologically, because of the dominance of dominant men over those who in theory are supposed to control them. The late, disgraced Robert Maxwell is said to have observed that boards of directors should always be an odd number, and always less than three. Under his kind of leadership, no board can be trusted to ensure, as it should, that superb succession arrangements are in place when the presiding genius is in his prime. Boards should also insist on statutory retirement, with a clean cut-off in executive powers. They should give the hero only one vote, and never a casting one, in the selection of his successor.

All of that – and there's more besides – implies a corporate culture far removed from today's top-heavy norm, which exists even in groups whose sitting top tenants are blessed by neither heroism nor genius. Only an open culture, in which the chief executive works collegiately with others of equal ability, can protect the company from what Honda (where the great man's succession was managed brilliantly) calls 'insideration'. A true collegiate performance is needed, above all, when the succession system hasn't worked, and the board must decide not only the company's fate, but its own. More often than not, 'outsideration' is the only answer.

Outsiders like Bob Baumann, the American who turned Britain's Beecham into the transnational SmithKline Beecham, the world's third largest drug company, can perform very effectively. His appointment, from outside both the society and the industry, was a virtue made by necessity. The board, impelled into making the change by profits stagnation, had properly exercised its ultimate duty. The profits problem was the indirect, long-term result of a great general, Leslie Lazell, erring at the last: hand-picking as successor somebody who couldn't match his own brilliance in fast-moving consumer goods and had no close connection, either, to Beecham's second core in drugs.

That's the central issue. Whether the chief executive is monarch, general, ambassador or governor makes no difference: all the titles imply too much power for hired hands. They have no right to be more than first among equals, a genuine *primus inter pares*. The germs of such an evolution, towards a chief executive who is distanced from executive management by a colleague exercising day-to-day powers, can be discerned in the increasing influence of COOs, or chief operating officers – now scattered right across the spectrum of US industries.

The fact that two high-flown PC companies, Apple Corp. and Compaq, took the COO route as the 1990s began (see Chapter 49) is significant. The grown-up high-tech start-ups, dependent on brainpower and speed of movement, are starting to influence the way managements in other, slower businesses behave. For long, every worthwhile management authority has disliked the chief executive being chairman as well: chief executives don't, especially those who are also chairman, or intend to be. But truly splitting the roles means sharing power, which like hot air (and often accompanied by it), tends to rise to the top: so that an Iacocca, for example, can hang on to power long after he has ceased to exercise it successfully.

Chrysler lost the great man's appointed (but not anointed) successor as Iacocca stayed on – and on. In early 1991, when the chairman was nearing 67, *Business Week* reported that 'With Chrysler's outlook deteriorating rapidly, the board has extended Iacocca's contract indefinitely'. The day of retirement was only postponed, but the day of Chrysler's new dawn had also been put off, perhaps for ever. Iacocca's true task was to convert the company from perpetual also-ran into a true match for the Japanese. They have been crowding Chrysler for room in the US market, and still are. That's only one of far too many good (or bad) examples of why, for the good of the boss, the board, and the company, power needs to move decisively downwards – and stay there.

PART 5
HOW TO CREATE THE SUPER STRUCTURE

CHAPTER 25

Ford:
The Plutocrat's Puzzle

When Henry Ford II was making his long-term preparations for his own retirement and replacement, he commissioned the management consultants McKinsey & Co. to advise him on what should be done. Their advice included the following comment:

'You are seeking to institutionalise a permanent management system that encourages innovation and new ideas and allows intuition to co-exist with systematic thinking.'

That was in 1978, and the sentiments may partly have been influenced by the client: even after the end of his business days, Ford kept a copy of the General Motors organisation chart on his wall. The GM system created by Alfred P. Sloan had impressed Ford mightily as he wrestled with the shambles left behind by his grandfather. The grandson wanted to create a Ford system all his life, without knowing how to achieve that end.

He did, however, know many things, including how to pick people whose strengths offset his own deficiencies. His successor management did the old boy particularly proud. Under the leadership of Donald Petersen, Ford achieved an astonishing run-up from 16.6 per cent of the US car market to 22.3 per cent: the resulting surge in profits took Ford past GM for the first time, as net income more than doubled between 1985 and 1988. Outsiders had no doubt as to the cause. A sharp rise in quality and drop in costs, giving Ford a clear lead among American car-makers on both counts, had been reflected in a successful, team-managed stream of new products.

Yet Petersen left early at 63: according to a *Fortune* story in February 1991, he was pushed. 'The Odd Eclipse of a Star CEO', said the headline. But the odd eclipse of a star company is the real story. Ford's market share, on calculations by DRI/McGraw Hill, is heading for a fall from nearly 15 per cent in North America, Western Europe and Japan to 13 per cent by 1995. While that is only a prediction, it would follow logically from a fact. The average age of model lines, two years older than GM's in 1988, was now level at around five years; but Nissan, Toyota and Honda all clustered around two years or less.

The magazine reported that 'a 20 per cent chunk' was Ford's target cut in the white-collar payroll as the result of plans 'to eliminate staff positions and increase spans of control and the independence of people down the ladder'. The report noted that this was 'a big cultural leap for a large bureaucracy like Ford's, where vice presidents write memos on blue paper and everybody else uses white'. On the product side, the 'shortfall during the Petersen era, especially in new engines' had demanded a $7 billion-a-year catch-up programme that would have strained profits even without the car sales recession of 1990-91.

Just as bad, the team-based product development that produced the best-selling Taurus and Sabre models turns out to have been a one-off exercise. In 1990, an English executive vice-president, Alex Trotman, set out to break down 'the remaining barriers between Ford's huge functional organisations: design, product engineering, factory engineering and sales and marketing' via a single team of 50 line executives representing all the functions. For the new Mustang, Trotman formed a 'skunk-works team of 20 young designers, engineers and product planners. By putting them together under one roof, he hopes to cut costs by speeding communication and reducing confusion'.

At Honda, the corporate vision statement has three elements: quality, reliability and communication. The last, too, seems to have been sorely lacking at Ford; moreover, the new Mustang on which the skunk-works team had started communicating was the *1995* model – Japanese makers like Honda have already brought development time well below this level. That's because of the culture established by Soichiro Honda, who personally worked on new products while others managed the corporation. Yet Petersen had risen to the summit through his track record as a product planner.

Once at the top, however, his thrust seems to have evaporated into internal politics. His predecessor, Philip Caldwell, complained that 'the words were there, but words don't get it done. ... Instead of delegation, there was abdication'. That is a severe criticism of both men – and, for that matter, of the other non-executive directors who eventually forced Petersen out. After seeming to take the company a giant step towards Henry Ford's objectives, they allowed it to slip backwards.

The ideal is to achieve continuous progress. You will never get that from a system in which top managers can commit the company to such large errors of commission and omission like Ford's overpriced purchases (of which the £1 billion buy of Britain's troubled Jaguar was certainly one), or under-investment in engines, or leaving bureaucratic strangulation at work. Those are the kind of sins which the next management has to undo – while, very likely, because of the system, making similar blunders of its own.

That's fits-and-starts management, which will always occur until the culture of continual progress is built into the management system, starting at the top. That was the truth which Henry Ford II failed to grasp. In the 1990s, the 'institutionalisation' and 'permanent system' after which he hankered seem to be the antithesis of 'innovation, new ideas and intuition'. He was right to want the latter so badly. But they feed on impermanence – in other words, change and progress. The need is not that of 'institutionalising' innovation and new ideas, but of never institutionalising anything at all.

CHAPTER 26

The Direction Of Thrust

The direction of thrust must determine where anything ends up – from a projectile to a corporation. It follows that, if the end-result is unsatisfactory, like that of Ford after the first fine run of post-Henry success, something must have gone wrong with the direction of thrust. That is plainly the responsibility of top management. So what's the thrust of its own work? Is it inner-directed, centring round the politics and policies of the board and executive committee? Or is top management thrusting outwards?

Ostensibly, these days, it's outwards: every effort is devoted to satisfying or, better still, delighting the customer. This desire encompasses every activity from defining the market in the first place to following up a sale in the last. So much for theory. In practice, many activities in the higher management spheres have no relation to the customer at all. Most deals are in this category: though mergers and acquisitions are heavy users of management time (not to mention corporate money), very few are market-driven.

Except where purchases genuinely overlap, there can't be any benefit to existing customers. Even in overlap cases, benefit doesn't follow automatically. The elimination of competitors is as likely to abuse the customers as delight them. But if external wheeling and dealing devour time, what about the internal variety? Any effort that's directed, not externally towards the customer, but internally, towards management itself, stands guilty until proven innocent.

The case could be made that, since the organisational effectiveness of management ultimately determines the level of customer service and satisfaction, the internal preoccupations in the executive suite ultimately determine the effectiveness in the market place. That calls to mind the oft-heard justification for prestigious projects in aerospace – that the commercial spin-off foots the bill. That dodges the issue of whether the progress couldn't be better and far less expensively achieved by aiming at the primary target, instead of making it a secondary objective, and a dubious one, at that. Where, for instance, are the money-spinning spin-offs from the Concorde supersonic airliner?

To put it as baldly as possible, who is boss matters far less than what is bossed. Expressed more subtly, the difference between a well-managed company and a bad one is that, when managers change in the good business, nothing else does – nothing, that is, to do with the direction of thrust. In the more typical company, the new manager, as a matter of principle, abolishes or reverses all of his predecessor's work on which he can lay his hands.

To give one example, when the guard changed recently in the British subsidiary of a US multinational, so did the strategy with which the deposed boss was associated. He had tried to convert the sales force from selling single products to marketing whole systems; to create a collaborative, team-based management; to upgrade the customers' perception of the business from basic hardware to top-of-the-market, state-of-the-art leadership. His successor threw out the lot in favour of gung-ho, quota-filling marketing.

He also threw out many of the inherited managers – some within weeks. Experts in so-called outplacement, the euphemism for finding jobs for sacked executives, report that three quarters have had a new boss within the previous two years. The sacked managers, moreover, are on average abler than the comrades they leave behind – an ability they prove by their performance in their new companies. Maybe the shock of dismissal generates a higher degree of motivation. Nobody wants to be fired twice in quick succession, and damaged self-esteem needs to be rapidly repaired. But the picture is still alarming.

Managers capable of excellent performance are painfully and expensively removed from companies every day for reasons that have nothing to do with their capacity, or even with themselves. Their boss has changed, or policies have changed, or both. Or poor financial results have precipitated a cost-cutting drive. Or a bout of internal politics, the game of managerial musical chairs, has left them with nowhere to sit.

The essence of a consistently successful corporate culture is that changes in management do not produce sharp changes in policy or a chain reaction of appointments and disappointments. The overall direction of thrust is the same, not only from year to year and manager to manager, but from generation to generation. The result is steady-state expansion, in which Japanese companies have specialised to such profound effect. Its opposite is fits-and-start growth, to which Anglo-Saxon companies are extremely prone.

Some fascinating research by strategic consultants, the Kalchas Group, throws searching light on what produces both the fits and the starts. The consultants' object was to discover why some share prices went to a premium over the market, while others lagged. This isn't a matter which much troubles the dreams of managers on the Continent or in Japan, but in the equity-dominated markets of London and Wall Street the share price is a matter of grave concern – so much so that one multinational chief executive keeps a constant watch on this one number on a desktop terminal.

Yet the share price is almost the only corporate parameter outside management's control. The received wisdom on how best to elevate the price is to raise the rate of growth in earnings per share, which theoretically produces a multiplier effect: the higher the eps growth, the higher both the price and the price-earnings multiple, because the market especially values fast eps expansion. The problem is that it doesn't: using the share prices of 500 companies and five years' performance. Kalchas could find no correlation between rapid eps growth and the market rating of the shares.

So what does achieve a premium ranking? The answer is a fit, followed by a start. When companies lose their way, or are thought to have strayed, their shares go to a discount: in 1987, this averaged 9 per cent for one group of twenty companies. They were subsequently re-rated until, in 1990, they stood at an average premium of 21 per cent. A statistician would recognise the phenomenon at once: the variation round the norm is swinging like a pendulum, first down, then up, and the norm itself is shifting along with the underlying improvement in earnings.

But what produces the improvement and the swing? The twenty managements all made a new start. This meant following three simple principles:

1. They chose the businesses they would exploit and improve.
2. They disposed of others no longer wanted on voyage.
3. They aggressively invested and acquired to boost the retained companies.

The most immediate impact was obtained from the second and most negative of the policies: disposing of businesses. The mere announcement pushed up the price-earnings ratios – from 13.4 to 14.4 in the case of a sale called Reedpack. This packaging business belonged to

Reed International, which has built up massive US interests, led by its purchase of the Cahners magazine group, in its bid for media greatness. Reedpack was a July 1988 management buyout, or rather sell-out. Reed was made to look extremely foolish in 1990, when a Scandinavian company bought Reedpack, sold to the management for £600 million, for double that sum.

By any standards, that's inefficient wheeling and dealing. The criticism applies not only to sales, but to buys. Reed bought Travel Information Group for £525 million at 29 times earnings when its own multiple was 13; by thus diluting its equity, the management committed what the conventional wisdom supposes to be a deadly financial sin. But this vice is typical of the uprated twenty as a group. Their acquisitions, on average, were rated 13 points higher than their own shares. So much for the conventional wisdom.

The saving grace lay in the restricted size of the purchases, never more than 25 per cent of the buyer's own capitalisation, and their relevance. These were what Kalchas calls 'bolt-on' or competitor acquisitions, with buyer and buy overlapping in turnover by at least 70 per cent. In other words, the sales and purchases alike tightened the focus of the companies. Within that narrowed focus, the up-rated firms followed six other important guidelines:

1. *Financial conservatism.* Gearing was kept below 50 per cent.
2. *Continuous improvement in efficiency.* Net margins were raised by more than 10 per cent annually, and working capital days reduced by the same amount.
3. *Strengthening management.* Within an overall context of executive stability, they raised remuneration substantially and gradually introduced new talent at the top level.
4. *Raising investment.* Capital expenditure grew 10 per cent faster than sales, while more was spent on both R&D and training.
5. *Innovation.* Higher value-added products were launched to improve gross margins by more than 2 per cent annually.
6. *Market penetration.* Shares of major markets were increased by more than 5 per cent a year.

As a fresh start, this seven-point programme is certainly convincing, although, as noted, the impact on the market rating depended partly on the new start's contrast with the previous fit. That fit, though, almost certainly represented the ultimate failure of an earlier start which, no doubt, achieved equally good results in its time. Instead of continuity, successive managements create violent discontinuity – so that Reed, having started as a paper and packaging company which acquired subsidiary publishing interests ended up (at least for the present) as a media group with no paper and packaging at all.

What's gained on the swings (or the starts) is often significantly lost on the roundabouts (or fits). Initially, the post-Henry Ford regime followed much of the seven-point programme above. It missed out on an eighth. That point is far more important than all of them put together, for the simple reason that it does put them all together. The Ford successors did not create a direction of thrust that would carry the company forward beyond its short-term financial objectives – and indeed well beyond themselves.

The culture of the company was geared to the performance of the share price, as were the personal rewards of the top management: Petersen pocketed $18 million between 1986 and 1988, when profits had already peaked and were about to start on their way south. It goes without saying that these rewards were astronomically beyond the moderate ratio of top to average salaries (only 10 to 1 in Japan) that is believed to generate the best corporate performance – and that ratio is a real measure of the otherwise hard-to-grasp concept of corporate culture.

If the direction of thrust is the enrichment of the top management, together with the enhancement of its power, both will very probably result; but the consequences for the corporation can be calamitous. Look back at the seven-point programme for corporate revival, and you can see how badly Ford had slipped. The *continuous improvement in efficiency* seems to have stalled. *Capital investment* was allowed to become inadequate. The same was true of *product innovation*. The drift in *market penetration* which Ford has experienced on both sides of the Atlantic duly resulted.

The right direction of thrust starts at the top. That's why the world-class Belgian steel wire and cord manufacturer, Bekaert, was exceedingly wise in the way it began its Total Quality Management programme. At 100 years of age, Bekaert is more venerable even than Ford, but it has been better at learning the necessities of modern times and management. It kicked off with a project directed at improving the quality of the board's own work, coupled with a training effort that started with the chief executive and his immediate cohorts – and carried on the whole way down.

Those are the magic words. Carry that kind of thrust *the whole way down* and it will also carry the company into the future – a future that is seamless, both from year to year and throughout the business.

CHAPTER

27

Guinness:
A Tale of Two Boards

The board of directors sounds like a fine place to be, and so it is – provided the company is also fine. But as non-executive members of the Guinness board must have reflected during the long dark nights, after Ivan Boesky had blown the whistle on the scandal which sent their chief executive to gaol, even fine old companies can hit foul weather. Then, all the boardroom seats suddenly become very hot.

At Guinness, chief executive Ernest Saunders had recently become chairman, symbolising a personal ascendancy which was only ended by the scandal itself. Saunders and his war cabinet (including people who weren't on the payroll, let alone the board) committed the company to massive illegal payments in the battle for the Distillers whisky giant. The tale that unfolded in court had many ramifications, but it certainly reinforced doubts over how effective, even how significant, a board of directors really is.

A lowest common denominator united Guinness and Distillers. Both predator and prey had entered the 1960s in proud possession of what the 1980s deemed most precious assets: great, powerful, world-wide brands. Guinness stout was virtually a monopoly, brewed to different strengths for different world markets – at its strongest where the supposed aphrodisiac powers were most in demand. Distillers' whisky brands like Johnnie Walker, Vat 69 and Haig had been attacked successfully by rank outsiders, but were still reasonably powerful. Gordon's Gin reigned supreme.

By the 1970s, however, both the greatness and the power of companies and brands alike had been vitiated by management that, in retrospect, seems not only witless, but almost wanton. At Distillers, the cardinal sins were, first, complacent failure to react to competition from the outsiders; second, inept decisions when the competitive inroads become so severe as to force belated reaction;

third, the innovative inertia which missed opportunity after opportunity (for example, the birth of the single malt boom); and finally the lack of cohesion that redoubled the impact of these defects. Distillers became a classic example of reverse synergy, the process which makes the whole worth less than the parts.

A sure method of reaching that end is to add too many parts, like the 150-odd businesses which Ernest Saunders swept away at Guinness while getting down to two sorely neglected tasks: resurrecting the main brand and recruiting adequate management. Distillers, too, had embraced the seductive idea that, the greater the number of eggs, the more valuable the basket. The shared error was to view historic brand portfolios as liabilities rather than assets. Because growth in a mature business is constrained by natural forces, the two managements turned their attention to supposedly greener pastures.

Good marketers know that the most valuable customer in profit potential isn't the non-purchaser, but the purchaser. That's a fruitful analogy for brands. The old-established product offers the greatest profit potential, because all gains are incremental. The neglect of Guinness and of the world's once-leading Scotch brands extended, not only to weak strategies, but to feeble spending on promotion. When Saunders poured money into a crude but vigorous campaign for his stout, domestic market share immediately responded.

Still, any strategist could be forgiven for jibbing at one-product status, especially if that single product is heavy and sweet in a light and dry world. Doesn't everybody know that one-product companies are unsafe – that just Guinness just isn't good for you? Everybody knowing something doesn't necessarily make it right. Nothing can justify the consequent sins of Guinness and Distillers, even though they were no exceptions in overpaying for and then undermanaging diversifications, with the inevitably painful outcome. But where does the responsibility lie? In tactical execution, or strategic concept? With the top management? Or with the board as a whole, including its non-executives?

The answers must be 'both, yes, and yes'. Top management, acting with the board's knowledge and approval, is supposed to devise and/or approve the strategic direction and to ensure that the strategy is effectively executed. The road to the Guinness courtroom was paved by directors who had presided over long-run declines in shareholder value. For years the Guinness family, boasting several titles from Earl of Iveagh (the hereditary chairman) downwards, but wholly non-executive, had in effect presided over its own financial dissipation.

The family can claim credit for hiring Saunders from Nestlé and giving the new hired hand freedom to restore the group's fortunes – and how. Guinness profits of some £20 million and heading down were multiplied twentyfold and heading up within seven years. The family members moved smartly from merely rich to super-rich. Yet the recovery from the 1981 nadir only took earnings per share above the 1977 level after 1987. By then the hard liquor purchases, first of Arthur Bell, then of Distillers, had transformed the business.

That transformation, like the Saunders surge, was only possible because board-led errors had brought the brands so low. The lower they fall, the higher they can rise. But the evidence of the two conjoined cases indicates that even when powerful personal financial motives are at work in the boardroom, the structure and culture of senior management can be harmfully decisive. If Guinness and Distillers were isolated examples, that accusation couldn't be laid. But every bank failure produces another crop of non-executive directors who were apparently fiddling while their financial Romes burned.

The recurrent suggestion, in face of boardroom feebleness, is to strengthen the top through devices like greater investor intervention or more, and more powerful, non-executives. That would only reinforce the top-heaviness that created the problem in the first place. The true renaissance of the publicly-owned company will have to start much lower down, by liberating the energies of management below the top – the people running the part-businesses which make up the whole business. That must include vital cores like, in these two cases, Scotch and stout. The Catch-22 is that non-executives, whose duty can best be fulfilled by that liberation, lack the power to bring it about.

CHAPTER

28

The Non-Executive Nonentities

When corporate raider Carl Icahn was trying and failing to bend Texaco to his will, he put forward some nominees for the board. One of them admitted, in the true spirit of the boardrooms which are supposed to be bygone, that 'I know very little about Texaco, but I don't think an outside director has to know the business'. He didn't get elected. Did that matter, for good or ill?

Non-executives are only as effective as the information they get. If that comes from the executives (and what other source is there?), they can make it very hard to second-guess their decisions or criticise their actions. True, ignorance is no excuse: in 1985 all ten directors of one company were found personally liable for damages for an ill-spent two hours – that being the total time taken for the board to sell a rail-car leasing business in a hasty meeting (note) 'dominated by the CEO'.

The ten settled for $23 million, of which the purchasers paid $13 million and an insurance company coughed up the rest. At one point, not surprisingly, American insurers were running so scared of such suits that some premiums leapt by 9,000 per cent in a year. Corporate chieftains fretted not only about the costs, but about finding anybody willing to serve. They needn't have worried. Awards of damages against directors are very rare, and the chieftains have found no difficulty in attracting outsiders (often their equivalents in other major corporations) to drink from the unpoisoned chalice.

The insurance premiums have settled down – but the issue hasn't. If you think the non-executive should provide better control over the executive, and better results for the shareholders, how? The law is no answer. That $23 million settlement, for example, flowed partly from the fact that the directors hadn't read the sale contract before approving it. But if you're not a lawyer or an accountant you will spot only truly gross sins in a legal document, even if you can understand it.

Every day directors put their names to long and tortuous verbiage in the hope that the professional advisers know what they're doing: that advice is the shareholders' true protection, on which, as the spate of suits against auditors shows, they notoriously cannot always rely. In most cases, the work of outside professionals is far more important than the contribution, or non-contribution, which outside directors make to the company's business.

No matter what their personal distinction, the role of the non-executive directors is likely to remain the same: low on power, and high on responsibility that can't easily be met. Given this fact, the critics are baying for the moon if they want boards to become positive forces for better performance, urging companies on to prodigies of growth, efficiency, global enterprise and innovation. You only have to think for a moment, or sit on a board for a minute, to know that the idea is nonsensical.

A recent recruit to the non-executive ranks, Robert Waterman, co-author of *In Search of Excellence*, told me, when I interviewed him for *Management Today*, that he didn't think 'we [at McKinsey] really knew' what goes on in the boardroom; how 'groupthink' takes over as the great minds think (often wrongly) alike; how people 'picked by the CEO and usually vetted by the succession' aren't likely to kick over many traces; how the club-like atmosphere militates against abrasive behaviour, even if abrasion is needed.

The background of non-executives has a profound influence on their ability to be useful. Senior citizens associated with the company's past history, men who themselves run large groups, and representatives of minorities or the community are all hamstrung to various degrees: by their intimate past relationship with the present management whose culture they share; by the wish not to rock somebody else's corporate boat lest others rock theirs; by simple lack of business experience; or absence of management muscle. The lone woman on the RJR Nabisco board was former secretary of commerce Juanita Kreps. *Barbarians at the Gate* records her brief attempt to bring sense to the issue of F. Ross Johnson's buyout plan:

'After a few moments, Juanita Kreps spoke: "You know it seems a shame [that] we're forced to take steps like these, breaking up companies like this," she said. "On other boards I've been on there have been the same complaints about the stock languishing. The scenario elsewhere has been different. Managements look more to the future and beyond the immediate discounting of the stock. Why is it different here? Is it an issue of tobacco, with the decline in sales and the problems with the industry?" '

The lady's somewhat bemused question received a crisp, irrelevant and dismissive reply. ' "Juanita, I hear a lot of CEOs complaining about their undervalued stock but I don't see them doing anything about it," Johnson said. "This is something you *can* do about it. The other guys are afraid to do anything about it". ' And that, apparently, was the end of that.

In more normal circumstances, non-executives seem to have power through manning the most influential committees of the board: those which decide on grave financial matters, on major developments affecting the company's future, or on the pay of executives. Some measure of the ineffectiveness of these committees lies in the enormous rise in average chief executives' pay in the US since 1960 (from 11 times a schoolteacher's salary, according to *Business Week*, to 66 times). That partly reflects the scandalous amounts obtained by executives at the top of the tree (headed in 1989 by Craig McCaw's $54 million at the *profitless* McCaw Cellular).

It doesn't include those who fall off the tree, floating down under golden parachutes (none more golden than Johnson's $53 million) to which the outside directors have meekly assented. The American system has simply not evolved any countervailing power on the board to match the rise of professional executive management. But the age of the boardroom sinecure may be ending. The outside directorship has become notably less cosy for boards which preside over deterioration.

Stockholder suits for dereliction of duty, as noted above, may not cause much financial damage so long as directors are covered by insurance and the company against calamities. At Guinness, Ernest Saunders was ruined financially only because the family deserted its saviour in his hour of greatest need: the deserters suffered nothing worse than embarrassment – the noble Earl had a particularly torrid time in the witness box. Still, harassment and the threat of professional damage should be enough to spur much sharper attention to the duties of the director.

An era of accelerating upheaval creates many more opportunities for explosions that will suddenly load the non-executive directors with heavy fall-out. Grumble and temporise as they may, they can't unload that weight. In the last resort, only the non-executive can act as bulwark of the non-executive interests involved in the corporation – including all those now named in the jargon as stakeholders: the public authorities, the community, the investors, the employees. The trouble is that last resorts come last. The existing mechanisms don't do enough to ensure that the non-executive applies a stitch in time.

Non-executive directors are ultimately there to ensure that the chief executive fulfils what a Japanese counterpart would consider his prime responsibility: ensuring the successful long-term continuity of the corporation. In the Western context, that makes it important that outside directors should be true professionals – not in some other role, but as non-executives. The development of the modern corporation has unfortunately given the occasional director increasing trouble in this respect. He can't keep up with the pace of corporate developments and information. He can't fairly be expected to play any constructive part in the boardroom as the load both of responsibility and information increases.

In part this isn't entirely the amateur's fault. Existing methods of reporting and conveying information to the board are seldom suitable for sharp decision-making, or sharp awareness of what's actually happening inside the whale. But that sharpness is surely what the stakeholders (if they had both minds on the matter and voices) would demand from non-executive directors. The latter often don't even possess enough information to act on the data received. More often than not, they are compelled to be rubber stamps to the executives who supply the information and also determine how that information is delivered.

That can change radically with the electronic revolution. One day, quite soon, every corporation will have executive information systems (EIS) that provide full corporate information and the ability to dig down beneath it. The EIS sits on a desktop and responds to the touch of a few buttons. Some executives may well try to stop non-executives from turning these master-keys to the corporate business. But that will pose in concrete terms, and in a challenge which can hardly be dodged, the issue of whether the non-executive element, and the board as an independent force, can really do its supposed job.

The whole company must be strengthened by moves to improve greatly the quality and quantity of the knowledge which non-executives acquire about its affairs. Professionals with professional back-up can be as helpful to the executive work of the company as the excecutives themselves, especially if their relationship *isn't* arm's- length. David Norburn, the director of the Imperial College

Management School, reports that where non-executives represented the interests (and thus self-interests) of suppliers, outside investors, customers or financiers, the corporate results were far better than at companies with boards composed of the uninterested great and good.

The professional non-executive director is already an established life-form; it differs from the historical non-executive. In the first place, there's a clear limit to the outside responsibilities which the real pro can handle. Seven to eight boards is the practical extent of his useful workload – and that's pushing it. In the second place, to be any use, the pros must come expensive: the calibre of directors taken on in this function can't be any less than that of the people they are aiding and invigilating.

The fees offered to outside directors today are generally too low to attract the best talent. Not only are the fees too small; the opportunities are too casual. You know a man who knows a man (very rarely will it be more than a token woman). One study showed that 70 per cent of such appointments were personal contacts, which simply extends the bad old habit of filling the board with those you know, rather than those who know.

The *de facto* situation may be moving closer to what the backers of new *de jure* solutions want to see. Nominating outsiders to represent specific outside interest groups – including women and minorities – presupposes a selection, probably not very large, of people who are qualified to serve. The executive directors, however, have the ultimate say. If they have any sense, they will turn more and more to outsiders who have a special interest or can offer specialist knowledge.

In the professional role, the non-executive director acts as a permanent consultant. Interestingly, the ex-McKinsey man, Robert Waterman, felt that his best contribution and greatest insight into the corporate affairs came from a couple of days' consultancy in addition to his non-executive duties. The chief executive concerned was keen to perpetuate the arrangement. It foundered on the insistence of the other non-execs on getting their fingers into the same financial honey-pot. As that demonstrates, human nature is the largest single element in the boardroom outcome.

Overcoming its vagaries is especially tough in companies founded by entrepreneurs, developed along entrepreneurial lines and operating in entrepreneurial ways. There will always be tycoons, and tycoons will still be surrounded by people who are their underlings. These yes-men, or yes-persons, will in many respects still know as little as the tycoon about areas of management safely missed while he made his fortune: and yes-people, of course, will be ignored.

So will no-people, in proprietorial or corporate contexts alike. In most cases, when an outsider tangles with the insiders, as computer services king H. Ross Perot did at General Motors, it's the critic who goes and the criticised who stay – even if the dissenter, like Perot, is one of the richest men in the world, and a large shareholder to boot, and even if, as a GM veteran told *Business Week*, 'Most of the simplistic solutions that Perot proposed were absolutely right'.

The veteran went on to say that 'The problem with Perot is that he never understood the complexity of the organisation. Nobody can run General Motors. It's like a big blob that has a mind of its own and just kind of moves'. Yet Perot was a Superchief version of an emerging and highly promising species – the successful managers who finish with their first careers (as he had finished with Electronic Data Systems on its mega-sale to GM) and move on to proactive roles as non-executive boardroom experts.

It's essential that proaction should lead to action. It better had – for the big blobs 'that just kind of move' will never win. Whether it's in one, two, three, four or five corporations, professional managers who don't manage, provided that they don't fall into the laps as well as the pockets of the executive members of the board, could become a powerful new factor in achieving organisational vitality.

CHAPTER 29

McDonald's: Eating Its Words

That all-American and humble product, the hamburger, has come to typify the new global imperatives of world business. McDonald's, even more than IBM or Coca-Cola, is the paradigm of the giant corporation selling the same product or service in the same way to customers worldwide. Where IBM sells high-tech products to relatively few customers, McDonalds serves fast food to millions upon millions, from Miami to Moscow to Tokyo and all stops in between. Coke has a larger global franchise – but it isn't a global manufacturer or retailer: McDonald's, in effect, is both.

Yet according to *The Borderless World*, by Kenichi Ohmae, the McKinsey head in Tokyo, the McDonald's model of homogeneity isn't the shape of the global future. It's the disparate interchange of goods and services between companies and markets that has made global business a current reality. The enabling force hasn't been the corporation, but the customer. It's the customers' readiness (in consumer and industrial markets alike) to buy whatever they perceive as offering the highest value, whatever the source, that creates the global marketplace.

It follows that the driving strategic force for the global corporation can't be the old economies of scale. The way to growth and profit must lie through customer satisfaction – and the growth is essential, because costs (like those of research and development) that used to be variable are now fixed, and fixed at enormously higher levels. Ohmae is only taking another route to the same conclusion that all other gurus worth heeding have reached. In today's competitive battle, you win the customer to win the war.

McDonald's amazing global spread has been based on exactly that concept. Its core strategy is 'to offer the customer food prepared in the same high-quality manner worldwide, tasty and reasonably priced, delivered in a consistent, low-key decor and friendly atmosphere'. That's a *service* strategy, for in the new globalism product and service have merged indistinguishably. Sir John Harvey-Jones, when turning round ICI, deliberately redefined it as a chemical *service* company. Customers are simply interested in having their total needs met, whether they want a fibre for eventual manufacture into the latest fashion in designer jeans – or a Big Mac.

This concept was crucial in one of Ohmae's favourite cases, which is the resurrection of the compact 35 mm camera from graveyard to global success. Manufacturers had first to realise that the customer just wanted to take pictures with the maximum ease and best results, and didn't much care what met those needs. Since that breakthrough, the product has been endlessly refined by competing suppliers, developing new 'features', meaning new ways of defining and satisfying both new and old needs.

Ohmae makes the point that his native environment is admirably adapted to this 'sustained product-specific improvement', largely because the mature Japanese company is a community to which you belong: 'All you can do is try to make it better, to improve its products, to make incremental gains wherever possible'. The US, in contrast, is the paradise of the start-up: but the transition to maturity is so difficult and unrewarding that the time when the company goes public 'probably has the highest value for you'.

At that point, the wise American (and even more the wise Briton) takes his money and runs, and the country has lost another potential Ray Kroc – the McDonald's tycoon who not only created the strongest of all fast-food formats, but bequeathed a management organisation and culture that could sustain its worldwide expansion. Plainly, if this analysis is true, Japan has a huge built-in advantage in competing for global customers. Ohmae, however, thinks that much of the talk about competition between nations, trade deficits and currency imbalances is meaningless in what he calls 'the interlinked economy'.

In that interlinked world the corporation acts as 'a social institution whose responsibilities extend far beyond the well-being of the equity-owners to giving security and a good life to its employees, dealers, customers, vendors and subcontractors'. Whether this is pious hope or actuality, the statement could stand in for many of the mission or vision statements of global companies like McDonald's. There 'QSCV' reigns, standing for Quality, Service, Convenience, and Value – a doctrine whose spread is complicated by the fact that McDonald's depends so heavily on franchisees.

How are they and the employees in so many different countries bound together? In their book *Corporate Cultures*, Terrence Deal and Allen Kennedy stress first the need for heroes, a role which Kroc fulfilled admirably and apparently well understood: that was why he created lesser heroes and heroines, from the waitress of the month to the franchisee of the year. The authors use the Catholic Church as illustration for another aspect: the creation of a 'human institution' that captures qualities 'seen as soft and fuzzy by modern managers; soul, spirit, magic, heart, ethos, mission, saga'.

They attribute McDonald's absence of 'problems of sabotage or catering to special-interest groups in local areas' to the 'common spirit' built by the common values of QSCV, to the common symbols on which McDonald's rigorously insists, to the common training, and the common procedures – including not only the preparation of food, but reactions to problems as they occur. These are unquestionably telling factors. But pervading them all is the fact that the company eats its words: that management believes what it says, communicates the meaning of those words, and lives up to them, even to the extent of having its executives dine at an in-house McDonald's.

In a homogeneous global corporation, that formula can be readily, though not easily applied. But Ohmae is right in stressing that most global corporations are heterogeneous, and becoming more so as they respond to segmenting customer needs.

How does a hetero-corporation achieve homogeneity? Can it do so without losing the essential virtues of creativity and entrepreneurial drive? Unless that is achieved, the high ideals of the transnational company, as listed by Ohmae, will be betrayed by low performance. High performance is going to require innovation – above all, in the style of transnational management.

CHAPTER
30
Why the Matrix Lost Merit

'Top-level managers in many of today's leading companies are losing control of their companies.' That's the sentiment with which Christopher A. Bartlett and Sumantra Ghoshal began an important article in the *Harvard Business Review* (July-August 1990). The importance lies in their diagnosis – that grave loss of control arises from the form that most 'leading' organisations have adopted: the matrix.

The matrix, in its full glory, is multinational. Only the many-nationed group can order its multitudinous businesses on three dimensions – functionally, by product, and geographically. An individual national business will be part of both a regional and a product group or groups, while key functions of each business (finance, R and D, marketing, etc.) will belong to world-wide corporate structures as well. The authors aren't keen on the idea: they call it an unmanageable recipe for dual reporting, proliferating channels of communication (and committees) and overlapping responsibilities. That results, not surprisingly, in 'turf battles and a loss of accountability.'

But how else are managements to cope – to stay coherent and organised, while obeying the imperatives of decentralisation *à la mode*? That mode is the division, subdivision, and sub-subdivision of companies into discrete businesses, built around their specific markets, and entrusted to separate, autonomous managements. In theory, control is exercised by strict financial targeting and reporting, coupled with business planning. At the same time, creativity, entrepreneurship and marketing orientation are made possible, if not encouraged, by the combination of autonomy and accountability.

This organisation scheme is so widespread and widely approved that it counts as the consensus model of the corporate form. Under its aegis, the corporation can supposedly have the best of both worlds: discipline and freedom, control and independence. Much of modern management teaching hinges around this concept of centrally controlled decentralisation. Deep flaws in the consensus model would seriously undermine powerful and popular ideas like tying remuneration to superior divisional performance, or making sharp-end customer satisfaction the central point of sub-unit strategy.

So if some kind of matrix organisation is the only answer, whether Bartlett and Ghoshal are right or wrong becomes a fundamental question for all managers, for the trade-off between control and coordination, on one hand, and initiative and opportunism, on the other, extends well down the corporate scale. It has to be said, as a starting point, that one of the authors' main favourable examples lacks conviction. This is the assumed success of Philips, the Dutch electrical behemoth, as the result of co-opting 'previously isolated, even adversarial, managers into the corporate agenda'. Given the increasingly poor results of Philips over a long period, it's startling praise (see Chapter 31).

The problem starts with a basic question. If a company is a collection of independent businesses, what's the role, if any, of its central management? The question is actually circular: the role of central management must begin with – you've got it – defining its own role. Here practice is more helpful than theory. What do central managements customarily do in great corporations? The list includes:

1. Structuring and 'restructuring' the businesses.
2. Appointing to senior management positions.
3. Approving and disapproving capital investments above pre-determined limits.
4. Approving and disapproving the business plans of sub-units.
5. Monitoring the performance of sub-units.
6. Buying and selling businesses.
7. Making and unmaking alliances.
8. Deciding on rewards and punishments.
9. Raising and disposing of financial resources.
10. Representing 'the corporation' to the internal and external audiences.
11. Coping with corporation-wide issues.
12. Development and communication of a clear and consistent corporate vision and 'the integration of individual thinking and activities into the broad corporate agenda'.

The wording of the twelfth point is that of Bartlett and Ghoshal; the phrase describes one of the key directives, in their view, for managements that want their strategies to succeed. It begs two vital questions. Sure, it's what all central managements think they are doing, but: (a) how is it best done? and (b) how do you know when you've done it?

Look back over the whole list and one conclusion leaps out. The dozen functions are all translations into corporate terms of the behaviour of the absolute personal proprietor. That's how he carries on, no matter what the size of the business – recruiting and managing his people, masterminding what's made and sold and how, controlling the pennies and the dollars, making the final decisions, 'being' the business, establishing its commercial relationships, etc. All this, moreover, can be totally arbitrary.

The role of central management, then, is to be the proprietor writ large. In 1990-91 many multi-business groups resumed the effort to 'restructure', in the favoured euphemism. It means selling or closing businesses and plants, thus taking underperforming assets off the books and white and blue collars off the payroll. In much the same way, Unilever's top management in 1989 reshuffled its portfolio to concentrate on those sections where the senior management saw the corporate future in its vision – meaning essentially that of the three top executives.

All such designs sweep before them any individual ideas possessed by the individuals running the supposedly decentralised units affected. The arbitrary power may well be inconsistently applied, too. Yet the consensus model implies, indeed depends on, the exercise of proprietorial powers by the sub-management. Plainly, there's an inherent conflict between the two principles. But if Bartlett and Ghoshal are right, and top managers are 'losing control' and yet their sub-managers haven't picked up the reins, it's no wonder that so many Western companies have fallen short of expectations – and urgent need.

The remedy proposed by the two authors adds up to greater centralisation: the pendulum, in other words, needs to swing back. The hero corporation, in addition to Philips, is Unilever. According to the authors, the Anglo-Dutch management (with 17,000 managers in 75 countries), solves the strategic control problem by:

1. Building 'common vision and values' through an entry-level 'indoctrination' course.

2. Developing contacts and relationships by 'bringing managers from different countries and businesses together' for management training.
3. Spending as much on training as on R & D.
4. Employing the 'most promising overseas managers on short- and long-term job assignments' at corporate headquarters.
5. Transferring 'most of these high-potential individuals through a variety of different *functional, product and geographical* positions (my italics), often rotating every two or three years'.

Notice the matrix rearing its head in the italicised words. Floris Maljers, the chairman of Unilever NV, regards his group as extremely decentralised, and maybe the view from the bottom is the same as that from the top: maybe not. But is the Unilever recipe really so excellent? The process of 'Unileverisation' rests essentially on moving human pieces constantly round the corporate chessboard, sometimes for training, sometimes on detachment, sometimes into new jobs. That can't be consistent with the consensus model.

Suppose that, as a proprietor, you could get a guaranteed period of excellent service from every bright, capable manager you can find. How long would you want the guarantee to run? The truthful answer is probably for ever: certainly it would be much longer than Unilever's 'two or three years'. The old ITT principle, followed by many other conglomerates, was three-year rotation – on the following argument:

One year is required to master a job. In the second year, the incumbent is at the peak of performance. In the third year, interest begins to flag. But this rake's progress manifestly doesn't happen to successful, self-employed entrepreneurs, who often see out a whole generation. Three years, equally plainly, isn't enough to complete the deep immersion in every aspect of a business, its markets and its industry from which something of the utmost importance flows: experience and intuition.

Maljers noted, in a paper published in *Long Range Planning*, that far from making 'strategic decisions' only after exhaustive analysis of both the competitive advantage and the industrial environment '... many firms operate in a very different way ... Decisions are made quickly, based on experience and intuition as well as thorough analysis'. This is undoubtedly right, and so are the firms concerned.

'Experience and intuition' are a single quality. The former is the accumulation of knowledge which the mind processes automatically (operating in a mode every bit as efficient as methodical analysis),

HOW TO CREATE THE SUPER STRUCTURE

while applying other relevant inputs, to arrive at a conclusion – or 'hunch'. 'Gut feeling' and hunches aren't a substitute for organised, deliberate thinking; but neither is the latter a substitute for 'experience and intuition'. You need both: but while any brand-new MBA can do the analysis, it takes years of business practice to create the invaluable 'experience and intuition'.

Maljers quotes an interesting example, although it isn't overly apposite to his case. At one point, 'it was suggested that the expertise that had developed in monoclonal antibodies might also be applicable to humans. There was great uncertainty ... However, the consensus within Unilever was that the idea felt right ... As a result a revolutionary home pregnancy test was launched... in a form that was much more convenient for the user ... Unilever has now established itself as a world leader in this area'.

This was a case, common enough in research and development, where acquisition of further knowledge wouldn't have made the decision any easier. 'Go/no go' then has to hinge on intuitive assessment of (a) the chances of producing a commercial product (b) the size of the market if you do succeed. In other words, Unilever was demonstrating the value of 'experience and intuition' here, but not by choice: there wasn't anything else it could use.

A more relevant case is that of Timotei, a shampoo which originated in Finland from the perception (which could well have been intuitive) that there was a market for a soft shampoo which women could use several times a week. That's now a world best-seller. Unilever's difficulty lay, not in selling the product to the market, but in selling it to the Unilever world beyond Scandinavia. As Maljers emphasises, strategy doesn't exist unless and until it is implemented – the nub of the Bartlett-Ghoshal problem. In the Timotei case, implementation meant patiently leading the various national horses to water (or shampoo) and waiting for them to drink.

Supposing, however, that there had been a Mr Timotei, a tycoon of the tresses. Would he have hesitated for a moment to spread his wonder worldwide – even without the enormous benefits of a universal network like Unilever's? The problem of transferring information, products and methods about the corporation is generally described as one of synergy – without which there's really little point in placing disparate businesses under the same banner. But the problem is better expressed as that of achieving the optimum proprietorial development of each business.

This may very well demand different treatment of each one: the prime strategic task for the centre thus becomes the creation of subordinate proprietorships which don't require central intervention to maximise growth and profits. Proprietorships demand proprietors. On this point Bartlett and Ghoshal are absolutely correct in supposing that the centre's recruitment and selection role is exceedingly important (see Chapter 50).

How you manage those recruited and selected matters even more. The matrix won't manage them properly because it can't: it's another doomed device to combine control with uncontrol. The only answer lies in letting go, rather than taking hold: in the culture, not in the construction. With their culture of in-built human controls, the Japanese have had little apparent difficulty in scything through the Bartlett-Ghoshal knot. Very obviously (and very fortunately), it can be done.

PART 6

HOW TO GENERATE STRATEGIC POWER

CHAPTER

31

Philips Electrical: The Light That Failed

Small companies hit big difficulties in large numbers every day. That's the nature of the beast. But decline and fall in a great company is both puzzling and awesome. 'The shares would be worth a good deal more ... were the company dissolved ... the shares can no longer be assessed in terms of earnings ... The lamps grow dim at Eindhoven'. The name of the town in these quotes from the *Financial Times* gives away the company: the $32 billion Philips Electrical. How could the mighty be so fallen?

The possible causes of large-scale corporate calamity aren't that numerous:

1. The company could be selling the wrong products (poor research, development and design), or...
2. ... making them in the wrong way (too costly, too sloppy), or ...
3. ... marketing them wrongly (bad targeting, pricing, distribution and promotion), or ...
4. ... overreaching and stretching itself – through runaway overheads, excessive debt, misbegotten merger, or ruinous overambition, or (very likely) some combination thereof.

All these sins are just as readily and ruinously available to the smaller fry; but these weaknesses in great companies should be drowned in their strengths. With a Philips-type powerhouse, the potential strongpoints of competitive advantage are formidable. It takes decades of success to build a strong global brand across many product and geographical markets; to span the world with distribution systems, and build a wide reputation for value in consumer, professional and industrial markets; to sustain depth and quality of R and D over many technologies, basic and leading-edge; to create deep financial resources, well-sited plants, a huge corps of skilled managers and specialists. Throw in a well-defended base in the solid European Community, and what could go wrong?

There is only one possible answer: management. The weaknesses listed above haven't permeated the whole of Philips, but in some of its too many businesses, they became endemic. In other subsidiaries, largely immune from the viruses in question, performance fell far short of potential year after year. And in one area, computers, the group has pursued at horrendous cost a quarry that has eluded every other major electrical group: a profitable, expanding, self-generating business. Add together money-losers, underperformers and a bottomless cash drain, and you have a sure-fire recipe for crisis.

The fall of Philips into a chasm of cutbacks and losses ($2.5 billion net in 1990) has also been partly created by an overcentralised bureaucracy. That overload has not only stifled the efforts of operational managements to maximise their portfolios, but has imposed unsupportable strategic burdens on the whole corporation. Oddly, this contrasts totally with the picture of Philips painted in the *Harvard Business Review* (July-August 1990) by Christopher A.Bartlett and Sumantra Ghoshal (and referred to in Chapter 24).

The authors say that management 'knew that its national companies' long history of independence made local managers reluctant to take orders from Dutch headquarters in Eindhoven'. But only fifteen lines on they contradict this image with a quote from a senior manager, summing up the new, liberated feelings of US managers: 'At last we are moving out of the dependency relationship with Eindhoven that was so frustrating to us.' Yet, according to the *HBR* article, the frustration worked the other way around.

The authors blame North American Philips (NAP) for refusing to launch the V2000 video-cassette recorder. NAP argued that the Beta and VHS formats were already too well-established – and 'As a result, Philips was unable to build the efficiency and credibility it needed to challenge Japanese dominance of the VCR business'. But NAP was right, of course – and the fact that the rival formats were so entrenched (and would have made the V2000's task ferociously difficult) was Eindhoven's fault. First to produce a VCR, Philips lagged hopelessly behind Sony and later JVC in creating a business system capable of exploiting its lead.

Paradoxically, the consequences of its managerial lapses have placed Philips in a strong position to make a stirring comeback. By escaping from its computer Black Hole and shutting other unprofitable operations, the new regime at Philips was able to achieve enthusiastic coverage in the business media by 1991's big swing from loss to profit, or from crisis to stability. Those are two of the three turnround stages identified by Professor John Whitney, the third being transformation.

Whether or not the notorious Philips hierarchy can attack its own layers and numbers, other easy pieces abound in any large company (and many small ones). But that's not transformation. The key to the future lies less in stopping losses than in replacing ungotten gains – like the lost VCR market – with gotten ones. The penalties of such mismanagement don't show up in current figures, because they aren't there: the lost business, the one that got away, isn't contributing to either losses or profits. Nobody will ever be able to measure how much Philips has lost, for example, by having to beat a humiliating retreat from the vanguard of Europe's microcircuit efforts.

That retreat came after publicly committing itself to tackling the Japanese head on in all crucial areas of high technology. Thus can bad short-term figures ruin good long-term strategies. But Philips has always prided itself on relating its bean-counting to the longer term. Well before anybody else took the matter seriously, the Dutch company adjusted its figures for inflation, so that nobody, inside or outside the group, should be deceived by unreal profits. The actual counting of the beans, though, slipped badly. When profits virtually disappeared in the first quarter of 1990, the group director of accounting made a remarkable admission. He was 'astonished' by the news. But even if Philips' reporting system had been respectable, would it have told the management – or the world – what really mattered?

CHAPTER

32

The Figures That Don't Count

Business isn't only beset by economic cycles. Whenever great corporations are forced to restructure and rationalise – which has happened to some of the world's largest (not only Philips in Europe, but American and British giants from General Motors and IBM, and BAT and ICI, downwards) – the determining force is at least as much internal as external. The traditional cycle of success, stagnation, crisis, rebirth, success, stagnation, etc. is caused in large measure by internal pressures.

Rousseau's impassioned observation that man is born free, but everywhere he is in chains, applies far more strongly to modern managers and companies than they realise. The chains range from the historical legacy of the culture handed down by a founding father or fathers to the real or imagined constraints imposed by the industry or the market. But the heaviest chains of all may lie where few managers suspect their existence, because all managers live by the very instruments that enslave them

The enslavers are reporting systems. No company can be managed effectively unless its management accountants produce regular, rapid and accurate information about income and expenditure, for a start. Moreover, a fundamental concept of management over the postwar era has been that of making the reporting system the key to performance. Year after year, the number of managements subscribing to this concept – that of linking reported results to managerial appraisal – has swollen, until the system has become as widespread as sets of lights in controlling traffic.

The numbers control the manager, by enabling his superiors to monitor the results of his performance: they raise the level of that performance by embodying targets against which those results can be measured. In many companies this concept was elaborated into a system, blessed by the name of 'management by objectives', which sought to tie the corporate ambitions and individual performance into a seamless whole by the mechanisms of corporate planning and targeting, reports and appraisal.

The heyday of MBO was mercifully brief, since it substituted a rigid and bureaucratic formalism for the informality and flexibility which are now rightly seen as the better way to achieve dynamic corporate results. MBO imposed a set of chains, with the best intentions in the world, but without the best results. Its influence does more than linger on. The financially ruled companies which were so rampant in the 1980s all operated to a system of management by financial objectives – often crude, often lacking the appraisal element of MBO, but effective all the same.

By common consensus, though, the effectiveness is limited. The charge levelled against such companies is that, however efficiently they squeeze profit out of current operations, their systems don't achieve equal prodigies in generating new growth. In another form, the accusation is the same as that levelled at big American companies in general by one Japanese critic: that they manage ineffectively in the long term because of overconcentration on short-term results.

The long-term debilitating effect of obsession with short-term performance and financial targets is no secret. Nor is the solution esoteric. One manager who went to work for a Japanese manufacturer, after spells with several Western employers, including an American giant setting up a plant in Britain, found that answer at first hand. From the word go, the Americans demanded frequent reports on the standard financial ratios – from return on net assets downwards. The Japanese showed no interest in these ratios at all; they were, however, obsessive about cost figures.

This produced an extraordinary contrast. In the American company, and in his other Western employments, this manager had found accountants breathing down the line management's neck, demanding figures and checking on variances all the time. In the Japanese firm, it was the other way round: the managers were constantly badgering the financial people for more information so that the management job could be done more efficiently.

The financial shackles on corporate creativity can also be removed by creative thinking. One chief executive, who had pondered profoundly over how to set the organisation free from its reporting system, came up with a simple and arresting solution. He refused to look at the monthly financial reports. They were, of course, still scrutinised by his financial control bean-counters. But all the boss wanted to know was whether current performance was 'there or thereabouts'. If it wasn't, the question became much harder and more insistent: why hadn't he been told that things were going awry *before* the monthly figures routinely appeared?

This radical management thinker continued to hold monthly meetings with his managers, but not for the usual hashing over of the historic figures. His questions were never about the past or the present, but only about the future. How, he wanted to know, are you going to improve your business, area by area, and what will be the results if you do? The psychological pressure for business creativity was built into the process, for no manager was likely to admit to having no plans for improving his business performance.

The theory was as elegant as management by objectives, but avoided the MBO trap of seeking to tie corporate ambitions and individual performance together in one neat package. Did the scheme work any better than MBO? That chief executive nearly doubled his market share (from 11 per cent to 20 per cent) and was able to increase his prices at the same time; for once, market share wasn't won at the expense of margins. But what did this real-life experiment prove?

The boss had realised that nothing is to be gained from living in the past – even a past as recent as the previous month. Every top manager knows how, with the best will in the world, attempts to confine board or executive committee meetings to strategic issues rapidly degenerate all too soon into the same old *post-mortem* discussions, seeking explanations (and getting excuses) when targets are missed, patting backs when the business is flooding in. The only way to avoid that trap is never to have the monthly figures on the table at all.

In a well-managed company (though not apparently in the Philips of 1990) that can be done in near-perfect safety. An imperfectly run firm is another matter – but plainly there are faults other than one month's performance which need to be addressed, and that right soon. The figure-bound meeting, however, has another drawback, also familiar to every experienced management hand: the phenomenon of flux, the way in which January's problems are never the same as February's, which won't be the same as March's, and so on – and on.

The reason is that management is always running behind the action, and looking over its shoulder while doing so. That's no way to win races. Forcing managers to look and think forward means that they will anticipate the future, and, far more important, act to create it. The mechanics adopted by that crafty boss, though, aren't the only reason for his success. All corporate systems give signals to those who inhabit them. The secret is to create a system whose signals are the ones you truly want.

In a strict financial-control business, the chief executive may be desperately keen on dynamic organic growth and adventurous investment – and may even say so. But his people will react more strongly to action than words. They feel the hot breath of the short-term figures down their necks, and they know why their colleagues get fired – for not 'making their numbers'. Psychology operates in the same direction: just as managers told to report what they are doing to improve the business won't want the embarrassment (let alone the pain) of saying and doing nothing, so those in tough financial regimes don't fancy putting forward plans which will be savaged by the accountants and their superiors.

In the latter regimes, people aim only for targets they can hit, which may be a far smaller ambition than the company actually needs to achieve. In other words, reward systems must match the management needs of the company, not just its reporting and control requirements; and so, emphatically, must the information systems. In many companies, maybe most, historic accounts represent almost all the regularly available information. It's a palpable and potentially lethal inadequacy.

Managements which haven't taken radical approaches to escaping the chains of historic reporting may know well that the future, not the past, is where the destiny of the company lies. They may also know that the path to that destiny is paved with the intelligent use of the right, the real and the rewarding information – including, but only among much else, the right figures. There's a danger, however: managers being bombarded with messages about the importance of information may forget the purpose of that vital commodity.

The aim of the electronic revolution is to replace that risk with the opportunity of turning unprecedented quantity and quality of data into a strategic armoury. The new software makes full use of the new and increasingly powerful and convenient hardware to make management more effective. It can both improve internal operations and greatly raise the degree of responsiveness to the outside world. That means, among other things, moving away from the concept of being 'market-led' or 'customer-led'.

Those phrases have become clichés, in the way of all good management ideas: every other corporate mission statement probably includes some such words. It has long looked sane to change the emphasis in this direction: companies which had always given the customer what the factory wanted to make, rather than what the customer wanted to buy, truly had to change. The models to imitate become companies like IBM, although the would-be imitators forgot that a *sales*-led company may think itself *customer*-led when it is nothing of the sort.

The phraseology, and the orientation, encourage the passivity which you get by concentration on monthly historic reporting. Instead of making things happen, adopting a *proactive* stance, the 'market-led' company *reacts*. Companies, like those managers with the radically minded boss, need to be forced to look forward, to anticipate market trends. Anticipation and forward thrust enable them to lead the market, not the other way round. That is the traditional role of the great entrepreneur.

People were buying portable radios before Akio Morita and his co-founder, Masaru Ibuka, came across the transistor and bought Sony the rights from AT & T for a paltry down-payment of $25,000. They saw that the market would make a great lurch upwards if they led it by taking advantage of the new technology to miniaturise the set. In just the same way, Morita led not only the market but his own reluctant marketing men, when he and Ibuka later sensed that, given the chance to buy their own portable hi-fi, millions would don the new lightweight headphones which made the whole dream possible.

Entrepreneurs lead markets by instinct. Managers inside companies are unlikely to have the same qualities of intuitive creativity. What instinct cannot provide, information can stimulate and nourish. Leadership is far more than market share, for example; future share depends not on the present penetration but on factors like relative perceived quality and service, on value for money comparisons, on which competitor (in reality, not in the management's own eyes) leads in innovation and technical specification. Without full information on how they rate today, managers can't even guess intelligently at tomorrow.

They also need full understanding of the trends which will shape the environment and the reaction of the markets. In many non-consumer markets (and in some consumer industries) the mistake has been to identify the market with the buyers who actually place the orders. That error led the British aircraft industry, locked in overmatched competition with Boeing, into the trap of satisfying its monopoly domestic customer. Too late, the planemakers turned to meeting the needs of the real purchasers of their products – not only other airlines with different route structures and requirements, but the ultimate customers: notably the transatlantic and intercontinental traveller.

Markets have moved on far and fast since those days. That only increases the premium and the reward for getting ahead of markets and staying in that true lead. The danger of looking at the wrong numbers, and missing the right ones, is that the cycle of success, stagnation, crisis, rebirth, success, stagnation, etc. will peak at lower and lower levels – as at Philips.

After announcing that a fifth of the Philips employees would lose their jobs, the new president, hastily installed in July 1990, Jan Timmer, gave the *Financial Times* a deeply depressing interview. 'He was not interested in questions such as what kind of company Philips should be in the 1990s. The task now was to produce profits by improving stock control and making employees more aware of the competitive market place.' You couldn't ask for a clearer example of either the journalist or the interviewee grasping the wrong end of the stick.

How could the employees be unaware of competition in industries like lighting, home electronics and semiconductors? In Philips, the systems and signals alike had failed. Point the information systems of the company, including its bean-counting, in the direction of vitality and real growth, and not only will the managers get the right signals from the company, so will all its markets.

CHAPTER 33

Toshiba:
The Hidden Agenda

Look down on a Tokyo park in the very early morning and you may see it dotted by people mysteriously performing their exercises in perfect time. Somewhere in the park a peerless leader is leading the drill, which is transferred by those who can see him to those who can't, and so on, until all the exercisers are in perfect unison. That epitomises the Japanese management approach which has achieved such startling leadership in industries where, originally, the Japanese were led – and by large margins.

In the electrical industry, for example, the US achieved leadership at all the beginnings: the inventions of Thomas Alva Edison spawned the industry's development all round the world, just as in a later era the semiconductor pioneering of Bell Laboratories and Silicon Valley moved the entire global industry into the new era of solid state electronics. Yet in the 1990s only one US electrical company is in the world Top Ten by size; the biggest, General Electric. Four of the others are Japanese; their combined sales are three times GE's.

The largest, Hitachi, close enough to GE for the latter's advantage to be wiped out by some unfavourable movement in the dollar, endeared itself to me by an ad campaign headlined 'the 2,000 years of Hitachi'. That long view is echoed by what happened fifty years into Matsushita Electric's brilliant history. The great Konosuke Matsushita, who originally formed his corporate plan in the 1930s, covering the next 250 years, called his team together to celebrate their success over the first fifth and to discuss their strategy for surpassing that achievement in the next fifty years – a period that he was very certainly not going to see unfold. He died in 1990, probably in perfect confidence about his company's worldwide encore.

You can't separate Japanese corporate strategy from these long-sighted visions or from the culture which permeates them. In their study *Strategic Control: Milestones for Long-Term Performance*, Michael Goold and John J. Quinn took a look at Toshiba to compare its strategic planning with that of Western companies, including GE, and found, for a start, that while there is a formal planning system, it doesn't create strategy.

Instead, 'decisions are reached through collaboration between levels and represent a consensus between them. Building the consensus involves frequent informal meetings, subtle hints and thorough staff work'. In other words, there's a hidden agenda: strategy is inseparable from the culture of a company which (so its philosophy declares) 'contributes to a richer and healthier life and to the advancement of society through the creation of new values based on human respect'.

That lofty declaration meant, among other things, providing 'staff members with the opportunity to realise their full potential and cultivate their abilities'. Fine words indeed, but, as the British say, fine words butter no parsnips. The Toshiba experience in Britain, however, shows how effectively the fine words are backed by deeds. Taking over a money-eating factory previously owned in partnership, but still working through a British chief executive, the company utterly changed the culture.

Out went the hierarchial canteens as uni-status dining and uni-status hours, holidays and pensions took over. Individual offices vanished. Everybody donned the same blue Toshiba jacket. In went Japanese ideas on good housekeeping. The new owners took it for granted, in Plymouth as at home, that production equipment would be the best available; that inventory levels would be rigorously controlled; and that financial management would be as neat and exemplary as the premises. (Repainting the factory was one of Toshiba's first and most symbolic acts.)

That, too, is standard national practice. At Fort Dunlop, once the citadel of outdated British management practice, the Sumitomo tyre company promptly instituted the four s's: *seiri, seiton, seiso* and *seiketso*, or sorting, orderliness, cleaning and cleanliness. The chairman (a Briton, note) commented: 'Our factories have been cleaned up, and are kept that way, not by a team of cleaners, but by the workers themselves. Their machines have been painted in bright colours; and every item is allocated to its appropriate place'.

The good housekeeping is of a piece with applying the 'simple and obvious' (to quote the same Brit) to every aspect of the company. The same principles run all the way from the man at the machine to the boardroom strategist, from the stores to the labs. All are tied together at Toshiba by what Goold and Quinn call 'a long-term vision for the company that looks forward into the 21st century but is primarily concerned with the next decade'. Future changes in society, the economy and technology are covered in a statement which maps out the aimed-for structure and mix of all Toshiba's businesses.

Brilliant breakthroughs, like the laptops which took Toshiba from nowhere in the global computer market to leading position in its fastest-growing and most profitable sector, are generally the work of project teams; they are set up 'to convert broad ideas ... into more specific plans. Toshiba's vision was first drawn up in 1984, but is subject to revision and updating. As Goold and Quinn comment, 'The most important elements of control stem from a corporate culture in which people work together in teams to achieve shared goals. This sort of culture cannot be built through formal control processes'.

One of Toshiba's managers in Japan worried to the *Financial Times* that 'The spirit of the corporate warriors is dying' as 'Western-style schemes for pay and promotion by results' infiltrate Japan 'to accommodate a greater sense of individualism among young Japanese'. As the newspaper comments, though, corporate loyalty is being reinforced by still higher levels of company benefits, like housing, sports centres and resorts. The combination of the corporate *samurai* and the youthful individualists could result in greater, not lesser power. It is, after all, the ideal combination after which the best Western managers are striving.

In a real sense, Toshiba's vision statement even has a musical rendering. When its employees sing (heartily, so it is said) 'Let the boon of science Spread our tide to towns and villages Planting new culture Toshiba the honoured, Fruits of science, May Toshiba prosper – for all eternity', they mean what they sing, especially the eternity.

CHAPTER 34

The Everlasting Strategy

Tactics could be defined as the social inferior of strategy. Where tactics is merely 'the art of placing or manouevring forces skilfully in a battle', according to one dictionary, strategy is 'the planning and directing of the whole operation of a campaign or war'. In other words, to switch to a more peaceful metaphor, strategy is like the bidding in contract bridge, which sets the framework in which play can proceed, while tactics is the play itself, whose skill or ineptitude will determine whether the contract is made.

That, however, presupposes an achievable contract, which is where the management difficulty arises. To paraphrase Alexander Pope's infamous sexist lines about women and character, 'Nothing so true as what you once let fall. Most business has no strategy at all'. Lack of strategic thinking has been rightly regarded as a key weakness of Western business. That means a key weakness of top management, since that's where strategy starts for a business of any size.

Every company needs a plan which, as management professor Brian Houlden says in his book *Understanding Company Strategy*, describes what kinds of activity it will engage in, the resources needed, the main steps, the people responsible, the key signals or 'milestones' and the external factors to be reviewed. Every manager must decide how to measure progress and success; the handful of measures with which Houlden personally starts are growth in turnover, profit margins, return on capital employed, and level of borrowing – all of them, of course, financial controls.

While Houlden would be the first to say that strategy must go into countless other non-financial dimensions, that points to a fundamental question. In their study on *Strategic Control*, mentioned in the previous chapter, Goold and Quinn insist that, if you don't have that, if you don't have 'strategic control', you might as well not bother with strategic planning. The controls, moreover, must use targets that measure strategic progress, not something else. Managers must agree on their strategic targets and be rewarded for doing so. That's all obvious enough; yet all too many companies do nothing of the kind – their strategic controls stay loose to the point of laxity.

By revealing contrast, financial controls are often very tight. But 'exclusive focus on financial results and budgets does not encourage managers to invest and build for longer-term competitive advantage'. Hence the dilemma. The board is responsible to the shareholders for the financial performance of the business. How does it best combine strict execution of this duty with developing true strategy? As Houlden stresses, 'Organisationally, growth businesses need greater freedom to grow vigorously and more direct access links to the main board ... entrepreneurial enthusiasm should not be discouraged by over-zealous criticism ... '.

There's an evident, grinding conflict between the centre's desire to manage – to be responsible for the success of the 'growth business' – and this need of unit managers to maximise growth by behaving as effectively as *good* owner-entrepreneurs. The 'good' is italicised because, brought down to fundamentals, that's the centre's true role: to act as team managers and coaches for developing good businessmen. If the centre accepts that role, it can perhaps produce more effective results even than the cut and thrust of the unprotected entrepreneurial experience.

But success in this role presupposes that the 'coaches' know, either from their own experience or from deep study, what good entrepreneurial management entails. In many boardrooms and executive suites, this know-how is conspicuously absent. Nor is it easy to identify in real life. *In Search of Excellence* has been criticised in many places, including this book, for the fact that so many 'excellent' companies exploded during or after the long process of publication: but that's an occupational hazard of those (including me) who seek real examples of successful management from the only possible source – real companies.

You could, in perfectly good faith and authority, have praised Jaguar (as Houlden did) for its progress on four correctly identified strategic issues. However, the apparent advances concealed severe relative decline in productive efficiency, human relations, innovative prowess and much else, which led to large losses and loss of independence to Ford. The progress on those four issues could not be taken to ultimate resolution and success given Jaguar's independent structure, which left it far too small to compete in the big leagues, and its existing management, whose horizons had been narrowed by too much initial turnround success and praise.

Likewise, the Goold-Quinn study of BAT Industries, the owner of Brown & Williamson and much else in global tobacco, has been overtaken by events. Dramatic change of strategy was enforced by the unsuccessful and ill-judged attempt to break up the group, led by the predators' predator, Sir James Goldsmith. Two of the four main activities or legs on which BAT stood at the time of the study were divested by the BAT management itself, including US retail interests like Saks. That prompted an inevitable question: if break-up to concentrate on tobacco and financial services was the correct strategic choice under threat, why wasn't that strategic view apparent beforehand?

Goold and Quinn also speak well of Xerox's 'unusually strong commitment to benchmarking', or comparisons with other firms, with planning leading to data collection, analysis, integration, action and finally to 'maturity'. The object was that 'Xerox should be the leading company as measured by the benchmarked parameter'. But is that truly strategic? Or is it tactical, the way the plan is carried into execution?

All the benchmarking in the world, while it undoubtedly soaks up man-years, won't resolve strategic issues such as Xerox's true role in an age when straight copiers must die; or the proper, productive relationship between its various multinational parts and functions; or how to exploit the innovative strengths which (see Chapter 58) have sometimes withered on the vine. To stress the point, you could have terrific benchmark performance on every count, and still fail through aiming the wrong product at the right market, or *vice versa*.

Moreover, the benchmarking process smacks of bureaucracy – and there's another rub. Goold and Quinn list the potential advantages of strategic control processes in a way that makes you wonder how any company can ever do without them:

1. Greater clarity and realism in planning.
2. Higher standards of performance.
3. More motivation for business unit managers.
4. More timely intervention by corporate management.
5. Avoiding 'back door' financial control.
6. Getting more effective decentralisation through clearer definition of responsibilities.

But the catch or trap is that systems aiming at these dreams can end up as bureaucratic nightmares. Formal processes require a heavy seasoning of informality, a realisation that over-explicit objectives may ignore nuances and cultures, people issues and crucial matters of timing. In this context, Houlden uses the phrase 'company cement' to describe what, in a sense, is indescribable: the combination of factors which makes it possible to direct and manage a large group effectively, and to establish relationships between subsidiaries that take advantage of opportunities to add value throughout a business system.

The problem won't go away. You can achieve better motivation through decentralising, stronger profit performance through financial controls, and greater central impact on development through strategic controls. But you may still have sub-unit managers chafing at the bit, anguishing about the neglect of long-term strategic development – and such chafers can surely be found even at the best-managed of Western giants, like General Electric. Would similar carping be heard among the West's Japanese competitors?

Those words quoted by Goold and Quinn about Toshiba come to mind: 'Building the consensus involves frequent informal meetings, subtle hints and thorough staff work'. Note the words 'subtle hints'. In the end, strategic success is achieved by intangibles that can't be set down on paper, though the tangibles suggested by Goold and Quinn (for which the computer is heaven-sent help) are certainly important enough:

1. Avoid large staff departments and lengthy reports.
2. Make sure that the normal operations of the business generate the information required.
3. Meet to discuss strategic issues face-to-face.
4. Combine formal process with informal, wider-ranging discussions.
5. Don't let the process prevent or interfere with an 'effective and speedy line management decision process'.

Toshiba's planning process confirms and enlarges this five-point programme. Good strategy must start from separating out good businesses. At the time of the Goold-Quinn visit, the company had ten, one of which ('Information Group') subdivided into four others. That meant sales of nearly $3 billion per business; the average of the ten, in other words, was the size of Toshiba's laptop competitor,

Compaq. All too often, breaking down apparently large companies into their components shows that the individual businesses are globally insignificant – and you can't build a strong strategy on weak foundations.

The ten Toshiba businesses report through the 'General Officials Committee' or *Keiei Kaigi*, to the executive vice-presidents, the president and, above them, the chairman and the board. The formal relationship matters far less than the informal. Of course, each of the ten, bearing in mind the vision statement, presents a broad three-year plan (reviewed every three years) and a detailed, one-year operating plan. In principle, Goold and Quinn were told, 'the business head is free to implement the plan once it has been agreed with the board. In practice, they check back frequently'.

The authors add that 'three or four non-financial objectives or commitments may be agreed between each business group and the corporate centre ... these emerge from an *informal* [that word again] negotiation between the business group and the corporate centre'. Things can get tough if the going does, which would be revealed at monthly performance reviews with the top dozen corporate managers on the *Keiei Kaigi*. According to one manager, if 'a business is showing significant variances from the plan, the top management will put pressure on the team in question to improve the results'.

And if they are still not satisfied? 'They may call in corporate staff to provide additional advice. This is not so welcome' – no doubt, a massive understatement. In a corporation built on face-to-face encounters ('Toshiba encourages extensive discussion and wide consultation between the levels of the company') and 'close relationship' between the business group heads and corporate executives, nasty surprises and nastier reactions are unlikely. It's a system in which 'individual personal responsibility and accountability for strategy' was 'replaced by a more collective, shared responsibility'.

In this climate, the leaders, from chairman downwards, can more properly fill the crucial role of head coach and coaching team. They can also concentrate on the longer view: for the crucial difference between strategy and tactics is time-scale. Strategy governs a series of events unfolding far into the future, while tactics are more immediate. To express that another way, to go for better benchmarks or Total Quality Management or higher sales force productivity is a *sine qua non*: laying the foundations on which strategic success can be built. It's a tactical effort, like military training, that you dare not neglect.

Outside the world of high-tech, where a company like MIPS Computer Systems, designing and making the most advanced microprocessors, can soar from $14 million of sales to over $100 million in two years, strategies generally take time to blossom. And even a MIPS has to operate on long time-spans itself: when the company introduced its 64-bit chips in early 1991, it wasn't aiming for the existing market but for the applications that would be required in the middle and late 1990s. For lower-tech businesses, strategic time-scales can be longer still.

Building a truly significant business can take a generation. That's fine for an entrepreneur starting in his 20s or 30s, but it means that the typical professional chief executives can't expect to see more than the seedlings of any forests they plant. With only a decade or so in power, their capacity for doing harm, by pushing through misplaced deals and developments that will be identified with them at once, is larger than their ability to create lasting good. Their greatest strategic contribution must be to build on their predecessor's bequests and leave a much strengthened inheritance for their successors.

That demands the collective and collaborative style of a Toshiba. Humane, intelligent, open, ambitious, flexible, long-sighted, painstaking, imaginative and informal management is the ultimate strategic asset. Those are the qualities that ensure that strategy will be better designed, will fit the corporation and, above all, will be turned seamlessly into an everlasting reality.

CHAPTER

35

Berkshire Hathaway: Buffett's Beating

What makes a good investor is a highly relevant part of another question: what makes a good chief executive? The answer includes the ability to spot an investment opportunity and go for it (otherwise known as being an entrepreneur). It also includes the ability to spot a good business (and, by definition, to exclude a bad egg). And it most certainly takes in personal judgment: the ability to assess the quality of individuals, whether as colleagues, employees or business associates.

The bizarre behaviour of the banks in throwing good money after bad (and to bad risks) without even knowing that the commitment was already addled missed out on all three attributes. Their personal judgments were particularly at fault. Over-lending to men like Campeau, Maxwell, Bond, Trump and many others reached epidemic propotions. Does this mean that the judges were especially weak (or weak-minded)? Or is the game of spotting honest, sustainable, high-class managerial and financial talent too tough to win?

If the latter is true, then the past record of Berkshire Hathaway is hard to explain. Its great contrarian investor and leader, Warren Buffett, looking for 'value' (or more accurately under-value), made his killings from stocks which the inefficient market had unwisely shunned. But he also built a portfolio of long-term investments in seven businesses partly on the basis of his judgment of the people running them. This was demonstrated by an ability to generate such astonishing returns that Buffett calls them 'the Sainted Seven'.

The saints, like the Nebraska Furniture Mart in Buffett's base city of Omaha, at one point collectively achieved a 57 per cent return on equity capital. That was one of the reasons for Buffett's faithful Wall Street following, and for the sensational rise in his shares, from $12 a share in 1965 to $8,900 at the peak. Small wonder that investors in turn backed Buffett. Their judgment, reinforced by the results achieved remorselessly every year, was that he was the nearest thing to infallibility in picking winners. As Buffett himself has said, his stock market winners were no more important than the winning managements in whom the maestro put his own trust.

The number on which the investors pinned their faith was earnings per share, or more precisely their growth: for the first 23 years of Berkshire Hathaway, the compounding proceeded inexorably at 23.1 per cent. In 1989 the magic stopped. Earnings grew by only 12 per cent, which still left an impressive ten-year average of 25.1 per cent. The markets were evidently not impressed. From late 1989, the shares notably under-performed, plunging to $5,550. Berkshire Hathaway's holding in Capital Cities/ABC dropped by 24 per cent in the process, and that company was headed by the chief executive Buffett most admired.

A huge holding in Salomon Inc. is one of the other reasons why Buffett's own shares fell below book value for the first time in many years. Buffett backed Salomon partly out of the faith in chief executive John Gutfreund that was finally proved to be misplaced by the bond scandal of 1991. It was a confidence which any student of the fiascos and foibles delineated in Michael Lewis's best-selling *Liar's Poker* must find very hard to understand. The contrarian move into a Wall Street investment bank was easier to follow, especially if you thought the 1990s would be a honeypot for the sector. They won't – according to Salomon itself.

Its researchers in early 1991 saw real estate 'price declines of 10 to 30 per cent in the major world financial centres over the next two years'. They sarcastically called this 'great news for the banks that have drunk so deeply at this well'. Not that the other news for financial services was any better: 'the scramble for market share ... has resulted in deteriorating asset quality, failing profitability and inadequate capital'. That was at a time when, on Salomon's Wall Street, profitability had fallen practically to vanishing point.

Buffett became justly celebrated for his patience, stalking the right opportunity for years and sticking with the purchase for whatever time was required for the big payoff. But his later crop of such holdings (Salomon, Gillette, Champion International and US Air) looked much more problematical than past hits such as Disney and American Express. 'White squire' investments like Salomon (so called because they help to save the incumbent managements from aggressive bids) are also different in nature from Buffett's earlier coups.

So sceptics could make what Wall Street analysts call a fundamental case for the Buffett buffeting, based on specific events and fears. But that could be beside the real point. The fact that Berkshire Hathaway sustained an astonishing run on the strength of its growth in earnings per share fits the conventional wisdom. Many managements would regard earnings growth as their primary corporate target, and many investors would judge companies by its delivery. But what if the Buffett rise were itself an anomaly, an over-valuation as opposed to the under-valuations from which he created his billions?

In Chapter 26, I mentioned research by the Kalchas Group of strategic consultants. Using a sample of 500 companies, the study could find no correlation, using five-year comparisons, between a high rate of earnings growth and the kind of premium rating which Berkshire Hathaway so long enjoyed. A scatter graph showed that even in the higher, above-Buffett reaches, with annual growth of 40 per cent and upwards, the below-average market ratings far outnumber the above-market figures. The highest price-earnings ratio of all 500 shares was achieved by a company whose annual growth barely cleared 10 per cent.

In contrast, a growth record of nearly 70 per cent per annum was rewarded with a strictly middle-of-the-road rating. The mass of firms grew earnings by between 10 and 30 per cent: overwhelmingly, they fell below the average rating line. Has the conventional wisdom got it wrong? And if growth in earnings per share isn't the true measure of excellent management, where should the chief executive turn? The answer very possibly lies close to Warren Buffett's heart – in the performance of the Sainted Seven.

CHAPTER 36

The Right Measure of Management

In pure logic, the choice of earnings per share as the management target, and the apple of the board's collective eye, seems perfectly defensible. The object of the board is to deliver value to the shareholders. However great the value in the balance sheet, the shareholder sees none until it is converted into a higher price for the stock. What can be wrong with the proposition that, the higher the earnings, the higher the price? Raise the earnings, and you raise the value – subject only to the market's varying assessment of those earnings.

That's a very large proviso. Select any three companies with the same price-earnings ratio and you will probably find that their industries and outlooks alike are very different. Those seeking a sensible foundation in the absolute level of earnings per share seek in vain, which is what any gunslinger would say. Absolute earnings are not his ammunition. Dynamism is the supposed key to a dynamic share price. The faster earnings per share grow, the higher the PE ratio will mount. Multiply a rising absolute by a leaping ratio, and the results must be wonderful.

That's why the Kalchas research mentioned before is so significant. The topsy-turvy results arise partly because 'a decade's growth' in earnings doesn't take place over a decade. It is the difference between earnings in Year One and earnings in Year Ten, divided to result in an average figure. A company which earned 100 in Year One and expanded steadily to 300 in Year Ten would thus rank equally with a company that had suffered eight years of losses in between. The reason why high earnings growth isn't associated with a high rating is that views of the stock will have changed between the beginning and end of the series.

Another crucial point is that, even in the most stable of decades, the value of the money in which earnings are measured depreciates over time. In the decade to 1989, the *Fortune* 500 recorded huge increases in sales and substantial rises in profits. But after adjusting for inflation, the rise in sales came down to a barely visible 7.1 per cent – over ten years, remember – while net income was actually 3.6 per cent lower. Growth in real earnings per share, for most big US companies, was *negative*: a stark and revealing contrast to the quadrupling of the 500's net income between 1954 and the onset of the 1970s.

The inflation problem applies to another conventional argument for earnings: dividends. Earnings are the basis of the latter, which are another way in which shareholders can get their hands on the company's creation of value. Since earnings per share are the source of the dividends, the higher the former, the greater the latter can be. Presumably, too, some relationship exists between the level of dividend and the price of the shares. You wouldn't normally expect a doubled dividend to result in an unchanged share price (unless, that is, the market had already anticipated the dividend boost). But what if the doubled dividend were paid out of unchanged or lower or even non-existent earnings?

The question didn't seem to bother seven of ten leading money centre banks in the US. According to Joel Stern of *Corporate Finance*, the seven nakedly financed their dividends in the years from 1983 to 1987 only by issuing new equity. That was the very same practice that led the Rolls-Royce aero-engine company to ruin and nationalisation in 1971. But engineers aren't expected to understand elementary finance: if bankers don't understand that, can they understand anything at all?

The policy is plainly disastrous. Worse, it is wholly unjustified, according to the researches of Chicago's Merton H. Miller. Since he won a Nobel Prize for his thoughts on the matter, belief in his findings makes sense – and so do they. He stresses that the worth of a company (which is what the investor is buying, whether purchasing 100 per cent of the equity or a mere sliver thereof) is unaffected by its financing arrangements. As quoted in *Fortune*, he thinks that 'if you take money from your left-hand pocket and put it in your right-hand pocket, you are no better off'.

In other words, the more paid out in dividends, the less is available for other worthy purposes – like building for the future or reducing borrowings. Moreover, retained profits are free of any financing costs or any banking fees, though this point seems to have eluded, of all people, the chairman of Citicorp. John Reed informed a bunch of analysts that holding back on dividends was a 'highly inefficient' form of financing. If the remark made any sense at all (doubtful, since Citicorp cut its dividend two weeks later, anyway), it lay in the possibility that the lower dividend, by reducing the share price, would raise the bank's overall cost of capital.

As *Fortune* notes, however, 'Empirical studies have shown that real-world returns to shareholders are not raised by paying dividends'. The article calls as witness companies which have rewarded investors handsomely while being Scrooge-like or worse with the dividend. The only named example, alas, is Berkshire Hathaway, which (as noted previously) was underperforming badly at the time. That last fact, though, only goes to prove the lack of solid, fixed relationships between earnings growth and shareholder value. Rather, the relationship is essentially volatile.

If investors conventionally consider that a fast-growing earnings per share figure will lead to a superior performance in the share price, they will invest accordingly. They will then, by definition, be joining the crowd, who all think likewise. The falsity of the proposition, however, will sooner or later be demonstrated: and at that point investors will become disenchanted – not with the proposition, but the shares. Disappointment, sooner or later, leads to disposal. That only makes matters worse, especially as the crowd (again by definition) will be moving in the same direction.

Hence the apparently paradoxical behaviour of the Kalchas scatter graph. In correlating market behaviour with earnings performance, you are simply not comparing like with like. Do corporate statistics yield a better measure of shareholder value? An important element must be continuity, or consistency. To be significant, moreover, the number would have a better predictive value than earnings growth, which cannot safely be extrapolated from past results. So the measure must relate strongly to present performance and be self-sustaining: that is, give reason in itself to suppose that good figures will be maintained.

Another *Fortune* list, which caught my attention in April 1984, used just such a criterion. Very few companies could pass the test – and that strongly suggests that its results are valid. The magazine could find only 13 companies in the 500 which had averaged at least a 20 per cent return on year-end stockholders' equity over the decade to 1983, without ever dipping below 15 per cent. The 13 were Coca-Cola, Merck, American Home Products,

Dow Jones, Mitchell Energy, SmithKline, Kellogg, Deluxe Cheque Printers, Worthington Industries, Maytag, Nalco Chemical, IBM and Dover.

Move on five years from 1984, and how had those companies fared in 1989? Eight of the group reported returns in excess of 20 per cent; a ninth, Dover, just missed the cut at 19.3 per cent. Four had slipped badly: Mitchell, Maytag, IBM and SmithKline, which was forced to accept a British embrace. Note, however, that its new mate, Beecham, was among only eight big British businesses (out of 250) that had achieved more than a 17.6 per cent average return on invested capital over the decade to 1983, without ever falling below 13.2 per cent.

When *Fortune* repeated its exercise, using 1988 figures, the same eight 1984 survivors were among 21 with a decade of consistent performance. As Carol J. Loomis pointed out, the increase in numbers was fortuitous. A record peacetime expansion made life easier, the Federal government cut corporate tax rates, and greater leverage, as debt levels rose, tended to enhance return on equity. For all that, 21 companies out of 500 is a very select group; and the standard of financial performance is matched in most cases by the non-financial achievement; witness the Excellent Eight.

Kellogg's handling of the breakfast trade has been a consistent masterpiece of marketing; so have Coca-Cola's defence of its global brand leadership and the handling of a wide brand portfolio by American Home Products. Merck's pre-eminence in pharmaceuticals has been won by all-round excellence. DeLuxe was one of the first American companies to cotton on to quality of service. The *Wall Street Journal* is a symbol of Dow Jones's conservative adherence to quality and integrity of product. Maytag, another quality freak, makes 71.4 per cent on the assets it employs in its soft-drink vending machines.

That's higher even than Philip Morris makes on tobacco (64.1 per cent) and than the 57 per cent return on the equity of Berkshire Hathaway's Sainted Seven. In his praises for the latter group's performance, Warren Buffett is wholly justified, for that is the true definition of giving shareholders value – investing their money and then making on those funds far greater returns than the shareholders could achieve for themselves.

The return on equity figure can, true, be fiddled – both by leverage and by creative accountancy legerdemain, which in 1988 added an estimated $1.8 billion to the profits of General Motors. That raised GM's return on equity from a terrible 8.6 per cent to a barely respectable 13.6 per cent. But the reality can't be falsely represented over the long term, which is why the consistency test is so important. It doesn't, of course, have much appeal for managers whose performance is assessed against annual budgets and who are placed under severe pressure (or place it on others) if quarterly results go wrong. Those all but universal devices cement short-termism into the management system. So does concentration on the share price, which isn't even an annual figure, but an hourly one.

Chief executives who keep an hourly watch on the share price are practising management short-termism with a vengeance. There's no doubt that the blame for short-term (and short-sighted) policies lies there, not in Wall Street or the City. After all, the share price is about the only parameter that the chief executive and his friends can't influence at all – except by jumping out of the window, and even then the effect wouldn't last for long. In Japan, however, that last observation would be no joke. The chief executive is held very directly responsible for performance, even though his main role is strategic, not operational; and if he fails, he jumps.

Such failure would be assessed not in short-term results, but in weakening or damaging the company's efforts to achieve long-run success. The Sainted Seven and the Excellent Eight have alike demonstrated that a company which earns high returns on its equity capital generates the means to sustain its profitability and enhance its growth. The measure is static: stringing together a series of these static measures year after year, though, creates a powerful dynamic. You would expect this to be reflected in the share price, and for once such expectations are not disappointed.

In 1989 the Excellent Eight averaged a 33 per cent total return to investors. That calculation takes in both the dividend and capital gains, but the latter overwhelmingly account for the outcome. The fine figures for 1989 brought the return for the whole decade to 22.4 per cent. Both figures compare with a median of around 15 per cent for the *Fortune* 500. That's an imposing differential. The eight produced a decade's return of nine times the original stake against four times for the 500's median. Even the five dropouts from the list averaged a median return to their investors.

The correlation is as powerful statistically as in logic. But a high and consistently maintained return on equity isn't the only parameter the chief executive has to watch. The non-financial figures that contribute to consistent high returns come first in every sense. Among those, market penetration has plainly had a deep influence on the performance of the Excellent Eight. Merck, Kellogg, Philip

Morris, Dow Jones, Coca-Cola, DeLuxe, Maytag and Nalco Chemical all occupy core market positions that are dominating, sometimes to the point of virtual monopoly.

Much the same is true of 1980's 13 newcomers to this Hall of Fame, like the Washington Post, Tambrands (the makers of Tampax), Anheuser-Busch in beer and Bristol-Myers in drugs. It's also true of Warren Buffett's Nebraska Furniture Mart. Look after the true return on equity, and nourish the market share, and the stock price will look after itself. And if it doesn't today, it will tomorrow.

PART 7

HOW TO MASTER THE NEW MODES

CHAPTER 37

Robert Bosch: The Founding Obsession

When it comes to quality, the Europeans are building on some even longer traditions than the Japanese – like those of Robert Bosch, whose founder wrote this in 1919:

'It has always been an unbearable thought to me that someone should inspect one of my products and find it inferior. I have therefore always tried to ensure that only such work goes out as is superior in all respects'.

To this day, the same spirit animates a company which by 1989 had risen to $16.3 billion of sales. That not only made Bosch larger than one of its most famous local customers for automotive parts (BMW), but was three times the size of Dana, the nearest US rival. The German company, though it has long made domestic appliances as well, first caught the public eye when fuel injection started to replace the carburettor. Bosch became, and has remained, the world's leading supplier of the new wonder. Its chairman could once boast that among European car-makers 'the only alternative to Bosch is Bosch'.

Today the German firm finds itself supplying customers who not only have alternative sources of supply but have themselves been forced by their own customers to become more and more exacting. The result, according to Hansjörg Manger, a member of the board of management at Bosch, is a huge change. 'With the globalisation of the market, the suppliers from Japan are delivering to our traditional customers, and they are comparing us with them. What was unbelievable five years ago is that they ask that we have failures of under 100 parts per million.' As Manger points out, in 1985 Westerners would have laughed at the idea, saying 'that is ridiculous, it is not possible'.

With the strengthening of world competition, Europeans 'have to improve quality because of pressure from the outside more than pressure from the inside'. Manger thinks the process has now gone so far that 'quality is the competitive factor in the world company'. But it isn't the source of competitive advantage any more. 'Quality is getting more and more equal all over the world, products are getting more and more equal, the procedures by which they are produced are more and more equal, even the machinery on which they are produced is more and more identical'.

His conclusion is that, since the quality and specification of the product are 'more and more the same', that leaves only 'quality of service' as a competitive weapon, which 'may be decisive'. Manger's view is close to becoming the conventional wisdom, and it's very hard to argue with the logic. You have, however, to possess all three dimensions of quality for the third to decide the issue. And that, at Bosch, means living up to a dozen principles of Total Quality Management, or TQM. The dozen are distributed to all employees (which, in the polyglot world of German manufacturing, means in eleven languages – Turkish, Swedish, Portuguese, etc.). In précis form, these are the principles:

1. We want satisfied customers. The highest quality of our products and services is one of our major objectives.
2. The customer is the judge of our quality. His or her opinion on our products and services is decisive.
3. Our quality goal is always 'zero defects' or '100 per cent right'.
4. Not only do our customers assess the quality of our products, but also the quality of our services. Deliveries must be on time.
5. Inquiries, offers, samples and complaints must all be dealt with promptly and thoroughly. It is imperative that agreed deadlines be met.
6. Each and every employee in the company contributes towards achieving our quality goals.
7. All work must be without defects from the very beginning.
8. Not only defects themselves must be eliminated, but also their causes.
9. Demand the highest quality from our suppliers, and support them in adhering to our mutual quality goals.

10. We have introduced numerous and proven methods to identify defects at an early stage. These methods must be rigorously and consistently applied.
11. Ensuring that our quality goals are achieved is an important management duty.
12. Our quality directives are compulsory.

That last word means what it says. Bosch believes that its middle and top management have been converted to the total quality cause, but that the remaining problem is with the motivation of the worker on the shopfloor. As American companies have found, that demands a change of culture. That's where Manger feels his Japanese competitors have the advantage: 'When I visit a Japanese shop floor I feel the workers are more motivated than in some of our own plants.' No doubt, that's partly the result of those eleven languages: but there's more to the problem than that.

If the deficiencies are felt deeply in a company like Bosch, where 'total quality has been part of our philosophy' from the beginning, and which believes its founder created TQM ('although at the time it was not known as this'), the problems, and the necessity, must be enormous in the more typical firm. Bosch wants to go from 'an acceptable failure rate of half a per cent or so to zero defects'; many companies still have 20 per cent of rejects and rework – for them zero defects is as far away as the moon, if not Mars.

But the journey must be started. Outside Japan 'there are still people who believe that zero defects is impossible, that it costs too much even to attempt, and that it is much more economical to allow a certain failure rate and just replace the failed parts to your customers'. Actually, zero defects isn't realistic, but that makes no difference to Manger's argument. 'Let's come close, 20 defect parts per million, 10 defect parts per million, without the target of zero defects we will never get there'. And there is where the Western company, like it or not, has to get – and can.

CHAPTER

38

Quality's Total Impact

Two elements are immediately prominent in Robert Bosch's quality manifesto. First, improved value for the customer is both the objective and foundation of Total Quality Management. Second, this is a 'hard' discipline, not a 'soft' statement of aspirations. That truth hasn't been seized by sceptics who wonder whether TQM isn't just another passing fashion, like Management by Objectives, say, or long-range planning, that will have its day and then make way for the next fad.

The Japanese have been practising their versions of TQM for 40 years now; not only is that far too long for mere fashion, but the results obtained by the Japanese are far too good for anybody to ignore. Indeed, that's what has inspired the upsurge of interest in total quality on both sides of the Atlantic. In the case of Hewlett-Packard, it was especially hard not to heed the message. In 1982 its Yokohama offshoot was the winning division competing for the Japanese Deming Prize, the world's premier quality award.

The prize was based, as always, on hard and hard-to-achieve results. Rafael Aguayo reports that, before the division instituted quality methods, its defect rate was four parts per thousand. When the Deming Prize was won, the defect rate had fallen to three parts per million. Eliminating a few defects out of a thousand might sound too infinitesimal to make much difference. But one of the first rules of modern quality is that such small improvements are magnified enormously by the time they reach the bottom line. Yokohama became the most profitable of Hewlett-Packard's divisions.

In fact, the improvements may not be that small, as shown by the results at Xerox Corporation since it started attacking supplier quality in 1983. By 1988, the proportion of defective parts had fallen from 8 per cent to 0.03 per cent (that is, 300 parts per million, or a decline of 99.625 per cent). And it doesn't stop there: the target for this decade is 125 parts, with zero defects the ultimate objective. These hard achievements rest on equally tough technical work. If you want to win America's prestigious Malcolm Baldrige National Quality Award, according to its director, you must have eight essentials:

1. A plan to keep improving all operations continuously.
2. A system for measuring these improvements accurately.
3. A strategic plan based on benchmarks that compare the company's performance with the world's best.
4. A close partnership with suppliers and customers that feeds improvements back into the operation.
5. A deep understanding of the customers so that their wants can be translated into products.
6. A long-lasting relationship with customers, going beyond the delivery of the product to include sales, service and ease of maintenance.
7. A focus on preventing mistakes rather than merely correcting them.
8. A commitment to improving quality that runs from the top of the organisation to the bottom.

Whether or not it wins the prize, any company that can genuinely boast these eight excellences is going to be a formidable competitor. The man-hours expended on chasing the Award (14,000 in one case according to an article in *Fortune*) may seem excessive in themselves. But the by-products of hardened management listed in the article are more than worthwhile. They range from eliminating weaknesses (like loose linkages between IBM functions) to strengthening technical capacity (like forcing the top executives of Milliken, the textile manufacturer, to master statistical process control).

Talk to European executives (like Bosch's Hansjörg Manger) who are leading the drive for total quality, and you see exactly the same development: greater technical mastery of the basics of hard management. Europe too has a quality award; perhaps typically, it's notably less rigorous than the Baldrige or the latter's Japanese model, the above-mentioned 49-year old Deming prize. Aguayo sums up a crucial element in quality philosophy in an exchange between Deming and a seminar delegate: the latter said that he only needed 'to know the minimum level of quality necessary to satisfy the customer'. Deming observed, 'So much misunderstanding was conveyed in so few words.'

That's part of the difference between the pre-Deming philosophy of quality and modern-day practice. Another is that total quality is applied to every activity in the firm – the Belgian steel wire and cord firm, Bekaert (winner of the 1990 European Quality Award), is using TQM in manufacturing, marketing, R&D, engineering and administration. If all these functions are achieving near-perfect quality, the products and/or services supplied to the customer should automatically follow suit. But here's the point where total quality enthusiasts must have a care.

First, Peter Drucker's distinction between efficiency (doing things right) and effectiveness (doing the right things) must never be forgotten. That's where the softer work of strategy comes in: to take the famous case of marketing myopia mentioned in Chapter 16, however wonderfully Gillette had made its carbon-steel blades, the failure to exploit the advantages (to the consumer rather than Gillette) of stainless steel – with which the then British-owned Wilkinson Sword made huge inroads – would still have done great harm. Here, the analytical frame of mind created by work on the hard disciplines and systems of TQM should provide good protection, but grave error is still possible.

Ford Motor was one of the first American companies to latch on to quality, and has won many plaudits for its achievements (including runner-up rank in the Baldrige). But in producing the new Escort range, a £1.5 billion investment, the company's European management relied heavily on customer feedback in designing a car which the British magazine *What Car* rated lowest of six competitors, slating it for 'bland mediocrity' and 'selling its buyers short'. These widely echoed criticisms meant that Ford would need all its celebrated distribution strength, and more, to stop its market lead from eroding further.

Feedback from customers should, of course, be part of any quality programme – and all intelligent marketing. But in new product development the supplier must always seek to lead, rather than follow the market. In terms of taste, that quest for leadership is certainly 'soft' – that is, the best-laid plans can founder. But in terms of comparison with existing products, seeking the lead is diamond-hard. The common Japanese practice, for example, is to list all the measurable attributes that influence the perception of the product and to match or preferably surpass the best benchmark. Thus Toyota, in making the Lexus luxury car, aimed to have the lowest internal noise level, and duly succeeded.

The payoff for such efforts was an almost universal chorus of praise for the maker's success in making a machine at least equal to Mercedes-Benz in quality (and selling in the US in Mercedes numbers). In contrast, Ford's overly soft approach to the Escort left it bottom of *What Car*'s comparisons in performance and economy, low in handling and ride and accommodation, and top on not a single criterion. The TQM principle of benchmarking must be carried through the entire business system, which may mean (though not in the Escort's all too obvious case) seeking comparisons outside the industry.

The Baldrige inspectors, according to *Fortune*, found that IBM was deceiving itself by comparing its distribution efforts (favourably) with those of other electronics companies. The target has since been changed: IBM now measures itself against L.L.Bean, the mail order champions. That's where the second warning note about total quality must be sounded: self-deception is eminently possible, not only over the level of excellence that has been achieved, but over the value of the actual achievement.

At the Dutch airline KLM, a $20 million quality programme started in the 1980s asked 700 employees for ideas on how to improve quality. Their 13,000 ideas included 80 per cent which could be implemented without significant expenditure – for instance, new bill designs that showed travel agents their commission at the top. But in the wake of the airline's three-quarters plunge in profits in 1990, the management could only fall back on the tired argument that results would have been still worse but for the programme; that argument is never good enough.

The profits setback has forced the airline's management to look to its laurels, a phrase that encapsulates the whole issue of hard and soft management. Looking to those laurels – querying whether good is good enough, searching for continual improvement, eradicating weaknesses – is the essence of hard, genuinely scientific management. The laurel-looking mentality, though, is soft: an attitude of mind without which the big benefits of hard management can't be won. Neither the hard nor the soft has succeeded unless payoffs come in the marketplace and the financial results – and in the fiery competition of the 1990s, those payoff victories have to be refought over and over again.

Anybody doubting that truth need only look at Jaguar Cars, turned into what its former chief executive, Sir John Egan, called a 'money machine' by what was supposed to be triumphant modernisation from top to bottom; energising the labour force, boosting education and training, restoring the strength of the company's engineering, greatly improving its models and, above all, vastly uplifting the quality vital, not just to a luxury manufacturer, but to any car firm in the new age. The first signs that Jaguar was slipping – in the slide that led to losses and takeover by Ford Motor – included a fall in US quality ratings.

That fall doesn't sound in the least surprising when you consider this quote: 'I have been to car plants all over the world. Apart from some Russian factories in Gorky, Jaguar's factory was the worst I had ever seen.' Thus spake Ford's William J. Hayden, talking to *Car* magazine about what he discovered on taking over as Jaguar chairman. According to *Business Week*, Hayden found a company 'starving to death for lack of investment ... a small and dispirited engineering corps ... new versions of older models light years away'. The only new product, the much-trumpeted sports car, was 'immediately shelved' as 'underpowered and prohibitively expensive to make'.

That reads like TLQM – Total Lack of Quality Management. Plainly, either the Jaguar resurrection was a mirage or, having indeed risen spectacularly from the dead, Jaguar suffered a signal and horrifyingly fast relapse. The latter must be the more probable explanation. Business transformation is an endless task, which demands 'continuous renewal': that being the phrase used by the European Foundation for Quality Management, to which Jaguar used to belong until Ford took over and subsequently cancelled its membership. The movement is led by European manufacturers like Robert Bosch, Sulzer, Fiat, Dassault and Volkswagen, and includes several US subsidiaries (among them the British offshoot of the above-mentioned Milliken).

Such companies, which have crucial stakes in the battle for world markets, have correctly identified total quality, not just as the means of success, but the *sine qua non* of survival. They have correctly understood that total quality doesn't refer only to the excellence of the delivered product. Like the US leaders in the Baldrige contest, these managements know the vital truth expressed above: that product quality is one prime consequence of raising standards throughout the organisation, whether in service or manufacture, to the highest attainable levels.

Using a combination of quality systems, technology, design, training, functional integration, cultural change, etc. to that end is a demanding, long-term process which requires the highest commitment from on high, and can never stop – hence the 'continuous renewal'. This is precisely the kind of programme to which British boards have historically been averse. It scores low on short-term pay-offs, high on current spending: the benefits can only be won by demanding, unremitting professionalism at all levels, starting at the top.

The aversion (literally 'turning the back') has a name: 'managerial short-termism'. It's enshrined in reward systems, with individual managers targeted and assessed on short-term performance, and in investment appraisal, through too high and too early target rates of return. If you believe (quite wrongly, as shown by all research to date) that your investors are only interested in short-term performance, that's what you will try to deliver. This creates a closed loop, from which there's no escape, other than the total breakout, as achieved by the best total quality exponents.

At Bekaert, the hundred-year-old Belgian firm making steel wire, steel wire products and steel cord, TQM training extends from the top right down to every new employee. It includes an annual visit of 25 people to Japan – for Japan is inevitably both the source of the driving necessity and the outshining example for the total quality movement in Europe and the US. If that driving necessity isn't felt with sufficient urgency, the game is lost before it starts.

The urgency was certainly felt by Bekaert president Karel Vinck, and to admirable effect: gains in market share, world leadership in steel cord, higher productivity, better satisfied customers and improved relations with suppliers. Vinck's drive for total quality had involved seven years' hard labour by 1990, with no end in sight – ever. That kind of long-term endeavour and competitive performance, not a sparkling short-term profit figure, is what's needed to create grateful customers and a great future.

CHAPTER

39

Coca-Cola: The Mightiest Mega-Brand

Many great companies can lay claim to the title of world marketing champion. When it comes to champion brands, though, there's only one contender for the global summit: Coca-Cola. In the 1990 list of the world's ten leading brands published by Landor Associates, not only did Coke lead in Europe, the United States and world-wide, but only one other brand, Kodak, featured in all three lists. That brand, however, has suffered painful competitive erosion. Globally, Coke has withstood all onslaughts, including the largest self-inflicted wound in the history of marketing.

When New Coke was launched in spring 1985, the judgment of Pepsi-Cola, the only real rival to Coke and a most formidable contender, was instant and indisputable. The champ had in effect voluntarily withdrawn the leading brand from the US market. How badly Coke had shot itself in the foot was emphasised by the enforced return – not so much by popular request as by popular outrage – of the original formula as Classic Coke. Bifurcating a great brand, especially when faced by tough and close competition like Pepsi's, is potentially lethal.

For a while, Coca-Cola's new-broom chief executive, Roberto C. Goizueta, seemed to have undermined the greatest inheritance in world marketing. Yet not only has the brand survived, along with Goizueta: under the latter's leadership, the company has inexorably advanced. Every year the *Fortune* 500 ranks performance on six measures: net income as a percentage of sales, assets and stockholders' equity; the previous decade's growth in earnings per share; and the total return to shareholders in the previous year and over the past decade. In the 1990 rankings, Coke's positions out of the 500 were respectively 7, 10, 18, 51, 21 and 51.

That gave the Atlanta company an average placing of 26, well ahead of Merck, America's most respected drug company and, more, the most respected US corporation of any kind. Even if you ignore return to stockholders, which is heavily influenced by movements in the fickle stock price, Coke comes out only marginally below Merck. Here's a soft drinks business matching the king of ethical pharmaceuticals, which have long led industry world-wide in their richness of return.

The crucial word in the last sentence above is 'long'. Great brands and companies, like great wines, get better over time – provided they are cared for properly; and the time and trouble go together. Long-term care evidently results in extraordinary long-term results. Coca-Cola and the six other manufacturers in Landor's US Top Ten brands (see next chapter) averaged a 21.5 per cent total return to shareholders over the decade to 1989, despite the poor performance of two big brand companies, Eastman Kodak and Black & Decker (which gave its investors hardly any return over the period).

That 21.5 per cent average, doubling investors' money every 30 months, was four fifths higher than the median in the *Fortune* 500. The common characteristics – or common virtues – of Landor's Fabulous Five add up to a description of Coca-Cola. Their older-line and generally conservative policies are built around a formidable, usually Number One position in a long-term, solid, non-fashion market. Values and virtues have been reinforced over time, generally in a well-defined specialism. The brand or brands on which these strengths are founded are exploited intensively to maintain high market shares. This provides an abundant flow of cash, profits and continuous investment.

The proof of this rich pudding (the right metaphor, since all the Fabulous Five, averaging a 23.5 per cent return on stockholders' equity in 1989, are in food and/or drink) is the long run of success. Highly praised companies, singled out for past performance, have a sorry habit of falling and failing – on some estimates, that fate befell three quarters of the companies marked out for their excellence in the McKinsey studies which Tom Peters and Robert Waterman turned into an unprecedented best-seller. *In Search of Excellence* was published in 1982, and plainly its selections suffered from looking at intangible attributes rather than tangible results.

Brands are both tangible and intangible. They are tangible in the sense that they are always attached to something physical, whether a roll of film or a bottle of Coke. Brands are intangible in the language of accountancy, because their worth can't be accurately measured (though specialist consultants and hopeful accountants have lately been trying hard to do so). The plant and equipment that makes the Coke essence and bottles the final product can be valued, of course: but without the brand, their worth is very little.

The brand's value may hover somewhere in the region that lies, say, between $8.3 billion (the worth that Coca-Cola placed on its assets at end-1989) and $24.3 billion (at which the stock market valued the whole company at the end of September 1990); or maybe the brand is worth even more than that mighty gap. Many companies thought that way during the final phase of the last takeover boom. Brands of confectionery like Suchard and Rowntree, to name two sweet buys, were the basis for enormous bid premiums over market valuations.

When you buy such a brand, the argument goes, you buy not just present profits, but the fruit of years and decades of marketing expenditure and customer satisfaction. In the case of Coke, that past investment is so towering that no corporation in this universe could hope to near its might, starting from scratch. Moving down from those Olympian heights, the argument still lies in favour of acquisition, rather than organic growth, because buying a brand is supposedly cheaper than building one. But that entirely misreads the case.

Brands like Coke only maintain pre-eminence because the company never stops building them, never abandons the pursuit of organic growth within the brand – whether it's through successful variants like Diet Coke or abortive upheavals like New Coke. Because the management knows the inherent and vast value of the past, it stays within the traditions of the brand while continuing to expand them. In other words, it adopts an old-fashioned, unvarying overall stance to govern the ceaseless new development necessary to meet the volatile end-century marketplace.

The new marketing is built, as all pundits pronounce, round the concept of satisfying, gratifying and delighting the customer. That's how the old mega-brands were built in the past – and what the best marketing Superchiefs, none more effectively than those led by Coke's Goizueta, go on doing in the present to ensure their corporate futures.

CHAPTER 40

The Old Magic Of Marketing

There's an intimate and fundamental relationship between the new and the old. The creation of brand-new businesses is the most exciting and satisfying of all management activity. But for all the headlong drive of new technology and the quickening tempo of markets, new businesses are heavily dominated by the old, right across the world. For example, after Coca-Cola, and as again measured by Landor Associates for 'familiarity and esteem among customers', what were the top ten brands in Europe, 1990?

The answer is Sony, Mercedes-Benz, BMW, Philips, Volkswagen, Adidas, Kodak, Nivea and Porsche. In every case save Sony and Adidas, the brands date back before the Second World War; with those two exceptions, the brands have been powerful market forces in Europe for at least three decades. Some are as old as their industries.

In the US, the dominance of the old is just as remarkable: there Coke's runners-up were Campbell's, Disney, Pepsi-Cola, Kodak, NBC, Black & Decker, Kellogg's, McDonald's and Hershey. Of these, only the fast food champions are post-war breakthroughs – and the Big Mac's rule also runs world-wide.

Across the globe, the top nine below Coca-Cola were Sony, Mercedes-Benz, Kodak, Disney, Nestlé, Toyota, McDonald's, IBM and Pepsi-Cola. The high ranking of Sony is especially remarkable, given that the 57th largest corporation in the world started from scratch in 1945. All Sony's success has been won by innovation that both created and built the brand.

Look at the other names in the three lists, however, and two conclusions leap out. One is that brand strength and strong corporate performance are not one and the same. Kodak, IBM, Philips and Campbell's have all had rocky journeys in recent years. Others went through serious vicissitudes somewhat longer ago. The other obvious point is that size and market image don't necessarily go hand-in-hand; only seven of the world's 50 largest groups feature in the Landor lists – both General Motors and Ford, the world's two largest industrial companies, were beaten out by the Europeans and the Japanese.

Ford came 64th out of 300 companies in the US brand list, a fact which should have both Henrys turning in their graves. The explanation lies in the same under-performance which has seen Japanese brands dominate the quality rankings for cars on sale in America and, increasingly, the sales leagues themselves. Even strong brands manufactured and marketed by powerful companies will be weakened by failure to match the market's changing and rising expectations for the attraction and quality of product and/or service. That's the very foundation of good marketing: tying the customer to the company by golden opinions of its offerings.

You can place a modern gloss on this concept, talking about customer value and delivery chains, etc. But the idea is as old as marketing itself. All the great brands listed above owe their greatness, not to the skills of modern practitioners, but to the arts of founding fathers. They understood, intuitively or deliberately, that any advantage won by product attributes is liable to be eroded over time. What remains is part branding, part 'service'. The two, however, are self-evidently linked, for customer expectations and experience create the strength of the brand, and service contributes heavily to both expectations and experience.

AT&T has been stressing this truth to managers in the thick of the telecommunications revolution. The company quotes research into market leaders which shows that, if you are perceived as providing excellent service, you keep 90 per cent of your market share. Even if your service is ranked as good, the difference between excellent and good will cost you 40 per cent of your share; 'fair' keeps only a quarter of that share; 'poor' puts you out of business. As the continuing strength of brands like those of IBM, Philips and Kodak shows, it takes time to accomplish these awful losses, but leave the situation uncorrected and the erosion takes an irresistible toll.

With fast-moving consumer goods, the service issue only hits the manufacturer, as opposed to the retailer, with complaints, though that's a vital area. Dealing with complaints is a crucial factor in retaining custom. Figures cited by Performance Research Associates show that, where complaints are minor, 63 per cent of those who don't actually complain will not buy from you again. Among 'minor' complainers, 54 per cent are lost if their complaints are unresolved. The percentage lost falls to 30 per cent if the complaint is resolved to the customer's satisfaction: do that quickly, and only 5 per cent of the customers depart.

With major complaints, 91 per cent of non-complainants disappear. Fail to resolve a complaint, and 81 per cent of the complainants go. Resolve it, and the loss is held to 46 per cent. Resolve it quickly, and only 18 per cent are lost. Ron Zemke of PRA comments that complaint analysis 'most definitely underestimates the magnitude of service quality problems'. That's because of the non-complaining factor mentioned above: PRA reckons that 'only one in six receivers of bad problems will complain'.

As the consultants say, complaints analysis is 'absolutely necessary for top management to get a better picture of what customers are complaining about'. That doesn't help too much when the service mostly experienced by the customer is that of the retailer. Obviously, it's in service businesses that quality of service has the decisive impact on consumer choice: because the service is the product. One hotel chain or airline can be distinguished from another only by its service – which is all there is to sell.

But perceived levels of service in commodity operations like transportation and banking cancel each other out just as effectively as product attributes – and provide an edge only as long as they remain unique. Not only do service levels become more or less equal, but the reactions of individual customers to a given supplier will vary capriciously, and from occasion to occasion. How many times have you heard people declare, of this airline or that, that they will never again fly with the carrier? Probably they will, for choice of services depends heavily on what is available, where and when.

But note how all those golden oldies above have defied the product life-cycle: they have prospered by exploiting the *brand* life-cycle, which is infinitely extendable – if it is supplemented by quality of service. In most industries the *service* life-cycle doesn't exist: innovate strongly enough in the service mix and the edge will be embedded, not only in immediate buying decisions, but in the everlasting strength of the brand. Harvard's Michael E. Porter offers thoughts on the edge-creating 'differentiator' that are too powerful to ignore. They include the injunctions that:

1. The differentiator must be easy to understand, important to the customer, worth a premium – and not a 'me-too'.

2. It must be promised first *by you* and provided first *by you* – a differentiator that comes in second doesn't differentiate.
3. It may well come from studying your own Strengths, Weaknesses, Opportunities and Threats – and not just from doing this SWOT analysis on the competition. The latter course, while sensible enough, can lead to me-tooism and delay.
4. Spend (and spend big if need be) on the few differentiators that meet your key criteria, and cut or hold costs where differentation isn't decisive.

Differentiation – or establishing reasons for customers to buy from you rather than anybody else – is crucial to the concept of brand and service strategy. Actually, the word 'service' is redundant, for it's difficult to think of any effective brand strategy today that isn't a service one. That's easy to understand, indeed obvious, for a fast-food company like McDonald's. As previously reported in Chapter 29, its core strategy is 'to offer the customer food prepared in the same high-quality manner world-wide, tasty and reasonably priced, *delivered in a consistent, low-key décor and friendly atmosphere*'.

The italicised words describe what Zemke calls the 'distinction' – the strategic differentiator. The service strategy concept applies equally strongly to an engineering company like Otis Elevator: 'to provide any customer with a means of moving people and things up, down and sideways over short distances *with higher reliability than any similar enterprise in the world*'. And a chequebook supplier, DeLuxe Checks, also has no difficulty with the concept: 'to provide all banks, S&Ls and investment firms with error-free financial instruments delivered in a timely fashion'.

The distinction in DeLuxe's case lies in its definition: '*error-free means absolutely no errors; timely means a 48-hour turnaround*'. No strategy is worth the paper it's written on unless that differentiator creates measurable standards of comparison and achievement. So there are two questions every manager must ask. Does the organisation have (or if not, can it have) a service strategy that can be expressed in words, defining 'the key customer, the core contribution and the distinction' (in Zemke's words)? And can that strategy be factually tested for validity and execution? Does the business have a set of sound, hard and fast marketing principles?

Principles, of course, are all very well. But what about practice? How can top management ensure that bottom employees are living up to such high standards? Some Canadian research throws light on what happens when they don't. Out of 100 lost customers, 14 vanished because their complaints weren't dealt with to their satisfaction, and no fewer than 68 departed because 'employees were indifferent and showed lack of interest in the customer'. How to dissatisfy customers is thus obvious enough. But how do you know if customers are 'satisfied'? And is it enough to 'satisfy' them?

A satisfied customer, on one definition, is one who doesn't complain. But that is plainly inadequate, since many partly or even wholly dissatisfied customers won't complain, either. Harvard's Professor Ted Levitt believes that 'one of the surest signs of a bad or declining relationship with a customer is the absence of complaints. Nobody is ever *that* satisfied. The customer is either *not* being candid or not being contacted'. Silence, in other words, is not golden. Far better to 'delight' the customer – and that too can be defined.

For Karel Vinck, quality prize-winning chief executive of the Belgian Bekaert Group, delight means that the customer expresses his or her pleasure. As he points out, that's far harder to achieve. There's inertia of delight as well as inertia of dissatisfaction. To pierce through inertia to the essential truth you need channels into the marketplace. PRA lists seven: face-to-face discussion; formal research by investigators; front-line contact by groups of employees; customer hot-lines for both external and internal customers; consumer advisory panels; mutual education, with customers and employees attending the same training/education seminars; and comment and complaint analysis.

All the above new and old ways for pursuing tried and trusted marketing objectives are valuable – especially, as noted, the last. But Sir Colin Marshall, the chief executive of British Airways, pointed out in a letter to the *Harvard Business Review* that understanding complaints isn't anything like enough. Far better to stop them arising in the first place because (see above) you always lose a percentage of complaining customers, and 'It is a well-known business maxim that it is far, far harder – and more costly – to win back a dissatisfied customer than it is to win a new customer'.

That only enhances the argument for emphasising service. The magazine *Car & Truck Dealer* found that 68 per cent of car buyers switching makes (oddly enough, the same percentage as that of dissatisfied and departing Canadian customers quoted above) do so because they are disappointed in service and treatment. That compares with a mere 14 per cent who switch because of the product – thus seemingly implying that products don't count. But the statistics conceal a terrible trap: you can't cover up product deficiencies by wonderful service, and that 14 per cent means far more customers than you can afford to lose.

Merely reflect on that disappointing launch of the new Ford Escort in Europe: while pouring effort into quality of product, quality of working life and quality of dealerships, Ford lost European product leadership to General Motors. Ford has paid the price of a fall in UK market share from the 30 per cent of the early 1980s to 24 per cent, plus a severe drop in vital European profits. It's the same point as that highlighted by the pre-Gulf War travails of the Scandinavian airline SAS under chief executive Jan Carlzon. He won world-wide fame for his enunciation and execution of quality-of-service principles: but no one dimension of the business holds the key to eternal marketing success.

Everything must be continually got right – unless nobody else is in the game. Carlzon unblushingly told his employees that 'we make a profit where we face no competition and we make losses where we face competition'. Only brilliant ideas brilliantly sustained are likely to produce the first state of effective monopoly in these tough and toughening times; but the second state is simply unacceptable, and there's a simple way to avoid it.

Never rest on your laurels in any aspect of the market – if you want to keep any laurels. Apply that philosophy to every aspect of the brand, and you are likely to make good and growing profits even where you face tough competition. Which is what, today and tomorrow, you are more than liable to get.

CHAPTER 41

Levi Strauss: The Humanity of Haas

The blue jeans of Levi Strauss have circled the world, or at least its *derrières*. The company could yet become as famous for its management as its denims. After a relatively unhappy episode as a public company, Levi Strauss thankfully took itself private in 1985. After that profits rose fivefold in four years to $272 million on $3.6 billion of sales. That's enough to satisfy most managers' aspirations – but that word has a special meaning at Levis.

It boasts an 'Aspirations Statement' that is quite a read, beginning 'We all want a company that our people are proud of and committed to, where all employees have an opportunity to contribute, learn, grow and advance based on merit, not politics or background'. The words continue in the same humane vein: 'We want our people to feel respected, treated fairly, listened to, and involved. Above all, we want satisfaction from accomplishments and friendships, balanced personal and professional lives, and to have fun in our endeavours.'

The statement then talks about 'building on the foundation we have inherited: affirming the best of our company's traditions, closing gaps that may exist between principles and practices, and updating some of our values to reflect contemporary circumstances'. There follows a discussion of the 'type of leadership ... necessary to make our Aspirations a reality', covering new behaviours, diversity (of 'age, sex, ethnic group, etc.', not businesses – the public Levis diversified dismally), recognition, ethical management practices, communications and 'empowerment' – which means 'actively pushing responsibility, trust and recognition into the organisation'.

As an empowered example, the sewing machine operators at Blue Ridge, Georgia (one of the top 10 per cent of the company's plants), were set production goals, absenteeism and safety standards and left to make their own economies or productivity improvements. As chairman Robert Haas reported in an interview with the *Harvard Business Review*, 'They're taking initiatives and making things work better because it's in their interest and they don't have to be told'. The 'interest' was a half-share in any savings, with the result that Blue Ridge became 'one of the top two plants – after only nine months in the new programme'.

Haas also cites the success of Dockers – 'a brand-new segment in the casual pants market' – which became a half-billion dollar line without an initial business plan, thanks to managers 'who saw an opportunity ... and made commitments for production that were greater than the orders they had in hand'. The boss's conclusion that Dockers wouldn't have 'happened before this more collaborative, open style of management' can be neither proved nor disproved. Plenty of entrepreneurial successes have been rammed through unplanned by managers as collaborative as Joseph Stalin and in cultures as easy-going as ancient Sparta.

One tycoon even expressed his own equivalent of the Levi Strauss 'Aspirations Statement' under the title 'Ten Spartan Rules'. They run as follows:

1. Create work for yourself; don't wait for it to be assigned to you.
2. Take the initiative in performing your job, instead of playing a passive part.
3. Grapple with big jobs – petty tasks debase you.
4. Choose difficult jobs. Progress lies in accomplishing difficult work.
5. Once you start a task, never give up – complete it, no matter what.
6. Lead those around you. Leading others instead of being led makes a big difference in the long run.
7. Have a plan. A long-term plan engenders perseverance, planning and effort, and gives you hope for the future.
8. Have self-confidence; otherwise your work will lack force, persistence and even substance.
9. Use your brain to the fullest degree at all times. Keep an eye on all quarters and always be on the alert. This is the way we ensure satisfactory service.
10. Don't be afraid of friction. Friction is the mother of progress and the stimulus for aggressiveness. If you fear friction, you will become servile and timid.

What nation spawned this exhortation to self-motivation and abrasive effort? And what kind of business did its author command? Neither question is easy to answer: the business is advertising, which is more commonly associated with free-and-easy creativity than the lash of the hard taskmaster. As for the nation, it's Japan. The credo is that of Hideo Yoshida, who built the Dentsu agency into the largest in the world.

The Spartan rules are a useful antidote to the sentimental idea that Japan's corporate cultures achieve their result through humanely shared values: they are also cultures of hard work and harder words. Not for nothing did Kuniyasu Sakai, writing in the *Harvard Business Review* (November-December 1990), headline his article 'The feudal world of Japanese manufacturing'. For instance, when as a small supplier he visited the president of a big company, his sole client, 'to profess my sincere desire to support his company's growth and to ask for more work', Sakai got this reply: 'Your words are like an expression of affection from an ugly woman.'

In the West, which is less able than Japan to swallow the bad and the ugly with the good, dictatorial and harsh corporate cultures are notoriously short-lived. Western leaders like Haas are trying to create enduring and developing societies by moving well beyond the expression of humane corporate values into fitting deeds: matching empowering aspirations with empowering actions. At the end of one world-wide management meeting, Haas 'held up the Aspirations Statement and ripped it to shreds'. He told those present to 'think about what you want for the company and what kind of person you want to be in the workplace and what kind of legacy you want to leave behind'.

The boss told them that 'If the result happens to be the Aspirations, that's fine'. Otherwise, they were to feel free to form their own principles, and he would 'go with whatever you come up with'. That grand gesture was highly symbolic – I'd be astounded if Haas's offer had any result other than endorsement of the Aspirations, for they express most enduring forces. Its key words are 'building on the foundations we have inherited' and 'affirming the best of our company's traditions'. For a member of the Haas family, which started the business in 1850, that's easy to say. But what about late starters?

CHAPTER 42

The Value Of Values

Every businessman – including Robert Haas of Levi Strauss – knows the sovereign importance of the bottom line. That's where the profit, if any, is kept or recorded. But where's the top line? In accounts, that dignity is accorded to turnover or its equivalent. But the true top line isn't measured or reported in monetary numbers, though its contribution in financial terms may be immense. That top line is 'value'.

The word is vague or 'soft' enough to curl a hard-nosed manager's lip, and the actual words used in 'value statements' would score no points either. Or would they? A study of 20 companies that for at least a generation have lived according to a value gospel (of which the Levi Strauss 'Aspirations Statement' is a good example) found a 23-fold growth in net income. That compares handsomely with the two-and-a-half times rise in America's gross national product over the same period.

The *Harvard Business Review* in an editorial observed that 'values', whatever they are, are seen by some companies as a source of hard-as-nails 'competitive advantage'. If those companies are right, that means winning wealth from mere words. The American consultant Neil Miller, best-known for his nurture of high-achieving managers, lists a few examples of this value verbiage:

'Integrity in our business dealings. ... Respect for our customers and our employees. ... Excellence in our products and our services. ... Responsibility to our employees, customers, and shareholders.'

All good clean stuff, of course, with which nobody would disagree (not in public, anyway). But Miller is plainly right to ask 'whether these statements are to be taken seriously or if they are some upper level manager's fantasy about what is driving the organisation?'. The question is easily answered in one context: that of Japan. There, the managements are deadly serious.

Any self-respecting Japanese company (which means every Japanese company) would feel quite naked without some such statement. It can run to flowery and philosophical language, like that favoured by Konosuke Matsushita in setting out the guidelines for his great electrical enterprise:

'Happiness of man is built on mental stability and material affluence. To serve the foundation of happiness, through making man's life affluent with inexpensive and inexhaustible supply of necessities like water inflow, is the duty of the manufacturer. Profit comes in compensation for contribution to society. ... If the enterprise tries to earn a reasonable profit but fails to do so, it is because the degree of its social contribution is still insufficient.'

The company's 'Seven Spiritual Values' duly flowed from this concept:

1. National service through industry
2. Fairness
3. Harmony and cooperation
4. Struggle for betterment
5. Courtesy and humility
6. Adjustment and assimilation
7. Gratitude

Beside all that, the Mitsubishi Bank's aims for the 1990s sound distinctly prosaic. They start with 'To enhance our position as one of the world's premier universal banks, in both breadth and quality of services rendered to our customers'. The cultural solidity of Japanese corporations, and their longevity, which in many cases stretches over several generations, might make Western cynics query the statements as no more than gilding on the lily – a symptom, not a cause, of Japanese strength.

But you don't have to look East to query the cynics. Look West, and obvious examples of high-value companies strike the eye. 'Organisations with very strong cultures', write Andrew Campbell, Marion Devine and David Young, 'are those in which people hold strong opinions about what is right and wrong and what is the right or wrong way to do things. ... If the opinions are well-founded, the organisation will be highly successful, like Hewlett-Packard or Marks & Spencer'.

The argument, as stated in the authors' *A Sense of Mission*, is a tautology: success demonstrates that the opinions are 'well-founded' because well-founded opinions bring success, a thought which gets you nowhere. Their book suggests, however, that you best escape the risks of wrong-headed opinions if you 'formulate a well-founded mission with values that are timeless and a strategy that can be sustained for decades'. Once again, large questions are begged: the words are soft to the point of sponginess.

But something hard lies beneath them, as I discovered when chairing a conference about retail design in London. One of the speakers had been inspired enough to send researchers out on the previous Saturday, asking shoppers which stores they thought best designed. The overwhelming answer from both genders, all socio-economic classes and all age groups was Marks & Spencer, the long-established, inherently conservative king of the high streets. All the other, newer, hotter shops weren't even in the race.

The M&S champion's stores, to put it gently, lag behind modern ideas of striking retail design. What the customers meant was quite different: they knew what the stores would stock, they liked what they knew, they thought the merchandise good value, they knew they could find it conveniently, they were sure they would be served efficiently. In short, they know what Marks & Spencer stands for, and they like it. So, of course, do the employees; and that's what corporate value means.

Note that M&S has never had a 'formal written mission statement', in contrast to Hewlett-Packard, whose *The HP Way* has 'been rewritten at least four and probably as many as ten times'. The latest version to my hand consists of eleven points, ranging from the high-minded (1) to the mundane (5):

1. Belief in people: freedom.
2. Respect and dignity: individual self-esteem.
3. Recognition: sense of achievement; participation.
4. Security: permanence; development of people.
5. Insurance: personal worry protection.
6. Share benefits and responsibilities: help each other.
7. Management by objectives (rather than by directive): decentralisation.
8. Informality: first names; open communication.
9. A chance to learn by making mistakes.

10. Training and education: counselling.
11. Performance and enthusiasm.

Written down like *The HP Way* or not, the values of both businesses were thrashed out in long discussions between two partners: Simon Marks with Israel Sieff, and Dave Packard with Bill Hewlett. The latter pair, inordinately wealthy, were still around to guard the values while others managed the business as the 1990s began – when, according to the *Financial Times*, 'the much vaunted "HP Way" had fallen by the wayside'. At 78 Packard actually 'emerged from retirement' in 1990 to help chief executive John Young 'devise a new corporate structure' (and a new *HP Way*, given the unofficial slogan, 'This is not your grandfather's HP').

The necessity was harshly expressed by Packard: 'There has been a build-up of unnecessary bureaucracy in the company ... a lot of emphasis on a matrix management structure in which responsibility and authority are so confused you don't know who the hell is responsible for what.' Others talk about a 'top-heavy' company that wouldn't let individuals 'make a difference' as 'management by committee' took control of the decision process. All that silting-up could have occurred while people hewed to every principle of the '*HP Way*': the values were enough to drive the company to formidable technological prowess, but not enough to exploit that base to its full and great potential.

The company was probably lucky that its founders were still around in its hour of need. The persistent quality of M & S under non-family control, however, shows how a strongly value-driven proprietorial regime outlasts and possibly even outdoes its creators. Like a strong brand, strong values can survive even long periods of straying from value management – witness the dominant $3 billion business that H-P created in PC desktop printers in the later 1980s, and its huge lead in Unix mini-computers; witness, too, the comeback of Levi Strauss from the years when it lost its way.

But can traditions like those of the Haas family be manufactured by latter-day professional managers? Must you have a founding father (or mother) to set the style, the values? Do you need a Robert Haas – or a Robert Bosch? The Bosch quality principles summarised in Chapter 1 are the equivalent of the Levi Strauss Aspirations Statement, an assertion of values that are deeply embedded in the culture of the company.

Many contemporary managements, without any such tradition at their backs, have tried to tread in footsteps like those of the two

Roberts. According to Miller, they fail because 'what top management says and what it believes is happening somehow gets lost as it is translated down through the organisational ranks'. His firm, Miller/Ginsburg, did surveys whose 'findings indicated simply that the actions of senior management and the management practices employed were often quite contrary to the expressed values'.

As Robert Haas says, his company 'is not going to be shaped by me or even by the Aspirations Statement. It's going to be shaped by our people ...' The value-driven company is neither top-down nor bottom-up, but both. The Miller/Ginsburg surveys indicated that values won't become 'living things, instead of mere words' unless six necessities are in place:

1. The board is fully involved.
2. The chief executive is the committed architect and first-level supervisor of the values.
3. Definition of the values, their priorities and a common language exists from top to bottom.
4. Values find their way into each management process used to lead the company.
5. Management is not the judge of its own success.
6. Values are taken into account in how people are paid.

Drop just one of the six essentials, says Miller, and you've blown the lot. The last two especially go against the contemporary grain. Most managers love being both judge and jury – and paymaster. And isn't paying people for above-average financial performance the way you get the latter? Haas doesn't agree: 'What happens there is you end up using pay to manage your company. But pay shouldn't manage your company; managers should.'

In his book on W. Edwards Deming, *The American Who Taught the Japanese About Quality*, Rafael Aguayo strongly endorses that point: today's 'reward system destroys any possibility of teamwork by incorrectly distinguishing the above-average from the below-average when the difference is due to chance'. Decades of practical work by Deming have established that in the factory the 'system' determines most of the results of the individuals working within it – up to 94 per cent, in fact.

The first conclusion from this principle, which applies as tellingly outside the factory, is that special rewards should only go to truly special performance – that is, outside and above the predictable range. Generally, group incentives work much better (as at the already good Blue Ridge plant where Levi Strauss got much improved results). The philosophy behind group rewards is embodied in the second, and far more important, conclusion: to obtain truly better performance, you have to raise the entire system.

The objective of value-driven management is just that. One M & S manager, for example, told Campbell, Devine and Young that the company's 'standards were much higher than those I had worked with before. It appealed to me and I became hooked. Before I had set my standards to conform with the group of people with whom I associated'. That's what a better system means and does, from shop floor to strategy, of which Haas remarks that a 'strategy is no good if people don't fundamentally believe in it'. Strategy has an essential relationship to the value system: the stronger the system, the stronger the strategy.

That system doesn't, indeed dare not, neglect profit. The Mitsubishi Bank, for instance, wants 'to achieve the highest possible levels of profitability in return on assets and equity consistent with the Bank's universal service mission'. As noted, Matsushita was insistent that profit followed social contribution ... 'Thus profit is a result rather than a goal'. Other companies, however, regard profit as a first aim that should therefore be put first.

Out of no less than forty thoughts put before its employees by Dana, the automotive parts maker, Number One is 'Remember our purpose – to earn money for our shareholders and increase the value of their investment'. At Rolm, the telecommunications company, the statement of 'goals' began bluntly with: 'To make a profit' – something Rolm conspicuously failed to do in its brief years as part of IBM (*en route* to becoming part of Siemens).

That grand old man Matsushita was correct, philosophically and in practice. The right values will drive profit along with every other aspect of the company. That sentence holds the secret. Unless every aspect of the firm is involved, management has missed out on the most driving value of all.

PART 8

HOW TO WIN PRIME PERFORMANCE

CHAPTER 43

United Technologies: The Carrier Bag

The threefold thrust that animates much of modern management theory is 'flatten the hierarchy, empower the workers, and get close to the customers' (in order to satisfy them). That's how the trinity was articulated in the words of Bob Daniell, the chief executive of United Technologies. In a conglomerate long dominated by the genius of Harry J.Gray, Daniell was calling for a massive shift of culture from the founder's style.

The old culture was epitomised by Gray's last-ditch struggle against retirement. His resistance led to massive boardroom indecision: according to one report, '55 per cent are conservative, 20 per cent haven't made up their minds, and 25 per cent say the king must go'. But go the king did. As his successor, Daniell undertook major reconstruction that amounted to corporate re-education: more than 5,000 senior and middle managers were given at least 40 hours of classroom work in an effort which *Business Week* characterised as 'train, train, train'.

The pay-off could be measured by a slaughter of unnecessary paper. After the destruction, if a design improvement was wanted, the engineer on the spot could decide, with only three sign-offs required – so average response time came down from 82 days to ten, and the backlog from 1,900 cases to under a hundred. At Pratt & Whitney, whose jet engines form UT's best-known and pivotal business, field representatives were set free to authorise multi-million dollar warranty replacements without waiting for head office approval.

So far, so very good. But the intimidating scale of the work which faces groups embarking on such programmes is emphasised by another *Business Week* report on another company – which also happens to be one of Daniell's very own. His Carrier subsidiary, the major US producer of air-conditioners, was the chief villain of this description of a tragic fall from grace:

'US manufacturers of this product long controlled its world market. They invented the snazziest new models. And their sheer size dwarfed rivals across the sea. Cosseted by a home market that was the world's largest, they could ignore foreign consumers and competitors. Then those foreign competitors turned up with models of their own that were cheaper, better made and more efficient.'

The Japanese were greatly aided by US failure to invest in a new American technology, the ductless split: the Japanese made no such mistake. That technology now accounts for most of a 38 per cent world-leading market share. Daniell's division, which has seen a 90 per cent home market share dwindle away, does boast the largest US share in Japan – but it's just 1 per cent. Carrier was let down not only by past under-investment, but by poor present quality and service. Sadly and significantly, those are crucial aspects of Daniell's trinity.

Yet Carrier isn't part of an old-line bureaucracy like General Motors, whose constipation is predictable. The air-conditioner business belongs to a one-time gee-whiz conglomerate growth star. How could UTC allow Carrier to (1) ignore the Japanese market, now the world's biggest, (2) neglect that US-invented technology that largely took Japanese firms to world market leadership, (3) let former massive dominance of the market wither away by the time-honoured means – under-investment and bad quality?

Business Week quotes a commercial developer who buys from Carrier and its major US rivals: 'The only difference is which of their boxes rusts out the most'. Add to this mish-mash the fact that UTC only made Carrier get rid of a trout farm and a dumpster business in 1990, and the disease points very strongly to its cause. If major markets are being missed, major technological changes not being followed, major declines in market share not being resisted and strategy not being focused, something is desperately missing at the summit of both the corporation and its affiliate.

Where was top management's collective mind while Carrier's deterioration was developing, not overnight, but over many years? With the writing on its wall, the company at last responded, but many years too late. It cut its white-collar overhead, modernised its products, earmarked $100 million for an automated plant to make a new compressor, and raised its technology spend to $30 million.

That effort deserved to be wished every success, but the previous failures point to an invaluable lesson. You have to change what has become a pejorative word: the Organisation.

There's good reason why the harmless word 'organisation' has won such negative connotations. In both the business world and the Mafia (which, come to think of it, is itself a business), the Organisation looms over its inhabitants. It can't be bucked, beaten or broken – and it's sinister. That may be unfair. Is disorganised crime any more satisfactory to the victim than the organised kind? Certainly disorganised business is deeply unsatisfactory to everybody: workers, managers, customers, and suppliers alike.

'Superbly organised' is a great compliment in anybody's book. The superbly organised business does exactly what is expected, when it is expected. But it won't deliver the results desired by the customers (and, presumably, the managers themselves) without something more. All three aspects of the Daniell trinity – empower the workers, satisfy the customers and flatten the hierarchy – are equally important in theory. But one is clearly much more equal than the others in practice. You won't get empowered workers and truly satisfied customers unless you do something drastic about flattening the hierarchy.

CHAPTER 44

Against The Organisation

The dreaded Organisation exists for internal consumption only. It imposes relationships and rules for no other purposes than its own. That is an excellent working definition of bureaucracy. Its procedures, manuals and charts mainly exist to bring comfort and convenience to the bureaucrats – and never mind the customers. One obvious answer, then, is to establish a new management principle. Nobody can work without contact with the *external* customer: delighting the *internal* customer, while valuable, is not enough.

The total quality concept insists that the accounts department, say, must satisfy the units or other corporate functions that it serves. The satisfaction is reassuring, but only partly relevant. What do the finance people know of the world beyond? What do they contribute to the company's success out there? The more that internal departments are externalised, the more effective they are likely to be. But that doesn't solve or resolve the problem of the Organisation. The authority of the bureaucracy is conferred. Its dead hand is created by live hands.

The crucial issues are: who has authority in the business? and how is it exercised? The questions have become more urgent because of modern ideas about corporate structure (for which read organisation). You've gone to all the bother of setting up subsidiary operations with discrete managements who are supposed to manage their businesses independently, or autonomously. So to what extent should the chief executive's own function (as it must) diminish, restrict or interfere with the exercise of the autonomy?

Whatever the answer, the relationship makes the offshoot not autonomous but semi-autonomous, which looks like a contradiction in terms. Yet many divisions of middling companies, let alone giants, are far larger than most independent businesses. What distinguishes the management of the independent? Only that the latter has shareholders (probably him or herself), while the subsidiary has superiors – or, to be more precise, superior authorities. In most companies, anything the inferior (*le mot juste*) may decide can be either blocked or supported from above. What price autonomy?

This fundamental management issue is too rarely aired. That's probably because the subordinate manager has no leverage, and the superior (like most corpocratic managers, unwilling to change until forced) no necessity. Actually the real, unexpressed necessity works in the opposite direction. The superior should really have to prove that he is necessary, that the assortment of businesses he controls would perform less well without him. That is, of course, unprovable, which won't stop the incumbents from trying to prove it.

With the conglomerates, the case is easier. Their whole existence hinges round their founders, and if they lose their founders (like Ferranti or Litton Industries, say), they often lose their steam. The reasons are in the nature of the beast. The conglomerate exists to exist. The great and lasting companies exist for a definable purpose which in many cases is summed up in the lasting power of their brands. When that power outlives that of the management system into whose stewardship the brands have fallen, either the system must change or the whole house will eventually collapse.

Change became a dominant concern of chief executives as the 1990s loomed, for that very reason. One after the other, they either found change wished upon them, or wished themselves to change the business. Their twin anxieties are, first, the fear that without change in the organisation decay will follow swiftly in a fast-changing environment; second, that without change in its competitive capability and performance the company will rapidly be left behind by its markets and competition.

The anxieties are well-founded. In a case like British Telecom, events have conspired to force tremendous change, and need for more still, on the corporation. Once a nationwide monopoly telephone utility, staffed by an army of near-civil servants, it is now a more competitive company, battling for global market share across a much broader front. The business is fragmenting around a core domestic phone service that has itself seen dynamic technological change, shifting customer patterns, different regulations and product proliferation. Left to themselves, BT's managerial thousands would change, but too slowly for anybody's comfort.

In such widely mirrored circumstances, change programmes have become mandatory. Whether corporate change is enforced or voluntary, one dominant factor applies: the change must have a purpose. That's true of all management activity, tactical or stategic, of course. But change programmes are often ill-focused. They seek such noble ends as the creation of managers who are more innovative and more receptive to new ideas. The object is to remove the organisational blockage, enshrined in the bureaucracy, that impedes creativity. But creativity, innovation, receptiveness, etc., are not ends in themselves. They are means to an end.

The most effective programmes use change to transform performance. I described some in Chapter 38, telling how companies seek to identify and then compress the time-cycles in the business system. Success in meeting these precise and measured objectives automatically both demands and arouses innovative and novel thinking: the medium is the message. Moreover, practical programmes defeat the problem that change seems to offer more negative disturbance than positive rewards.

If, as at the Japanese diesel engine company, Yanmar, labour productivity over a five-year period rises 1.9 times, and net asset productivity doubles, while product line variety multiplies nearly fourfold, the rewards of successful achievement are dazzlingly plain. Becoming more receptive to new ideas achieves nothing: it's turning the new thinking into successful action that makes the personal and organisational upheaval worthwhile.

Those companies whose change programmes include total quality or some other drive towards the perfection of internal and external performance (as seen in the customer's eyes) show great sense. New thinking applied to the existing business is the essence of effective change. Organisational blockage is the opposite. It arises not only from the deep conservatism which is half of human nature, but from the very fact that established businesses have been able to stay so powerful so long. Nothing puts off change more effectively than a good cash flow. It underpins established internal perceptions of the quality of a company.

Those are often considerably (sometimes dangerously) higher than the views held by the outside world. The top management trying to institute change to meet challenge must fight its way through the blockage of vested interests that, in the first place, see no need to change and, in the second, drag their feet. The problem is still graver if an enlightened management wants not to meet challenge, but forestall it. If people won't take action even with the wolf at the door, they certainly won't when they can't even hear it howling in the forest.

The necessity is to develop the action culture that will flow from a true change programme. The company, whatever its size, must have a clearly defined and articulated purpose which can be broken down into crisp, measurable financial and non-financial programmes and targets. The semi-autonomous managers must be given full autonomy so that they can produce these sub-plans and execute them, and generate strategic purposes applicable to their sub-businesses.

All these pieces of counsel are truisms. So is the general view of the necessity of *Teaching the Elephant to Dance*, and the idea that wonderful things will happen *When Giants Learn to Dance*. The dancing behemoths in these two titles, respectively by James A Belasco and Rosabeth Moss Kanter, are, of course, corporations – specifically the American ones that despite huge multinational spread have been so vastly outgrown in the years between 1975 and 1990. Initially the inroads were made by the European giants. But they, too, have been overtaken by the world-wide charge of the Japanese.

The necessity of liberating the behemoth from its own encumbering weight and making it trip the light fantastic is clear enough. Even Rosabeth Moss Kanter's research, vastly deeper than Belasco's, still comes up with too many idols whose feet are heavy with clay. Pillsbury had fallen off its pedestal (on the way into the arms of the British company, Grand Metropolitan) before she finished the book; Philips Electrical tumbled into loss; American Express's fusion with Shearson Lehmann Hutton was an unremitting disaster – and so on.

Even the two supposed dancers with whom she begins, Apple and Eastman Kodak, have tripped over the odd foot since her book's publication. What the organisation does is far more important than how it's done. The point isn't that the end justifies the means. Rather, if the end-result isn't good, the means don't justify themselves. The cause which both authors advocate is heartily endorsed by every serious management thinker. Everybody wants to eliminate hierarchy, achieve collegiate relationships, free individual energies, get closer to customers, raise quality, reduce costs, boost innovation, combine competition with collaboration, empower the workers. But will this form of dancing work any better than earlier corporate footwork?

Both these writers are really in the *In Search of Excellence* tradition. Both believe that the large American corporation, by adopting the new ideas and methods just mentioned, can make a comeback as triumphant as Mohammed Ali's. But modern competition isn't a boxing match, which starts from scratch and finishes with the final bell (or knockout): it's a continuing race, in which you may run (or dance) faster, but the other contestants may run faster still.

Kanter's diagnosis of the social, economic and technological pressures that are making giants dance more, willy-nilly, is acute and founded on that solid research. She has a little fable, however, which rivals any of her real-life cases. That is of the corporate manager who invents a Better Mousetrap. 'But first, the Mousetrap Department manager, her boss, and her boss's boss insist upon thorough reviews, each one asking for some changes before taking it to the others, and then the whole thing goes to the vice-president of the Mouse, Mole and Skunk Traps Division (MMSTD). ...'

And so it goes. Overhead costs get slapped on, turf battles develop, wires get crossed, and the final product is not only too dear but too late. The fable, of course, has an unhappy ending (closure of the project and firing of its champion). What are the odds that in any corporation, including those lauded by today's management authors, the Better Mousetrap tragedy isn't being repeated right now? That story is too often the reality, and neither setting up 'skunkworks' (nothing to do with MMSTD) to separate innovatory work from mainstream business, nor any other fashionable nostrum, will necessarily act as a corporate prophylactic.

As Kanter writes, 'Newstream need and mainstream management are ... in conflict'. The truth is that the Western corporation is constructed in the interests of mainstream management. That is dominated by the interests of the corporate centre, for nobody else can call the tune. If the leadership strikes up the wrong music, the other players won't sound good, least of all the second fiddles. And that is the problem: the changes in Western corporations have been top-down, instituted by top managements which have been working to expand and protect their authority and position, not to lessen and spread their powers. That is where the organisational blockage receives its ultimate sanction.

Yet Japan's even more hierarchial society produces elephants which have danced much more effectively. How? Kanter notes that Soichiro Honda used to work directly on new products with the young engineers. That was only possible because Honda had delegated all operational responsibility to concentrate on his vision of the future. Honda's corporate 'vision statement' reveals the essence of true organisational progress:

1. Quality in all jobs – learn, think, analyse, evaluate, and improve.

2. Reliable products – on time, with excellence and consistency.
3. Better communication – listen, ask, and speak up.

Nothing there about dancing, and no blue-sky visions either: it's a hard-edge action programme. Achieving the three ends of better quality, reliability and communication, especially against the high standards set by Japanese competitors like Honda, will of itself both need and create corporate dancers. Such success demands leadership, of course. But it's leadership at all levels of the corporation, orchestrated, and not dominated, from the top.

To return to the elephant metaphor, he won't dance if the mahout fixes chains on his legs. The paradox is that by imposing their own ideas of a change programme, too many managerial mahouts do precisely that. Solve the problem of organisational blockage by removing it at the top, and you have the key to managing change.

CHAPTER 45

Time Warner: The Rich Rewards of Ross

The media business, from Hollywood to magazines, has produced some of the ripe successes of late-century America. The cynic could say that this is one industry where the US faces no foreign competition. The less cynical would say that the industry depends overwhelmingly on the forces of ideas, imagination, individuality and innovation – the four I's of success in modern business, and the Holy Grail of modern management. All too often, the quest is fruitless because of the checks and balances on which the modern corporation insists.

In that context, there's an interesting description by Connie Bruck, writing in the *New Yorker*, of Steve Ross, the man who raised Warner Communications from a market value of $12.5 million in 1962 to $5.6 billion in 1988: 'Ross's credo is that it is sins of omission, not commission, that kill you in business, so he wants his people to be unafraid of error and comforted by his presence ("You have to be solid, you have to be a rock, you have to be a father – you have to encourage them to make mistakes, and they will, because they know you're there.")'.

One of his executives confirms that, if you do make mistakes, 'Ross doesn't dwell on them, but looks ahead'. If this account is true, Ross just asks 'What's on next year's slate?' In contrast, Nicholas Nicholas, co-chief executive at the merged Time-Warner until forced out in 1992, 'has been known to needle others for their mistakes for years'. Perhaps that is one reason why, according to an internal strategy report produced by the company itself, 'Time Inc. has become a well-managed organisation, but it lacks the palpable passion that once inspired creative energy throughout the company'.

The loss of passion had shown up less in bad performance than in mediocrity. Growth in earnings per share over the pre-merger decade was roughly in the middle of the *Fortune* 500: Warner, at 11.9 per cent, had averaged almost twice that pace. But one number at Warner exceeded anything at Time by far more: chief executive remuneration. The second-highest-paid chief executive in America over the 1980s as a whole was Ross. On 10 January 1990, reported *Business Week*, he 'pocketed $74.9 million in cash – nearly as much as he made over the past 10 years'.

That came on top of 1989 pay totalling $34.2 million. Nor was that all. Another $92.6 million of cash was sitting in a trust fund of which Ross was the beneficiary. Moreover, $17.8 million of Ross's January bonus was achieved only by the board agreeing to move up smartly from 'book value' to 'market value' for the shares involved. Small wonder that Graef S. Crystal, the Berkeley professor who is an expert on pay matters, called the whole Ross deal 'absolutely breathtaking' and said of the up-valuation: 'They may as well say, "Look, Steve, here's the blank cheque. Just fill in what you want".'

In 1987, Warner's outside directors voted against Ross's cheque, but were outvoted by the corporate insiders. The culture Ross built at Warner includes personal domination and personal greed – the total of the payments listed above, $201.6 million, surpassed the 1989 net profits of all but 240 US corporations. And Ross wasn't an owner (holding only 1 per cent of the Warner equity): he was a hired hand. Were the greed culture at Warner and the creativity two sides of the same coin, like the bureaucracy and constipation at Time? And are these contrasts inevitable?

The creative element you want is encapsulated in this quotation. The man in question 'was wonderful to work with. He was much bolder than most people realised. People in the studio tended to play it safe, and that drove him bananas. He'd go through the trash cans in the wee hours of the morning, or late at night, and if he found something adventurous, he'd stick it back on the drawing board and say "Go with that".' The man was Walt Disney, as described by designer Tony Walton in an interview with *The Times* – and Disney's company, too, went through the same mid-life, post-proprietorial crisis as the post-Henry Luce Time, Inc.

Bruck calls the latter 'a textbook case of the evolution undergone by many American companies as their leadership has passed from an inspired founder, to his anointed heirs, to latter-generation managers – and the companies' original sense of mission, and vitality, has become diluted'. Like Time, Disney turned for new impetus to inspirational leadership from outside, recruiting Michael D. Eisner and Frank G. Wells in exchange for contracts which brought the pair a combined $72.1 million in 1988.

That, pointed out *Business Week*, gave them 'far more money in a single year than the legendary likes of IBM's Tom Watson, Jr. or General Motors Corp.'s Alfred P. Sloan Jr. earned during their tenures as heads of American business institutions'. It also won Eisner second place in the magazine's least sought-after table: that of executives who gave shareholders least for their pay.

In 1989, Eisner's pay fell to a mere $9.6 million, which dropped him precisely one place in the least-for-their-pay league. His massive lucre partly results from a 2 per cent cut of all net income above a 9 per cent return on equity. Since that threshold is two thirds of the way down the *Fortune* 500, whose median was around 15 per cent for 1988, Eisner wasn't exactly being asked to aim for the moon – except, that is, in relation to Disney's previous dismal performance. Dismal results were involved in Time's merger with Ross's company, too: not before the deal, but *after*. The chairman actually advised shareholders that 'When it comes to valuing media and entertainment companies like ours, what matters is not profit but cash flow'. That was another way of expressing *BW*'s acid remark that, following the merger, 'earnings will disappear for several years to come'.

The price of acquiring Ross's charisma and creative zest (while also upstaging an unwelcome bid from Paramount) thus went vastly beyond pay that was enormous even by the standards of the decade. The 1980s saw the average US chief executive's pay rise from $624,996 to $1.9 million (some five times that of his average Japanese counterpart). That seems to place shareholders between a rock and a very hard place: either their companies languish in middle-aged mediocrity (or worse) or they pay through the nose for rescue after the damage is done.

The right management, creative without being greedy, and competent without being constipated, runs the right company and meets *Business Week*'s admirable prescription: 'The best way to head off criticism over high salaries is for Corporate America's performance to live up to the handsome pay its executives receive.' That's a more challenging task than it should be.

CHAPTER

46

The Right Kind Of Company

The midlife crisis of Time Inc. is a common corporate ailment. When soaring growth slows down, or worse, stops dead, the menopausal business gets stuck and can't produce a second-stage takeoff. That's when the critics and the vultures start to gather. Often, it's only when the midlife crisis becomes truly critical – if the company runs out of money as well as steam, or the predators pounce (as they did on both Disney and Time) – that the second stage ignites, sometimes too late in the day.

The corporate menopause is preventable as well as curable. Escapees that have won uplift after several years of going nowhere in particular show a marked pattern, according to research by the corporate strategists of the Kalchas Group. The consultants found 32 British companies which went through the same cycle. First, some kind of *crisis* set off the process; second, radical *review* of the business was followed, third, by heavy *restructuring* of one type or another. Invariably, that led to a fourth stage of tighter *focus*, dropping extraneous activities to concentrate on some chosen field.

The final stage was to build on these foundations by *development* of the business, investing in organic growth and/or acquisitions. After which, the cynic would say, the sixth stage would be another menopausal attack, another slowdown, another crisis, and here we go again. But there's another valuable clue in the Kalchas research. Some of the 32 take-offs were more successful than others: share prices of the A Group over five years increased by 21.2 per cent annually against 16.2 per cent for the B Group and 14.3 per cent for the market. That added up to the As performing against the market over three times better than the Bs.

Nor was this just stock market froth. Earnings per share growth for the As outstripped the Bs by even more – 30.2 per cent per year against 16.5 per cent. While the Bs doubled their eps over the five years, the As came close to quadrupling. Obviously, if some secret ingredient X explains the difference, it must be mighty magic. Michael de Kare Silver of Kalchas points to one important part of the secret recipe: acquisition policy. Buying other companies is a favourite corporate pastime, but the how could be as important as the what. To be precise, many smaller acquisitions, good; bigger single acquisitions, not so good.

Remember, however, that the consultants were only looking at successful companies: making too many small buys has laid low many a less adept management. If you know what you're doing, though, the small strategic buy, designed to reinforce organic growth, appears to offer fewer hazards to fortune than the great leap forward – especially if the leaper buys a whole company. When *Business Week* looked at the ten best and worst deals of the 1980s in the US, 90 per cent of the duds were whole-company buys: the wows were either purchases of divisions from less competent hands or (which comes to the same thing) buys of whole groups, swiftly dismembered to leave only the object of strategic desire.

The four cases where the purchaser bought only part of a much larger company were Grand Metropolitan's purchase of Heublein from RJR Nabisco, Rupert Murdoch's $2 billion acquisition of television stations from Metromedia, United Airlines' snip buy of Pan Am's Pacific routes, and Wells Fargo's removal of the Crocker National monkey from the Midland Bank's suffering back. The six other bests included Dow Chemical selling off less promising medical products after it bought into drugs; General Electric dropping huge chunks of RCA (for $2.5 billion); and Quaker Oats getting swiftly up to $125 million of annual operating profits from Gatorade sporting drink, which cost a net $95 million after selling everything else in the deal.

The explanation for the successes of these partial buys isn't magical. Buy a whole company, which in the dud cases was generally in a different business, and you may well be stuck with its culture, its top management, its shibboleths and (more often than not) its plunge into awful results. The bigger the buy, moreover, the greater the financial damage done by disappointment. Those ten worst US deals were on average 1.2 times the size of the acquirer: the best buyers acquired businesses averaging seven tenths of their own size, before any of those instant disposals.

Where the good and great deals sought, got and rapidly digested highly specific strategic gains, the bad deals ran the gamut. Rotten timing was the villain when Fluor bought a commodity business just before the 1982 prices slump. Its feat was emulated by Sohio when the oil company bought into copper. Strategic error led to Pan Am buying National for its domestic routes (which ran mainly North-South, instead of the required East-West) and thus setting itself up for the loss of the valuable Pacific runs. And there was ludicrous over-ambition, as in Blue Arrow's purchase of Manpower Inc. The British buyers couldn't manage the twice-as-large American business, and they wouldn't leave it to those who could.

The good-buy guys not only bought related companies, but absorbed them quickly into the culture and management of the new owners. They knew what needed to be done before the bid (because it had real strategic purpose), and they wasted no time over the next most important step – doing it. Another way of describing the guiding light of these successes is focus. The single-product company has a rotten name, largely because of the risk of being zapped by competition and changes of fashion, with nowhere else to turn. But for single-product, read highly focused, and the story is very different.

A piece of research by Nat Sloane, also of Kalchas, shows that the larger the number of 'primary business areas', the lower the stock market rating, from which it follows that the fewer businesses you are in, the more the market loves you. Since the market is by no means stupid (not all the time, anyway), there must be cause and effect, and there is. The more focused companies, with only one or two business areas, increased earnings per share over 1984-88 nearly twice as fast as the six-or-more business diversifiers.

The damage done to the latter by themselves is measured precisely in the *Harvard Business Review* by two McKinsey consultants. They report what happened when an incoming chief executive re-examined acquisitions that had cost the company $700 million in purchase prices and $100 million in further net investment. 'There was no doubt that the company had increased growth – but at considerable cost. In fact, the company's new business sectors had *reduced* shareholder value by more than $500 million ... shareholders would have been $500 million better off if the corporation had distributed cash to them.'

The two authors, David L. Wenner and Richard W. Leber, are scornful of anything that doesn't add 'economic value', which they define as 'net present value of expected cash flow discounted at the cost of capital'. Applying 'shareholder value analysis' (SVA) answers 'four fundamental questions':

1. *How well has the portfolio been doing?* (That's the question that threw up the $500 million *negative* value of the buys.)
2. *Does the company's planning make sense?* (In this case it didn't – because three businesses accounted for more than 90 per cent of the company's total economic value, while the Dirty Dozen remaining contained 30 per cent of the assets and devoured half the management's time.)
3. *How much better should the company be doing?* (If you look at ways to achieve the best economic value for each business, your attention is drawn automatically to ways of improving operations, cutting costs, lowering working capital, etc.)
4. *What should the priorities be?*

That last question can yield especially fascinating answers. The above company ran a series of alternative strategies through the computer, estimated and discounted the cash flows for each, and changed underlying assumptions one by one to see what were the 'value drivers'. The analysis showed that sales productivity was the most important driver; more, an aggressive growth policy was only the best choice if salesforce productivity really could be improved (as, in fact, it nearly always can).

Shareholder value analysis often only confirms what a half-blind management should have been able to see. To quote Grand Metropolitan, now the owner not only of Heublein but many more of the world's best liquor brands, 'We need market leadership and we can only get that in so many businesses'. The point is so obvious that you wonder how any managements, no matter how menopausal, could possibly miss it: yet they do. Dunlop, while on its tragic way out of the tyre business, had a fish-hook firm. Not to be outdone, Carrier Corp., lately clobbered by the Japanese in air-conditioning, had the fish farm mentioned in Chapter 43. Perhaps they should have got together. Dunlop never did escape from its crisis, and fell to takeover, while Carrier collapsed into a profit slump.

An earnings collapse is one of the three main instigators of crisis, along with downturns of the entire market (which will also collapse profits) and hostile bids. The post-crisis stages of corporate take-off are built into the corporate culture of the right company – starting with *review*. A couple of quotes gleaned by the researchers make the point: 'we are re-examining our business strategy in some depth' and 'we are looking again at everything we have taken for granted'. These are highly beneficial activities even for a very healthy company, and they may well lead to the next phase identified by Kalchas: *restructuring*. That has mostly meant closing down and laying off.

Ensuring that the business structure fits the long-term strategy will always involve chopping and changing: they are always far better done in good times than in bad. But what truly matters comes next, after restructure: not rebuilding, but *building*. It's not enough to escape from menopausal drift by getting a proper focus – although that's vital. Guinness made no sense at all as an anything-goes conglomerate run by booze-barons, but is logically secure as a booze empire managed by marketing supremos.

Many of Wall Street's disgraced favourites, the former entrepreneurial stars of yesteryear, made the same error. Like Field-Marshal Montgomery, who went a bridge too far at Arnhem, the hot-shots often made one acquisition (a big one, note) too many. Relatively early in their careers, they achieved an unnoticed mid-life crisis: behind the acquisitive growth lay inadequate organic expansion. For the driving truth is that acquisitions and original businesses alike can succeed only if their underlying growth is good enough – and the fact that all organic super-growth comes to an end is the fundamental cause of the profits plateau.

Buy a super-grower at the crest of its wave – like Xerox acquiring the long dead-and-gone SDS computer business for one third of its own capitalisation – and desperate efforts to justify the buy through extravagant expansion may well (as then) utterly destroy the purchase. If you can buy half a wonder-product's world rights, outside America, for £300,000 (as Rank did with Xerox), the problem naturally doesn't arise. But most corporate purchases are fully valued, if not overvalued, and thus only new growth, achieved in the *development* phase, ultimately justifies the buy.

Even that's putting carts before horses. The mid-life miracles mostly make buys to sustain the organic growth being achieved in their existing businesses. That self-same Rank, after dropping more than 100 now unwanted buys in three years, made several small purchases of less than £40 million apiece in pursuit of the policy of 'strengthening core market positions via acquisition'. Another mid-lifer put the issue another way when remarking that 'we only need to make small acquisitions because our organic growth is so strong'. Said another, 'our acquisitions were carefully planned and complementary to businesses we know about'.

What businessmen say and what they do, of course, are not necessarily the same thing. One man's 'complementary' activity may be another man's unrelated nonsense. The same subjective difficulty affects even 'strong organic growth'. How much depends on price rises, rather than adding value for the customer? What's happening to market share, accurately measured? What proportion of the rise merely or mainly reflects market conditions? – like the monetary over-expansion and lax controls that, far more than their financial genius (if any), created Wall Street's recent (or late) heroes.

The right company's management never deceives itself with good figures, or glib phrases, or anything else. It is only interested in real growth for the corporation, with management's own pay packets and prestige as secondary considerations. When it goes shopping for growth it makes sure that it buys the right company, in the other meaning of 'right': that is, one that has a genuine fit with the strategic purposes of the purchaser. And having bought a business, it manages it in the only right manner – to achieve major organic growth. That's the way, whether or not the firm is post-proprietorial, like Time and Disney, to achieve the best of all solutions to the mid-life crisis. Don't have one.

CHAPTER

47

Harley-Davidson: The Kick Restart

In his book *Well Made in America*, Vaughn Beals, chairman of Harley-Davidson, first of all tells the story of 'badly made in America'. Under conglomerate ownership, America's dominant maker of mighty motorcycles almost trebled its output in four years. Then, from 1973 onwards, the company saw its market share fall from 75 per cent to less than a quarter under the impact of relentless Japanese competition. There was no mystery about the decline. Harley-Davidson was competing with terrible quality against rivals whose own quality was flawless and who also offered far superior engine technology.

The resurrection of the battered company rested on two developments: the work of Beals and his management buyout team and a heavy helping hand from the Federal Government. There was no prospect of a comeback, however, unless Japanese quality and costs could be matched. Beals led a tour round Honda's assembly plant in Marysville, Ohio, which at last opened Harley-Davidson eyes. To quote Beals, 'We were being wiped out by the Japanese *because they were better managers*' (my italics).

'It wasn't robotics, or culture, or morning callisthenics and company songs', Beals continued, 'it was professional managers who understood their business and paid attention to detail'. After telling employees that 'We have to play the game the way the Japanese play it or we're dead', Beals led a stirring revival effort. Thanks to major steps forward, like redesign, employee involvement, statistical quality control and just-in-time inventory policies, the business doubled its market share, cut its inventory by 70 per cent and raised its world-wide revenue by 177 per cent.

Notice that it wasn't the opening of eyes that accomplished this result. Beals can't be proud of needing a Honda visit, as late as the

1980s, to awaken him to the way the Japanese play the game. But once woken up, he acted: and that's the real name of the game. For years, Western managers have talked about the high productivity and willing cooperation of the Japanese workforce as if it were an act of God, as inimitable as Mount Fuji, and therefore requiring no action or reaction on their part. But what was the truth?

A *Management Today* writer investigated the excellent labour record and productivity of Japanese firms which (like Honda) have turned to manufacturing in the West. She found, not surprisingly, that they had excellent management of people, which rested on elements that proved essential to the Harley-Davidson transformation. It was (and is) a wholly practical formula.

1. Numbers of employees are carefully planned and controlled, so sudden and disruptive hirings and firings are avoided.
2. Pay is good and progressive, so people are encouraged to enhance their skills and status.
3. Jobs are good, too, with plenty of opportunity for their holders to contribute to improvement of the job and its content.
4. That's all helped along by excellent training which makes sense of another plank...
5. Promotion by assessed merit – and merit alone.
6. Continuous and effective motivation programmes are used, revised and augmented.
7. Communication is equally continuous and constant, which becomes much easier when you have ...
8. Highly accessible management, and ...
9. Social equality within the company. Finally ...
10. Everything's bound together by the search for growth and constant change in products and processes.

Without that last quest, stagnation in markets and manpower policies alike is bound to result eventually. But those ten steps only put the building blocks in place. Implementation – doing it – is the real secret of Japanese success, and that demands not only understanding, but application by the 'professional managers' who so impressed Beals. 'Understanding your business and paying attention to detail' should be as American as Mount Rushmore. By mastering both, Harley-Davidson has ill repaid its mentor. Its domestic market share rose from 4 per cent in 1985 to 13.9 per cent in 1989, which is the biggest of all gains made from Honda's hide.

That great company's share halved in the period, as sales fell from $1.1 billion to $230 million. Instead of selling high-quality bikes at low prices – the mixture as before – Honda made a spectacularly ill-timed move up-market. It relied on hot technology to power its rise, and found that its assumption was wrong. While its crash proves (if anyone thought otherwise) that Japanese can make mistakes as well, or badly, as the next manager, the nature of the mistake is significant.

Honda's gaffe didn't stem from inattention or sloppiness, but from a heroically misguided attempt to adjust strategy to the declining US market. Nor was this so important an activity that much apart from pride was at stake: motorbikes are only a small portion of Honda's worldwide business. But pride is as important to a Japanese company as pelf. Honda will be back, and Harley-Davidson's task will never end. It has already shown that losers can win: if, that is, they are determined to win, no matter how much they have to learn from their competitors, by advancing remorselessly through thick and thin, in good times and in bad.

CHAPTER

48

Managing out of Recession

Achieving a turnround from long-run disaster like Harley-Davidson's differs little in principle from managing your way out of temporary recession. 'Managing out of recession' actually has two meanings which are quite different, but also very closely related. How well the business is managed in the fat years ('out of recession') has a profound effect on how successfully it can withstand the lean months – managing itself 'out of recession' into the lush valleys beyond.

Managing well includes, as a basic ingredient, the knowledge that some time the bottom will fall out of the market, the economy, the company or all three: the very combination that started to strike much of industry in the summer of 1990. Good management, by the same token, also includes the basic knowledge that lush valleys do lie over the horizon, and that the good times will roll again. Artful managements do nothing in their purple periods that would cause infinite regret in the dark; nor, in the depths of gloom, do they take any steps that might impair their capacity to enjoy the coming boom.

Human nature, alas, works in the opposite way. Over-reaction to easy living forces companies to meet harder times with dangerous measures that weaken their competitive ability for the vital years ahead. That certainly happened to British manufacturing industry during the years of relative decline: my strong suspicion is that US manufacturers have lost out in similar fashion. Certainly at Chrysler, cutbacks in engineering staff meant that, even had Lee Iacocca wanted to spend the necessary billions on new car and engine development, he didn't have enough engineers left to do the spending.

During the 1980s, this kind of blight spread to the service industries, previously thought immune to such troubles. The idea of retailers plunging into heavy debt, for instance, would have caused loud laughs once upon a time. With customers obligingly paying on the nail for goods whose costs were met two or three months later, who needed to borrow? But who was the hero, or villain, of what *Fortune* described as 'The Biggest Looniest Deal Ever'?

The magazine's story was all about 'How the wacky Robert Campeau and his fee-hungry bankers concocted a huge takeover that promptly went bust'. The subjects of the looniness were retail chains, including Brooks Brothers, for which Marks & Spencer proceeded to overpay, in a further fit of folly. The repercussions of the failure of this mad exercise in excess leverage 'clobbered businesses far and wide, and are still going on ... and on ...and on'. That puts in a nutshell what happened to the other services sector that created its own private recession ahead of the general epidemic. In financial services, 'fee-hungry bankers' led a world-wide rush into loans of gargantuan size and awful quality.

The larger the loans, of course, the worse their quality is bound to be. For every business that over-borrowed there must be a lender who over-lent – actually, many lenders, given the bankers' habit of spreading or 'syndicating' their risks. Since they are all taking in each other's dirty washing, this reduces their exposure not at all – which means, as in the cases of Donald Trump and Rupert Murdoch, that the lenders end up lending still more money so that the borrowers can service (and with luck repay) their existing, insupportable debts.

What leads financiers to advance funds in record amounts to dubious figures like Alan Bond (who borrowed the equivalent of $700 for every man, woman and child in Australia)?

Partly, it's greed – the hunger for fees referred to above: two investment banks got $14 million apiece, agreed in advance, merely for advising the board of RJR Nabisco on the conflicting offers for the company. That gives some idea of the free and easy money that sloshed around in Wall Street and washed away the normal canons of prudence and commonsense. Partly, it's fear – the fear that, if you miss this deal or that, you'll be left behind by more aggressive rivals. And partly, it's incompetence – the failure to do the sums properly, failure to keep the overall pattern in mind, failure to give due hearing to the Cassandras within.

Greed, fear and incompetence represent the taking to excess of three highly estimable qualities: ambition, opportunism and optimism. A Zen sage once proved his wisdom by advising, 'Never let an opportunity pass by, but always think twice before acting'. In booms, however, managers only think once, if that.

In recession, the three qualities get turned inside out. Ambition becomes a struggle for survival, opportunities are shunned, and deep pessimism reigns. As turnover heads downwards to meet the costs which, during the boom, were frothing upwards unchecked, the options are strictly limited. By definition, you can't hope to raise sales. So you attack costs, ranging all the way from 'restructuring' (the euphemism for closing plants and decimating workforces) to saving candle-ends: that's when instructions go forth about turning off lights, travelling economy (or not travelling at all) and otherwise delighting the hearts of the bean-counters.

The paradox is that the more you can save by these measures, the more extravagant your management must have been beforehand. If like IBM in recent years you need massive 'natural wastage' (not replacing and also encouraging leavers) to reduce your headcount, there must have been unnatural waste of expensive labour for years past. To cite IBM again, if at one blow the company can cut *$700 million* from global spending on travel, meetings, outside consultants and courses, the expenditure must have got wildly out of hand to start with. A properly balanced business doesn't build up that much adipose tissue, even in good times.

The balance must be wrong, too, if the company, like the Campeau cast-off Brooks Brothers in 1991, has to hang the Damoclean sword of a pay cut over its employees' heads – 25 per cent unless they contrived to beat new sales targets. That isn't something the new owners, M&S, would try at home. Efficient management budgets for expected sales, based on the most rational assumptions available, but also (a) plans for both shortfalls and over-performance and (b) constantly revises and monitors budgets as events unfold.

Royal Dutch-Shell has built (a) into its way of life, ever since the violent lurches in the oil world made nonsense of attempts at scientific forecasting. Inaccurate forecasts took managers off the hook: now 'scenario' planning, in which three alternative versions of the future, from great to grisly, are offered, forces managers to manage in advance, answering that crucial question, 'What if?' That way, nasty surprises are impossible within the predictable range of events, covering variations in the market that result either from competitive activity, or economic changes, or best-laid plans going agley. But is something like a Gulf War predictable? What do you do when business isn't so much damaged as destroyed?

One defence lies in lowering the oldest concept in business economics: the breakeven point at which revenue meets costs. Many managers are unblissfully innocent of its location. Once, not very long ago, the financial director of a large car company was speaking to a journalist when the chairman marched in. 'I'll tell you the key to making money in this company,' he said, interrupting the conversation, and drawing a line on a wallchart showing the number of cars produced. 'Just get production above that line' – and he marched back out.

The visitor noticed a strange expression on the finance director's face, and asked why. 'Well,' said the latter, 'that line he's drawn is at our maximum production capacity'. In such benighted cases, any downturn is catastrophic. But there's another motor industry example where absolute calamity led, not to collapse, but to splendour. The company is Mazda, which nearly went bankrupt in the mid-1970s, partly because its gas-guzzling rotary engines were invalidated by the quadrupling of oil prices.

The company didn't lay off workers: instead, it sent them out to dealerships to help sell cars. Meanwhile the factories were subjected to a massive effort, in which new models were rushed into production and efficiency was enormously improved. Annual output rose from 23 units to over 40 per employee. The workers were brought back as demand recovered (and were, incidentally, much better motivated and informed after their exposure to customers).

The Japanese have a genius for what they call 'cost-down', which has been used brilliantly to offset the surges of the yen. 'Cost-down' should be a continuous process in and out of recession, but human nature again plays its part: the best of managements sometimes need a push to make the next effort. But note that the efforts at Mazda were positive, based on expanding both the company's sales and its competitive powers. The key was ' just-in-time' or JIT, which brings parts into the plant only when and as needed.

As Corning group president Roger Ackerman told *Fortune*, JIT is a double defence against recession. If you're supplying people just in time, their orders should 'provide an early warning of recession' and lessen the threat it could pose. Corning's information technology has cut the supply chain from months to a few days, thus helping to avoid the biggest bugbear of recession: a pile-up of unsold goods, which grossly amplifies the impact of lower sales on factory output. As Ackerman says, 'It's getting blind-sided that does the most damage'.

That's only one of the many reasons why the magazine was right to advise 'Redouble efforts on all those up-to-date management tactics that should be second nature by now – total quality, self-managed teams, just-in-time, and speed'. In other words, to manage your way out of recession, accentuate the positive. Intensify cost-down, raise the perceived quality of service and product, and, whatever you do, don't cut back on training, new product development and marketing investment – because they create the future. Much of this spending will be self-liquidating, anyway.

The returns on total quality or installing JIT, for example, should be out of all proportion to the costs. Saving on the latter is thus the most false of economies – especially since the spur of recession shouldn't be wasted. It can be used to kick managers out of the deadly inertia which puts off until tomorrow what should have been done yesterday. Those deadly psychological forces, though, continue to favour inert responses to recession – like cutting back on advertising because the target is deceptively easy: the visible damage is inflicted outside the company.

The invisible harm of weakening the marketing offensive is long-lasting, though, while the benefit of gaining 'share of voice' by outspending competitors in recession is immediate. Obeying this obvious truth takes courage, true: more important, it takes money – and where's that going to come from? One source is recession itself. All general recessions conceal private ones. For example, the Gulf War's impact on airlines was compounded by an excessive investment in new planes. Over-capacity would have caused grief in any event.

Similarly, Wall Street and City institutions spent wondrous sums to create far more capacity than they, or anybody else, required. Such spending can go into reverse without any adverse impact on the future; on the contrary, as supply and demand come into balance, prices and profits will rise by natural law – until, equally inevitably, the next boom-time targets for market share add up to another impossibly large surplus of supply. Nobody budgets to be the loser, so everybody invests to achieve a triumphant increase in market share, which is by definition impossible. Hence the over-capacity.

All this comes back to the vital point about prudence and caution in your planning, working for the best while anticipating the worst. Delta Air Lines, for example, includes two sharp recessions in its ten-year plan – which in a cyclical industry is no more than commonsense, and which in Delta's case forces it to keep debt low enough (currently 34 per cent of capitalisation) to allow it to continue to expand through a slump. Fail to plan for recession, or fail to plan at all, and you end up, like many companies, under financial attack and trying vainly to raise the siege by saving candle-ends.

As noted, that isn't how the Japanese do it – or how they used to do it. In the early-1990s car recession, however, Toyota ordered a 10 per cent cut in office costs across the board. This might just possibly prove a portent (as the first IBM overhead cutbacks turned out to be) of how the mighty are about to fall. Programmes like the 10-point human relations policy outlined in the previous chapter are supposed to pre-empt '10 per cent off' economy drives by establishing a cost and attitudes base that will see off general recession, and prevent the private variety.

The evil that Harley-Davidson did to itself in good times created its bad ones. The task of any good chief executive is never to let that happen – and only a very bad one lets it happen twice. Recession, like crisis, is self-evidently and irresistibly the time for positive, prudent and realistic management. But so, *a fortiori*, is boom.

PART 9
HOW TO ACHIEVE THE IMPOSSIBLE

CHAPTER 49

Apple: The Hard Core

In January 1990, the top management of Apple Corp. suffered severe shake-up. That in itself was nothing unusual: upheavals and Apple have become almost synonymous. The despatch of co-founder Steven Jobs in 1985 was only the most conspicuous case of instability at the top. The 1990 convulsion, though, was special. The fact that, in the upheaval, chairman and chief executive John Sculley appointed a chief operating officer was interesting in itself. But the origin of the appointee is more interesting still – for Michael H. Spindler is German.

Once as American as apple pie, Apple Corp. has been globalised by developments in its domestic market and overseas. Slowing US personal computer sales reflect the maturity of the economy, while the relative vitality of business in Europe and Asia reflects both lower penetration levels and greater dynamism. Under Spindler, Apple's European sales whipped up two-and-a-half times in three years. He created a billion dollar business in a time that compared with the company's original record-breaking rise to ten-figure sales: a celebrated progress for which Apple had to thank American customers almost entirely.

Many older-line corporations now win around half their sales outside the US. Boeing, Caterpillar, Dow, Eastman Kodak, 3M and Merck are among a global élite with decades of build-up behind them, sometimes (as in Kodak's case) going back to the long-ago birth of the business. By those standards, Hewlett-Packard, which also gets half its business overseas, is a mere youngster. But HP is a grizzled veteran compared to Sun Microsystems: Sun moves two fifths of its work-stations outside the US, with special strength in the testing Japanese market. The high-tech upstarts like Sun, Apple and Compaq have found the overseas tail wagging a still young dog.

In 1991, Compaq followed Apple in appointing a German chief operating officer, Eckhard Pfeiffer (who before the end of the year was abruptly elevated to chief executive). Going outside US nationals for new leaders is a strong sign of the multinational times, and one which could perhaps have been expected from high-tech companies. Their high-speed growth, like that of guinea-pigs, makes them ideal for path-breaking laboratory experiments in management. In a few years they zip through stages of development that normally take decades, on a sometimes hair-raising ride. There have been some especially hairy moments at Apple, the company that gave birth to the personal computer, the icon of the 1990s and beyond.

When Steven Jobs and Steven Wozniak founded Apple in 1976, though, they had no idea of creating the ubiquitous tool of managers, knowledge workers and, increasingly, day-to-day lives. This wasn't a considered, careful and planned attack like that of Compaq (Chapter 2). The Steves ran their invention up the flagpole and found that people saluted the product so vigorously that, from 1977 to 1981, sales multiplied 432 times. Apple passed the magic billion in sales without needing to mature as an organisation nationally, let alone multinationally. Rather, Jobs was proud of his firm's anti-organisation culture, its free-and-easy, inspirational, impulsive ways.

The post-proprietorial phase was ushered in by the thunderous arrival of competition from IBM in 1982. For all the bravado with which Apple's ads welcomed the enemy, the threat was potentially lethal. It forced Jobs to relinquish authority, later power, and finally position to the professional management led by John Sculley, a successful recruit from PepsiCo. But without Jobs's very personal bequest, the Macintosh, Sculley's job would have been impossible. The Mac, above all its graphics capabilities, gave him essential muscle in both professional and truly personal markets.

That all stemmed from Jobs's inspired idea that the Mac should be genuinely easy to use. The results forced rivals wedded compatibly to the dominant 'industry standard', with its product-led philosophy, to imitate the user-led features of the Mac – what one computer writer called 'the real thing'. Without that real difference, Apple, the only non-compatible major in the PC world, would not have thrived, maybe not even survived, into the global 1990s. That's the hard core of a company which has an evidently deep survival instinct.

Its design philosophy achieved and maintained a Unique Selling Proposition, a differentiation strong enough to sustain a price premium over most of the young company's life. In 1991 Apple was forced to abandon premium pricing, through what amounted to swingeing price cuts throughout its range: but it wasn't only the differentiation that had supported Apple's survival to this point. The personal computer quickly became a ubiquitous, multinational product, selling to a distinct, borderless customer group: if the Mac could sell in America, it could sell anywhere. PCs are thus ideally placed to demonstrate a new economic truth.

In the past US firms could garner incremental growth, valuable but not overwhelming, in overseas markets. Now that European buying power has risen to American levels, US firms can create foreign businesses that don't just supplement, but match or outmatch the parent. Compaq's European sales, for example, rose to $1.2 billion in only six years: as at Apple, the growth rate far outpaced sluggish US performance. The high-tech management culture is intolerant of conventions and inescapably wedded to high-octane growth; hence the head office appointments of men like Spindler and Eckhard who have convincingly produced high-octane performance, no matter where.

As always for Apple bosses, Spindler faced a raft of problems when he took over. To quote *Business Week*, 'market share was dropping fast, investors and customers were griping, and workers, buffeted by continual churning in the executive suite, were demoralised'. Among the tasks faced by the 47-year-old Spindler were launching an entire new line of much cheaper Macs, recapturing lost high ground in technology, installing team concepts of management ('there will be no more prima donnas at Apple'), bringing down an absurdly high ratio of expenses to revenue, tightening controls, and recovering from a poor foray into laptops.

Significantly, Apple turned to a Japanese supplier, Sony, for its second and far more successful crack at the laps with its Powerbook range. The significance is not only that this broke an Apple shibboleth ('a year ago', one executive told *Business Week*, 'it would have been impossible to even discuss that'), but because it's yet another example of global interdependence. In that global world, where managers were born or where they have worked should be no more important than where products are sourced. Spindler and Eckhard could well be forerunners for the next generation of chief executives: multinational, multilingual and multifaceted – and ignorant of the word 'impossible'.

CHAPTER 50

The World-Class Manager

In his first incarnation, the multinational executive was generally an American, sent out, like Romans to Gaul or the British to India, to colonise foreign lands. Maybe the locals lacked expertise (for example, in production technology); maybe the parent simply felt much happier about control if its own people, seconded from domestic operations, were in command. In the latest multinational mode, the same factors still operate powerfully, but less in American subsidiaries than Japanese.

Now Oriental peace of mind demands that Japanese nationals command the outposts of their global economic empire. In many ways, it's a more impressive imperium than the American predecessor, partly because of the careful way in which most Japanese build their presence, with acute sensitivity to the diplomatic needs of alien bodies on foreign soil. The Japanese are, of course, far more alien than the Americans, rarely fluent in the local language, and coming from a business culture that differs profoundly from the West's.

On the whole, the new boys have adapted well to their environment and their Western colleagues (and *vice versa*). But the West knows little about the character of the Japanese multinational manager. Linguistic and cultural differences make it difficult to get past that smiling politeness. The separateness is heightened by the near impossibility of sending a Westerner back to the Japanese parent as a manager. That's something which presents no problems in the Anglo-American world, though such transfers, too, were rare in early multinational days.

Gauls and Celts weren't transported to govern Rome. Since they were also colonisers, the multinational managers were simply on tours of duty, and not seen as requiring particular talents or training.

Today multinational management has become a sophisticated and complex branch of business which is still changing – and in still more significant ways. As one magazine's front cover announced in May 1990, 'From Amsterdam to Yokohama, recruiters are looking for a new kind of executive'.

Intense competition in all markets (for this new kind of executive as well as for sales), global trends in business, increasing political pressures and sheer commonsense all militate against chauvinism. Global corporations need global, 'transnational' credentials; that image can't be sustained if all key posts are held by the nationals of one country. If the foreigners are Asian (and the Japanese company outside Japan is the fastest growing force in the world economy), it's not just the image that demands high local content: it's the local knowledge and language.

Finding suitable locals or suitable managers with excellent knowledge of, and adaptability to, local conditions has become a dominant concern of big business. Chief executives don't care how far afield the search runs, so long as the right executive, speaking the right language, is delivered at the end. But why should the manager recruited in, say, France, by an American-based multinational rest content with seeking and seeing his career only in French terms? The best managers, thinking themselves citizens of the corporate body, simply won't accept second-class status.

The training and experience provided by the parents have helped to produce a far better equipped breed of locals. Many have a sharp idea of their own abilities and rights. That's fine for the employing organisation, if, that is, it can retain these people. Employment is no longer restricted to a few fat-cat firms seeking overseas expansion. For many years geographical diversification has been the order of the day (though often disobeyed) even for middle-sized firms. International experience has become a sought-after, pivotal and transferrable asset.

Managers with battle-honours won in the European subsidiaries of IBM (only one example among many) have a saleable qualification that matches an MBA dollar for dollar. Despite the heavy setbacks of multinationals (including IBM) in various marketplaces, most managers believe that multinational work is among the higher forms of their craft. Consolidating and coordinating businesses across frontiers truly is more demanding, especially in the typical multinational, with product lines as diversified as its markets. The result has tended to be a heavy, possibly overweight build-up in management systems.

But exposure to overly systematised management is a healthy discipline both positively (teaching what to do) and negatively (teaching what to shun). The new generation of multinational managers are an advanced species. Like Spindler and Pfeiffer at Apple and Compaq, they can skip easily across frontiers, from function to function (though often they are wanted for special talents, rather than general ones), and industry to industry. When the British-based Saatchi & Saatchi was seeking global salvation, for example, the chief executive choice fell on a Frenchman Robert Louis-Dreyfus. No advertising man, he had made his bones running a medical market research firm in the US.

The mid-Atlantic English of these new men is often impeccable, their knowledge of management and management *mores* astounding, their flexibility probably the greatest displayed by managers at any time in business history, their ambition, like their experience, knowing no frontiers. Some have had four or five important jobs before the age of forty in their multinational speciality. The speciality, though, may still be their highest card. Multinational business isn't a separate world of its own: if anything, operating companies of multinationals have become more akin to national competitors.

The latter, forced along by having to battle with multinationals, have markedly improved their competitive powers. So have nationals running local multinational subsidiaries. These local bosses have heavily restricted influence over basic business and management decisions. Up to now, this hasn't been a blatantly great source of tension between the centre and the peripheries. Morale in multinational subsidiaries has mostly been high. But does continued ultimate and strict control from abroad, whether America, Japan, London, or anywhere else, make sense?

Many of today's American chief executives have at one time or another worked overseas, like Paul Allaire of Xerox Corporation, who once headed an arduous turnround of its UK operation. Will they give their overseas successors any more rope than they enjoyed (or didn't enjoy) themselves? Obviously, the overseas manager doesn't resent all of head office. Having a rich and technically well-equipped parent (with what one ex-employee of a US multinational calls 'all modern conveniences') has its points, especially in times of trouble. Often the complaint is the other way round: that subsidiaries can't get the help – in developing new markets, say – that the parent should provide.

The underlying issue runs very deep. In theory, multinationalism is the perfect set-up for decentralisation and delegation. Where languages, markets and frontiers differ, business success demands devolving decisions to the arena of action. It's a more extreme form of the essential dilemma of the 1990s for all management: how to combine control with freedom. Shifting international management from America to Brussels, or London, or Geneva has been tried as an answer. Like most halfway houses, it doesn't work.

Wherever you put head office, the psychological barriers against letting go mount high. Large companies love their control systems: often the reporting demands placed on overseas business are what most irk the multinational manager. There he sits, running the market-leader in its sector and country, wasting acres of time answering to a boss several thousand miles away. And there sits his nearest competitor, complete with his very own reporting systems, and subject to nó man. The fact that domestic servants of the same US master are in the same miserable boat won't make that multinational manager any happier.

Decentralisation offers managements simplified, better, more responsible performance; that being so, imposed and complex control systems are senseless. Developments in information technology are one solution. The overlords can now get much clearer and more detailed insight into far-flung operations without either leaving their desks or bugging their overseas managers – or making the latter leave their own work. Given more leeway to make their own decisions and mistakes, though, these people will need more entrepreneurial qualities, fewer gifts as bureaucrat and in-company diplomat.

Real difficulties remain about the power over money and the problems of coordination. No multinational can tolerate a situation in which two subsidiaries in different countries openly war in the market-place. Nor can any company, whether its base is Vevey, Minneapolis or London, allow national companies to pile up cash balances and allocate capital as if these gigantic sums didn't concern the parent. In practical terms, the parent management is the shareholding body: it stands at least one remove from true shareholders, but it has their authority, and their rights, to consider.

Moreover, the whole meaning of globalism is that purchasing and sourcing decisions can't be taken in each country unilaterally. Resolving such real problems will make extraordinary demands on multinational managers on both sides of the fence. The community of interest that exists between all the parties is potentially the foundation for high creativity. The parent management has only to resign itself to not managing: to becoming a facilitating body with a strong bias towards bankerly rather than operating functions.

This rings true even in a global era in which companies want to present a homogeneous image in different marketplaces. Coca-Cola has always to be Coke; Ford, having developed a European strategy ahead of anybody else, now has to make it global; a Compaq or Apple purchaser runs the same software on the same hardware world-wide. But you can achieve reasonable cohesion in marketing policies (as the Coke example shows) by ways other than riding corporate policemen on the backs of national managements. Parents who learn to lead from behind help their country managers to learn two difficult arts simultaneously: running a business of their own, while serving the interest of the whole.

The Spindler and Eckhard moves are outstanding examples of the increasing interchange round the world, with more foreigners joining the parent board in the US, and more non-Americans (following in the long ago footsteps of Jacques Maisonrouge of IBM) getting real influence inside a mighty American company. That's to the benefit of both parents and subsidiaries. If a Dutchman is the best man in the world to become financial vice president, why reserve the position for an American? For that matter, why should a Dutch company insist on having a Dutch group marketing director if its best qualified marketeer is an American in Brazil?

The strength of nationalism in a supposedly transnational age is still too great: multinationals are much less 'multi', transnationals far less 'trans' and both far more national than they like to pretend. Multinational parents lose much by trying to force their children into a corporate mould. Subsidiaries such as the sadly and badly reduced Hoover, once the leading appliance company in Europe, actually managed far better in their old days of near-total independence. True, what worked decades ago won't work in the 1990s, let alone the next century. But coordination and central direction are not synonymous.

The recipe is simple. Shift the balance more towards autonomy at the local level by revising control systems and delegating more authority: open all jobs to all-comers, right up to the highest parental level. That's good multinationalism and excellent management alike. The theory of delegation, nationally or multinationally, is to have each operation managed by the most able and suitable person. If that man or woman doesn't take the decision, but the boss does, where's the delegation?

You only need to look over managers' shoulders and countermand them if they're no good. Doing that makes them worse; second-guessing leads to third-rate management. The fact that, thanks to the IT revolution, the higher ranks of management can now be far better informed puts more ammunition behind their right and duty to say (with due discretion) what they think. They also have the right and duty to remove and replace managers whose decisions and actions fail. That's power enough for any sensible purpose. The right to interfere with the exercise of delegated responsibility is a contradiction in terms: responsibility without authority is no responsibility at all.

Implementing this truth demands more tact and self-restraint than most multinational bosses habitually show. Part of a multinational business can only galvanise or sustain the whole (as did the European operations of Compaq and Apple) if the branches have equality with the centre. Greater transnational equality is the inevitable trend, the only one that makes sense. Both sides gain greatly, whatever their nationality, by becoming one side, peopled by borderless managers who match Kenichi Ohmae's 'borderless world'.

One giant group selects its candidates for this role by applying the acronym SMILE. The corporation seeks Skill, Management ability, Internal flexibility, Language facility and Endeavour (described as vitality, perseverance in the face of difficulty). Significantly, SMILE comes not from a Western company, but from Matsushita Electric. The Japanese have achieved the impossible in world markets by their philosophy as much as their products. Given their inherent multinational advantages, Westerners can achieve even more.

CHAPTER 51

The Washington Post: What Katy Did

Many managers, some with genuine modesty, others with false, have declared that their predecessors have given them (to quote one example) 'everything but an easy path to follow'. Very few have said it of a woman, for very few have had that opportunity. That quote, however, was uttered by the heir-apparent at the *Washington Post*, Inc., one of the world's most deserving media groups. The heir was speaking of his mother, Katherine Graham, which doesn't detract from the sincerity of the tribute or the value of her achievements, corporate and personal.

The personal distinction can be gauged from one truly hard fact. At the start of 1989 only three chief executives out of the 1000 companies ranked by *Business Week* as America's biggest were female – and one of the others (Liz Claiborne) had founded her own company. As for Graham, she inherited her job on the suicide of her husband, Philip, who in turn had taken the mantle from Katy Graham's father, Eugene Meyer. A year later only Mrs Graham was numbered among the élite 1000, Claiborne having made a graceful exit. Not a single professional female executive had made it into the male Valhalla as the century's last decade began.

Yet nobody could deny Graham's professionalism or her success. Where women have stepped into business, either as principals (like Claiborne or Helena Rubinstein) or as consorts or widows, they have often shown brilliant ability. In researching my book, *The Age of the Common Millionaire*, I noted an extraordinary number, far higher than probability would suggest, of other media widows. These women, just like Graham, had taken hold of newspaper, broadcasting and magazine empires after the deaths of their husbands and outperformed them.

Helen Copley, the queen of the nine-daily Copley Press, credited with injecting strong commercial management into papers like the *San Diego/Union Tribune*, was a staunch tidier-up of holdings and a conservative empire-builder. Dorothy Stimson Bullitt was the first person to open a television station in the Northwest and the prime force behind King Broadcasting; in an uncanny parallel with Katherine Graham, Mrs Bullitt took over her father's bequest on her husband's death. Since that was in 1932, the King expansion has to be her doing.

That's also true of Oveta Culp Hobby's broadcasting interests, added to the *Houston Post* (later sold) which she inherited from her spouse, a former Texan governor. The billion or two value of these female-dominated family holdings is partly fortuitous: newspapers, magazines and broadcasting have made easy money for many males of no conspicuous management ability, like Walter Annenberg, former Ambassador to the Court of St James, who pocketed an out-of-this-world $3 billion from Rupert Murdoch for interests topped by *TV Guide*. That doesn't, however, invalidate the remarkable success of those four media queens.

But is their success really 'remarkable'? That can only be true if you start from the absurd proposition that women are unlikely to excel in business. The media widows were the forerunners of what are now hundreds and will be thousands of successes, and not only in the media. From the moment that a large pool of ambitious, educated women, interested in the diverse activities known as management, came into being, their progress into executive power has been inevitable. Timing is the only issue left in doubt.

The media have provided the perfect opening for talents like Katherine Graham's because of the peculiar structure of enterprises like newspapers. They maintain a generally clear division between editorial and business (the latter being the side, as the columnist A. J. Liebling once tartly observed, where they keep the money). The high cash flow of papers, paid for by customers on the spot, has made the preservation of proprietorial rights much easier to finance. With no need for deep reserves of management talent, or much managerial complexity, press empires are well-placed to avoid bureaucracy and, equally important, to promote creative independence and individuality.

Publishing managements fall quite naturally into a three-legged partnership, a *troika*, in which one boss sells the advertising, another edits the publication and a third, the publisher or proprietor, directs policy. A Katherine Graham binds together the whole, in part by appointments, especially to the two other positions, but above all by determining the ethos, setting the style, defending the established values. Dictatorial, Hearst-like power can easily be applied from this position: but it isn't sustainable, as the Hearst heirs found.

Within a non-Hearst culture, editorial people are free to express their own talents (without which the commercial side has nothing worth selling) within an unusually flat structure. From editor to junior reporter (as from the *Post*'s Ben Bradlee to Woodward and Bernstein in the Watergate exposure) you may find no more than two intervening ranks – more likely, one. In such a world of clearly defined, interlocking, non-hierarchical responsibilities, the top female executive seems quite natural, even to an editor who is male, as most editors are.

There's no longer a top female at the *Washington Post*, though. In 1991, the boss turned over the *Post* and her post to her son, after a job that was magnificently done but would never have been started save for accidents of birth, marriage and death. The freer and flatter nature of good publishing businesses makes the crucial point about what Katy Graham did. The exclusion of women from top management is a reflection, not of their ability or unsuitability, but of the outmoded, hidebound, uncooperative, hierarchial pyramids that male managers have built – which the best of them are now pulling down, doing so, if they are especially enlightened, with the help of wise women.

CHAPTER
52
A Regiment Of Women

Imagine the executive committee of General Motors, meeting in the year 2015. The chief executive is leading a discussion on how to consolidate the corporation's increase in domestic market share to 40 per cent – an advance taken largely out of the flesh of Japanese rivals, both American and home-based. She insists that her divisional managers institute plans now to reach 45 per cent penetration in 2020. With varying degrees of enthusiasm, the top managers around the table back the proposal. Half, like their leader, are women.

In the early 1990s, it's hard to say which is more fanciful: the idea of GM reversing the Japanese tide or the notion of this corporation, or any other Western giant, being headed by a woman, with other women occupying half the executive posts in the company. Yet women account for half the educated population. To expect their historical virtual exclusion from senior management to continue indefinitely is more unreasonable than to predict its end. Too many other bastions of masculinity have fallen for the executive suite to stay largely inviolate.

In 1988, IBM gave Ellen Hancock charge of one of its key operating divisions in a new structure designed to intensify the corporation's flagging competitive prowess. That's not exactly lightning progress: six decades after Thomas Watson set the company going and 35 years after it marketed its first digital computer. The odds, in an age of accelerating change, favour the arrival of still more women around the IBM summit in less than 35 years, let alone half a century.

The limiting factors aren't confined to male obstruction. Women may well want no part of commercial bureaucracies in which their upward path, because of gender, will be more strenuous than a man's – and taken with less prospect of reaching the top. In previous generations, Jewish men were likewise limited in an America whose racial bias extended well into the second half of the century. Similarly excluded by prejudice from corporate power, women have followed those male Jews by very sensibly opting for careers where prejudice is no obstacle: entertainment, the media, finance, service businesses, entrepreneurship, and so on.

But these denials and self-denials are not everlasting. Irving S. Shapiro, after all, did become chairman of Du Pont, a prime member of the American corporate establishment (rather endearingly, he acknowledged that his promotion was exceptional – because he was a businessman, not a chemist). Shapiro's elevation is still a rarity in American big business. But in an era when competitive conditions place an ever larger premium on talent, any company which in effect restricts Jews, blacks, women or any other human category is limiting its catchment area when it should be fishing in the largest available pool.

By the same token, those companies which encourage universal executive selection and promotion have a wider choice and, other things being equal, a better prospect. Anyway, open management, the dominant mode of the future, demands open recruitment and advancement. Openness to all-comers is practically a definition of the open corporation. But will sexual equality make any significant, real difference to management and the corporation in and of itself?

Psychologists have discovered that women's brains tend more towards the creative, right-sided talents. To the large extent that lack of imagination causes poor corporate performance, that promises a decisive contribution to business vitality. But it doesn't necessarily follow. The greater creativity of the female brain is an average: all women are not more imaginative than all men. Investing women with universal attributes falls into the same trap which their male adversaries have set for female intruders: generalisation as a cover for particular prejudice.

'Adversaries' is the word. Men who restrict women's corporate advance are opponents of the same stamp as the political opponents of the suffragettes. In both politics and business, the unexpressed but fundamental reasons for opposition are the same. If all posts of power were equally available to men and women, each male would mathematically have half the present chance of reaching the top. Generalisations about women have been the respectable form of job preservation for the threatened sex.

Take 'they're too impulsive', for example. Who are 'they'? The statement is as absurd as saying that all men are macho. Any statement that 'they' are 'all the same' is the beginning of prejudice, and maybe more than the beginning. Social pressures have served not only to keep women out of the managerial race. They have also been excluded or restricted in professional work, from the law and accountancy to engineering and civil aviation. In many of these professions (but by no means all, or all the way) the situation is now changing rapidly.

Management, as a conscious occupation, is a relatively late development, so it's not surprising that women have been especially late into this arena. The pool of female executive talent probably only began to form in the 1960s. It has been swelling year by year. Every graduating class from the business schools has released and is releasing a fresh flow of female talent. Eventually, it will not be denied. Already, the more direct the relationship between personal talent and corporate achievement, the faster the women have come through.

It isn't just the media widows who have contributed to the upsurge of printed publishing in what was supposed to be an electronic age. Helen Gurley Brown, with her uncovenanted resurrection of *Cosmopolitan*, opened the door to a flood of magazines aimed at carefully segmented marketplaces. One of them, *Vanity Fair*, is the editorial creation of another Brown, Tina, the earlier re-inventor of *Tatler*. Yet the magazine business, like most industries in the West, is still financed and managed largely by men. Likewise, men in Wall Street and the City of London have been forced by sheer need to hire female brains for high salaries, but have kept the levers of power in their own hands. Here and elsewhere, corporate conservatism has been mustered to protect the male monopoly of top jobs.

Prejudice, rigid structures, rigid ideas and stereotyped career paths are formidable obstacles. They are barriers, not just to the progress of women, but to that of the organisation itself. The general collapse of prejudices and rigidities under the weight of economic necessity makes it harder for male defences to hold. All the trends in society and management point in the same direction. Senior managers, after all, are mostly fathers. Their personalities will have to be severely split for them to deny promotion to other people's daughters when their own children are demanding, sometimes winning, a place in the corporate sun.

In many corporations large numbers of women are advancing along the same career routes as men. The women no longer need to rely on backdoor routes, like the traditional method of starting as secretary and elbowing your way across into the management mainstream. That transition in turn reflects a change in female thinking, which can be detected both inside corporations and outside, in the entrepreneurial world. Many women have chosen to start their own businesses. But inordinate female success in the marketplace isn't much more common than triumphs of women in the top boardrooms.

Anita Roddick of Body Shop (another of the cosmetic businesses where women have an in-built advantage over men) and her husband were worth some £150 million at the start of 1990. While Roddick's score is probably the West's highest among the new generation of women, entrepreneurs who create their own businesses are not the answer. The real issue is that of joining the top hired hands, whose remuneration represents a whole method of creating personal wealth from which women have been almost entirely blocked – except as spouses.

When the golden parachutes open, the wives float down with their over-rewarded husbands: but that isn't the kind of pay-off which either true feminists or right managers should welcome. The aim of both must be to take full advantage of trends that are giving the women of the 1990s opportunities denied to their predecessors. The increase in managerial mobility is a crucial development for both sexes.

In an age when job-hopping was uncommon, when managers joined companies expecting stable jobs for life, and when even two or three job-changes made potential employers suspicious, cracking the male phalanx was necessarily more difficult. Today, lifetime employment with a single company is becoming rarer, the company itself may mutate violently as a result of mergers and acquisitions, and experience of several companies is considered an asset rather than a liability.

The footloose male has removed one of the traditional arguments against hiring women for management posts: that they may become pregnant and quit. So they may. But there's no difference in corporate loss when a young woman leaves to bear a child, or a young man quits because a rival employer has offered him more money and a promotion. There is, though, a difference in the departures. The woman who has left carrying a child could well come back. The man who left for a competitor will very probably never return.

How will today's trends affect the male manager and the corporation itself? At the social level, change is inevitable. Women don't behave like men in different costumes and hairstyles. Their upbringing and their sexuality affect the way in which they approach their jobs and office life. Companies have become more enjoyable workplaces, anyway; an increase in female numbers accentuates the trend.

Less pleasantly for some, more women will make internal competition for jobs more intense. That's especially true of the earliest of the new waves of women. They need to be highly motivated, unusually able and extremely determined simply to succeed in what is still a man's world. Those same qualities make them formidable competitors, inside and outside the company. Once arrived at the top, they will be under no obligation to manage or organise in the same way as their predecessors. At first, though, they may do precisely that, just as the first Socialist Cabinet Ministers in Britain were at pains to ape their Conservative forerunners.

But like Margaret Thatcher in a later political generation, some of these women chief executives will have radical ideas and press them in a radical manner. Like her or not, the British Prime Minister extended her sway in a fashion no man had dared to attempt. It's hard to believe that the first women corporate leaders will all leave their companies just as they found them. The old-style hierarchial structure has outlived its usefulness, anyway. The old managerial order is dying with it. Any boost to the process of change provided by the injection of more women into positions of power can only benefit organisational life and achievement.

Like all such changes, it will take far longer than it should. Britain has been lagging behind the US, and the Continent behind Britain. Some indication of the barriers and backwardness can be seen from the entry into Insead, Europe's foremost business school, in January 1989. Out of a typical class of 200, only 30 or so were female. Against these facts, optimism has little on its side. Yet pessimism is not something which the West can afford. Its organisations are locked in competition with the East – a war which is steadily being lost.

The extent to which Japanese management is superior can be measured simplistically by the odds: a nation of 100 million people is outperforming 200 million Americans and 300 million West Europeans. To put it another way, an executive cadre drawn from 50 million Japanese males has proved more than a match for competitors drawn from 100 million Americans and 150 million West Europeans. Suppose that women were given equal opportunity in the West: would relative performance truly stay the same if the American rollcall of choice outnumbered the Japanese by four to one instead of two to one?

Female managerial brainpower is an underexploited resource of great potential value in the West. The economic suppression of women is a weakness in the Japanese super-economy. Not only do women play an even smaller role in the great corporations: they are kept out of business management right down the economic scale for reasons that run deep into the culture and the male psychology of Japan. On the face of it, Japanese women will still be excluded from direct managerial power (in family businesses they may wield decisive influence behind the scenes) long after true equality of opportunity has come to the West.

Windows of opportunity don't stay open for ever. All the arguments point towards accelerating the natural advance of Western women as part and parcel of the creation of a more imaginative, less traditional, more logical, more educated, less hierarchical, easier-going, yet more truly demanding management culture. If that is achieved, perhaps both impossible visions will come true: the executive committee of General Motors led by and half-composed of women and Japanese competitors hurled back by the right women joining the right men in the right management.

CHAPTER 53

Merck: The Magic Pill

Real quality of management will, for sure, show up in real quantities. Corporate virtue is not only its own reward, it creates rewards. The sight of these riches is generally the trigger that excites onlookers into fervent admiration, sometimes very wrongly. But an undeserving top management would surely not have been ranked in 1989 by its peers as the country's best on four out of eight key attributes – those by which *Fortune* magazine, every February, arrives at the title of 'America's most admired company'.

The next year, though, 1989's most admired winner added two more attributes to its roster of firsts, plus third place on two others, including, surprisingly enough, 'quality of management'. Why the surprise? What else must the company do before winning the latter palm? If top place in six out of eight key managerial attributes isn't top quality, what is? Or, for that matter, what is management? The company is Merck, Inc: one possible answer is that, in its industry, pharmaceuticals, management is different.

All management is different: every business differs from every other. But the pharmaceutical companies are truly peculiar. The businesses are led by research and innovation, which demand the employment of the best and brightest knowledge workers. Their lead products, for the most part, deserve their technical term of 'ethical', for they save and improve life. The companies are inherently profitable and thus financially sound, because of the fat margins between production costs and the prices that a monopoly or oligopoly supplier can charge a more than willing customer.

Their products are strong on quality, too, for if they fall short, the company dies (along, possibly, with several patients). Add to that the long patent or brand-protected runs of blockbuster and basic drugs, plus the care that management must take to keep the community on its side, and you can see that virtues are in a sense forced on companies like Merck. As evidence, three of 1990's ten 'most admired' US corporations were drug companies (the other two being Johnson & Johnson and Eli Lilly). But only Merck has appeared in that roll of honour ever since *Fortune* had the bright idea of its compilation; and Merck's edge over the other two is considerable – like its lead in profits.

In 1989, Merck's net income of $1.5 billion was half as big again as that of Johnson & Johnson (whose sales were over 50 per cent higher than Merck's $6.7 billion). Its lead over Eli Lilly was as long. The latter matched Merck in return on sales (22 per cent), but fell behind Merck's return on assets (also 22 per cent). Among all the world's drug companies, only Britain's Glaxo beat Merck's margins (with 27 per cent) and equalled its ROA. If profitability is the ultimate measure of management, Merck deserves its plaudits. But the praise is earned more by how the profits are made than by their size.

The now-dead British magazine *Business* noted that Merck 'has won gongs for being the best employer of women, the best employer of blacks, the most innovative company, the best managed company'. None of these achievements can stand alone. They all react on and reinforce each other in a culture which the career of chief executive Roy Vagelos itself illuminates. He is the knowledge worker personified: a qualified physician who became a professor of biochemistry and joined the pharmaceutical company as head of R & D, or chief of innovation.

His biochemistry background is credited with a vitally productive shift in focus to understanding the disease before selecting the compounds to be tested against the condition. The old game of 'molecular roulette', in which enormous numbers of compounds are tested, is both wasteful and chancy. The story of a great researcher, Sir James Black, shows the difference. His initial theory pointed to half-a-dozen possible compounds to tackle stomach ulcers. When these failed the test, 700 more compounds were explored fruitlessly before another scientist found that the wrong test had been applied. Going back to the beginning showed that Black was right.

The right result led to Tagamet, the world's first billion-dollar drug, and created magnificent profits for the old Smith Kline French, now re-styled SmithKline Beecham after the mismanagement which ran its bonanza back into the ground. Under Vagelos, Merck has produced its own first billion-dollar baby (Vasotec, used in treating heart conditions and high blood pressure). But that success contrasts with the Tagamet story in several respects. For one, Vasotec is no stand-alone, but part of a strong portfolio, containing a dozen other drugs with more than $100 million in annual sales.

That portfolio is also evidence of Merck's second strength: the ability to achieve high creativity (eight new products launched in two years, six of its own invention) through an effective management system. *Business* quoted a former colleague on Vagelos: 'Roy is a scientist, and he wants the business to be run along logical, scientific lines'. While Vagelos drives his people hard, he does so in a spirit closer to the academic than the businessman: 'all that crap' is how he describes the financial and legal matters he leaves to others.

The doubling of sales between 1985 and 1989, which was handily outstripped by the rise in profits, is directly linked to the surge of well-aimed research activity that Vagelos generated. A series of sane strategic decisions has been taken to defend and extend a leading market share (only some 5 per cent in a highly fragmented world). Alliances such as those with Johnson & Johnson in over-the-counter drugs and Du Pont in ethicals are designed to augment the basic strengths created by the 17 per cent of revenues flowing into R & D and by the high-powered sales force that markets its results.

Vagelos has an interesting question for the managers of this supremely successful effort, according to *Fortune*: 'Who have you recruited lately?' A head-hunter observes that 'There are plenty of good people around, but I wouldn't send them to Merck. I send Merck only people with world-class reputations'. The six attributes in which Merck's 1990 peers judged it to lead American business are innovativeness, financial soundness, quality, long-term investment value, and community and environmental responsibility – and one other, without which all the other firsts would be impossible: 'the ability to attract, develop and keep talented people'. That is truly the magic management pill.

CHAPTER 54

Motivating Beyond Money

'Attract, retain and motivate', three departments in which Merck is thought to lead America's corporate employers, are the Holy Trinity of executive selection and remuneration. If a company can't find the best managers to fill its jobs, something is wrong with the organisation, its conditions of employment or both. The same is true of retention: unless a company deliberately wants high managerial turnover (and few do), heavy fall-out is costly proof of deep problems.

In theory, attracted and retained top talent will prove its quality by motivating itself. So why so much fuss about motivation? As the psychologist and consultant Neil Miller of Miller/Ginsburg says, it shouldn't be a difficulty. The only unmotivated human being, he points out, is a dead one: alive, all people are bundles of most powerful motivations. The chief executive who has trouble motivating people simply hasn't found a means of making his ambitions, their ambitions and the company's work in the same direction.

In face of this insight, the old argument about the stick and the carrot looks out of place. Both have seemed effective motivators in the right hands and places. But the Theory X stick – the threat of firing or demotion or simply violent upbraiding – is out of favour, no matter how successful the result. The directly opposed Theory Y approach, made famous by Douglas McGregor, is justified on the grounds of efficiency and productivity. But is also embodies a general benign view of human relations. It is right to be Y, kind, supportive and understanding with employees; wrong to be X, harsh, demanding and ruthless.

The idea of the pendulum swinging back towards the authoritarian Theory X sounds ridiculous, and few would want it. The Y approach is here to stay and spread, all the way from shop floor to higher management. It rests heavily on the assumption that well-treated managers will motivate themselves. Yet the highly motivated manager is in the minority, outnumbered and often obstructed by the many who 'do their jobs' (and nothing more). The passing of the Organisation Man is reducing the numbers of mere job-doers, but has its flip side: old motivating bonds like corporate loyalty are weakening at the same time.

So is hierarchy, still the dominant form of organisation. Its slow withering away offers an irresistible opportunity to generate motivational drive that goes beyond hierarchy to create better corporate results, however they are measured. At General Motors, Alfred P. Sloan believed, in the words of Peter Drucker, that 'performance is the only thing that counts' (*Fortune*, 23 April 1990). How do you get it? Miller boils down 'high achievement' to five essential, hard-nosed motivational elements:

1. A committed chief executive supported by a knowledgeable and committed board of directors.
2. A company with common management language and concepts.
3. Tools to make the management process work.
4. Identifiable points of success.
5. A reward system that pays for success and never rewards adequacy.

The job of the manager, writes Miller, is 'to create opportunities for people to satisfy their drives within the organisation'. He tells the leaders to 'shift away from top-down decision-making', to involve their people in every aspect of the business, open up communications, empower subordinates to make decisions: and recognise that their own behaviour, and not the motivating of their subordinates, is 'the key to successful high achievement'. Sloan's stress on performance remains: but it won't be obtained if you cling to his further belief that it's 'the only thing that the professional manager is permitted to pay attention to'.

A post-Ford philosophy in the factory, where individual initiative is taking over from regimentation, is thus being matched by a post-Sloan philosophy in the executive suite. (The automobile has shaped managements as well as cities). Is this looking forward, or looking back? For a long time now the talk, and even the practice, has been of relaxing central control, and instead breaking corporations down into smaller identifiable units – just like the good old days.

Free-and-easy exchanges of views among expert colleagues are to become the new norm, too: again, just like the good old days of companies as they grew from small beginnings. They made their founders rich as they grew; there was no shortage of carrots. In the 1980s top managers went to considerable and often unconscionable lengths to make their own capital gains just as rich, but also fool-proof, and as little linked to genuine performance as possible. Like an automatic bonus, such schemes create nothing except wealthy managers. The idea that an enriched manager is necessarily a high achiever is as false as the old, exploded notion that a well-contented factory hand works harder.

By rights, as Miller says, financial incentives should be triggered only by excellent performance. When performance is either mediocre or bad, rewards (if not punishments) should fit the crime. That won't happen so long as schemes are left in the hands of greedy beneficiaries. If giving excessive capital rewards to senior managers – including enormous payoffs for losing their jobs and even their companies – was an experiment, the results are clear. America's corporate effectiveness hasn't benefited at all.

If you study W. Edwards Deming's thoughts, you wouldn't expect any different. In Rafael Aguayo's account, Deming challenges the idea that individuals need incentives to work and even more its corollary that 'people must be recognised for their differences in performance, otherwise they'll sluff off'. Do studies confirm that performance improves if rewards are based on individual performance? Not according to Morton Deutsch. He tested various reward systems in a series of six experiments with Columbia University students – including winner-take-all, 'a distribution proportional to accomplishment, and an equal distribution'.

Deutsch found that 'when the tasks involved could be done independently without help from any of the other students, the reward system had no effect whatsoever on the performance. A competitive reward system wasn't able to squeak out even a scintilla of better performance from the individual. But when the tasks required that the students work together, which is the essence of commerce, the reward system did make a difference. A system of equal reward gave the best results and the competitive winner-take-all system gave the poorest'.

That seems to contradict another hallowed theory of motivation – that people strive to win, so that competition is itself a motivating factor. Again, the empirical evidence is lacking. Achievement does not depend on competition. At Merck, a scientist told

Fortune that 'My sense of accomplishment is far greater in this setting than when I was at Harvard. My basic research is immediately applied to developing medicines'. The high achievement of the company and that of its people feed on each other – though both are also fed with plenty of financial reward.

According to *Business*, 'the lead developer of an important and successful drug could become a millionaire through stock options'. Nor have Roy Vagelos and his top executives been financially neglected. While his vice-chairman garnered $11.7 million, the chief executive earned $15 million in 1987-89: high reward, but *half* the one-year 1989 take of Steve Ross, whose company, Time-Warner, was simultaneously losing $256 million. In contrast to the get-rich-quick-and-easy boardroom schemes tolerated by American society, Vagelos & Co. were being paid according to Miller's prescription: exceptional reward for exceptional performance.

European and Asian norms are essentially different, but the Atlantic is a narrower divide in this respect than the Pacific. The American approach to compensation has been spreading thick and fast in Britain, and can't be kept out of the rest of Europe. Across the Western world, as global business spreads, more managers will get their pay in at least three parts: basic salary, then the two 'motivating' components of bonus and capital stake.

Leaving aside the extent to which these do actually motivate, another form of motivation has waned – the idea, in the immortal words of *How to Succeed in Business Without Really Trying*, that 'the company way is by me OK'. Once, that identified the individual manager, like some member of a knightly order, with total faith in, and commitment to, his organisation. It has gone right out of style. The need to belong, and to admire what you belong to, is still there, and still highly effective. But it plays a smaller part in the motivational mix, partly because of social change and partly because of painful experiences in recent decades.

Major corporations have had not one, but two or sometimes three massive redundancies in management ranks. Managers who have seen what insecurity meant to their dismissed friends are less likely to love the dismissive company. Anyway, organisational motivation is becoming more closely geared to individuals' personal drives. In an atmosphere of permanent change, or unceasing turbulence, they seek self-realisation. The company is not the be-all of their being: their work within the company is the source of satisfaction.

As such, work ranks more closely with outside interests. The thinking organisation has to be concerned with what kind of people its managers are outside the office, how aware they are of general social, political and economic developments, how open they are to new ideas and influences – from the outside as well as the inside. The company way is no longer OK even for the company. Individuals given more individualistic treatment will perform better in the freer, more collaborative style that is becoming mandatory.

Such a style answers the overriding question of how to motivate the collective, the company itself. This follows naturally and inevitably from Miller's prescription: the 'shift away from top-down decision-making' to total involvement, open communications, and empowered subordinates, with bosses who have stopped 'motivating' and adapted their own styles to the demands of the new age – one in which non-financial performance is no longer of secondary, but of primary importance.

What Vagelos has achieved for Merck is incumbent on all chief executives. They must win high scores on the non-financial factors, led by those, like quality of products and/or services and level of innovation, which determine the outcome in the competitive battle and the profit and loss account alike. Only aims that are linked to the attraction, retention and development of the individual manager are liable to be met. Only structures that allow the best-qualified managers to tackle the key tasks will be effective, meaning that positions can no longer be awarded on seniority alone.

The greatest managerial motivation of all, both for the executive personally and for the organisation, is the manager's ability to make his or her way to where work and talent can be most effective and most productive. As Vagelos says at Merck, 'Developing people as fast as possible is the way to have a vibrant and exciting organisation'. That means rapid promotion, and if necessary, ignoring hicrarchical steps in the process.

Not only do companies need 'vibrant and exciting' managers who can create profitable enterprises, but they also need heretics (maybe one and the same thing). The outsider, the maverick, is always the source of the new orthodoxy. Big organisations, by excluding the heretic in general, and the young heretic especially, have implicitly rejected new ideas, which is no way to win. The religious heretic is the 'free thinker'. So is the corporate heretic, whose free thought goes hand in hand with high quality of recruitment.

Ed Scolnick, Merck's R & D head, told *Business* that 'the better the people, the less you have to do. When you get good people who assimilate the culture, they pick the target themselves and once or twice a year you talk to them and see how it is going'. In the climate of the 1990s, the contrary orthodoxies of hierarchy are an unaffordable luxury in economic and motivational terms. If a major contribution (like one of Merck's new drugs) deserves especially high pay, logic says pay the money: if a senior position doesn't deserve a seven-figure endowment, logic says don't pay it.

If managers want to run a business successfully in their own way, don't make them conduct to someone else's tune. Concepts of authority and reward structures alike also have to become flexible to cope with the rise of managerial team-work in the shape of cross-functional and cross-departmental teams. Collective success demands collective reward, no matter what the bureaucrats prefer. Creativity demands freedom, without sacrificing the essential administrative tidinesses: Merck has shown that a business can be both inspired and run 'along logical, scientific lines'.

The difficulties are not organisational, but psychological. The men whose motivation gets in the way are those in power: women don't yet figure in this context for the same bad reason. The seniors have to surrender authority, hand over privileges, and earn respect and rewards all over again. Otherwise, the self-interest of the too high and too mighty coincides with the self-perpetuating urge of the company. That is still a formidable collective motivation. But in a turbulent age, permanence is impossible. Worse, pursuing it restricts the zones of possibility in businesses which must operate in a world where success depends on widening those bounds – and going beyond them. That's the most motivating force of all.

PART 10
HOW TO UNIFY ORGANIC STRENGTH

CHAPTER

55

Toyota:
The Legacy of Ohno

Hierarchy makes self-defeating outcomes more likely. No organisation can move from also-ran to best unless the emphasis on responsibility goes right down the line. The best person in the job must be seen to be doing it, and with the full powers necessary to enable him or her to succeed. These necessities were central to the brilliant Toyota Production System, invented by an inspired manufacturing director, the late Taiichi Ohno. He died in 1990, but his basic philosophy lives on – and not just in Toyota.

The world's Number Three car-maker has been the main beneficiary, but Ohno's ideas have spread across Japan (not least because of Toyota's network of over 200 closely knit suppliers), and to a large, if lesser extent round the globe. In the Arthur D. Little book *Breakthroughs!*, P. Ranganath Nayak and John M. Ketteringham give a remarkable account of the great man. The flavour and personality of this machine-age edition of the mighty Zen teachers can be gathered from one of his sayings:

'I feel strongly that the word *work* refers to the production of perfect goods only. If a machine is not producing perfect goods, it is not working.'

Pursuing this unarguable truth, Ohno installed machines with built-in sensors that stopped operations if there was a malfunction. He gave the worker just the same ability to stop the line when imperfections occurred. This stood in direct contradiction to the Western philosophy of keeping the line running at all costs: 'all costs' are generally excessive costs, and so it has proved. Despite the proof, Ohno's philosophy was still imperfectly understood and only sporadically applied in the West as the 1990s began, with the result that

Toyota could maintain the formidable competitive advantages Ohno left behind.

In the year to end-June 1990, Toyota earned 4.7 per cent net on sales, thanks to the highest operating margins in the business and to the returns from a $22 billion cash mountain. An innovative power-house, it could introduce six new models in little more than a year to strengthen its stranglehold on the domestic market. At its best levels, Toyota's production machine was churning out a car in about two thirds of the time taken by its nearest rival in Japan: at least that much faster than the best Ford plant, and still further in front of General Motors.

Joseph L. Bower and Thomas M. Hout charted the full extent of Toyota's advantage over Detroit in the *Harvard Business Review* (November-December 1988). New car development took two years less, cycle time through the plant two days instead of five, scheduling a dealer's order a single day against five. The inventory for the entire supply chain was turned over 16 times a year, twice the Detroit figure. All this flowed inexorably from Ohno's practice and preaching. He was even the first to foresee the breakdown of mass production in face of fragmenting consumer demand:

'It's a wrong notion to believe that mass production will guarantee you less cost. That was true in the 1960s ... Now production capacity exceeds demand ... We cannot depend upon a production schedule to produce cars.'

The Ohno innovations helped Toyota to lead the world industry into a system in which cars would ultimately be produced to customer order in only a few days. The elements of this system, like just-in-time (which eliminates inventory) and *kanban*, the system of coloured cards which travels with parts and regulates their movement round the plant, have become famous: so has the idea of 'quality circles', in which workers meet to discuss means of improving their work.

But as *Breakthroughs!* explains, you could understand all those three intimately without grasping the essence of Ohno. 'The Toyota Production system is no system at all. It is a philosophy. ...' It's a living philosophy, too, shown in the dedication of the 1990s management, under president Shoichiro Toyoda, to *kaizen*, or continuous improvement, all the way from small details of cars and production to major matters of manufacturing, management structure, and global strategy, including even the corporate culture to which Ohno gave such forceful shape.

HOW TO UNIFY ORGANIC STRENGTH

His bequest takes in not only *kaizen*, but the hugely important concept of *jidoka*. Giving the worker the ability to stop the line is *jidoka*: so is automation. They go together because Ohno's aim was to add intelligence to machines. That's the role of the sensors, and of a system known as *andon*.

You can see *andon* boards in any Toyota plant: their electrical displays tell managers and workers exactly what's happening in the plant, including what's going wrong and where, down to individual machines. The simplicity of the logic is as evident as its power, and its results. *Breakthroughs!* describes 'Ohno's triumph. With *jidoka* the assembly line *never* breaks down ... because, rather than consisting of machines operating automatically, it consists of people and machines working together intelligently'. To rub in the point, the workers are called *gino-in*, or 'skilled persons'.

The logic of just-in-time, like everything else Ohno taught, was to eliminate waste and inefficiency. Piling up parts, part-assembled products and finished cars enables you to go on running a poor-quality production process, covering up every kind of failure, up to and including a stoppage on the assembly line. Remove the inventory buffer and you enforce efficiency, and the more efficient you are, the more efficient you can get. Thus, Ohno got down the crucial die exchange time (sixteen hours in some cases) to three hours, then to under ten minutes, then to three, then to a minute – and still Ohno wasn't satisfied.

The West has been forced to acknowledge the strength of Ohno's legacy and to claim its share of the inheritance. But it's typical that just-in-time, for example, has been installed primarily as a system of inventory reduction, without any understanding of its wider implications. That is a downright contradiction of the principles which Ohno (like all the best Japanese management) exemplified: persistence, commitment and professionalism – PCP.

Managements won't get other people to work as they ostensibly want, with those very qualities, unless they display the same qualities themselves. The absence of PCP in firms is easily cured: not by motivational programmes, but by insistence on good performance and above all on *kaizen* – its constant improvement. That's the single most important lesson that the Toyota-led rise of Japanese productive efficiency has to teach the West. As Ohno's revolutionary decades of work showed, it's tough to implement – but it's terribly easy to learn.

CHAPTER 56

An Age Created By Japan

The record-breaking best-seller *In Search of Excellence*, which Thomas J. Peters wrote with Robert Waterman, was a recipe of comfort for the chief executive (especially the American one, since all the excellent examples were American). It enshrined the existing order. It looked mostly inwards (only one of the eight attributes of excellence, 'continued contact with customers', a fairly mealy-mouthed formula, looked outwards). It affirmed that you, the chief executive, could centrally command corporate success, making the company what you wanted in the way you wanted.

No wonder so many of the *Excellence* companies flopped. Today's necessity is to decentralise success, as recognised in Peters' own new creed, with its amazing change of emphasis from the earlier recipe. His latest inward-looking attributes number only four: flatness of organisation, trust in people, high reward for high levels of achievement, and intensive training. All four are indispensable in a concept for effective management of men and women which doesn't look back to the 1980s but forward to the next century.

The four are the foundation stones for the outward attributes: market segmentation, innovation, responsiveness, relative perceived quality (RPQ), and relative perceived service (RPS). In this list, the issue is not, as before, merely contacting the customers, but satisfying them by anticipating and serving their needs, and doing so better than the competition. Shifting the whole organisation away from the interior to the exterior, from the centre to the periphery, provides the best context for better management of people the whole way down: it gives the worker on the line, in the office, or in the retail outlet something near at hand to identify with, a centre of achievement.

This identification of man and activity, the concept of the business as a harmonious social grouping, has marked one of the major divides between Western and Japanese practice, and it's very hard to believe that the concept bears no relation to Japanese success in W. Edwards Deming's 'age created by Japan'. Yet the notion that they order things better in Japan has taken a strangely long time to sink in. Robert Waterman's book *The Renewal Factor* is subtitled 'Building and Maintaining Your Company's Competitive Edge'. But I could only find four references to Japanese companies or individuals, even though Japan plainly has the most to teach about competitive edges and keeping same.

Peters has more references in his far longer book, *Thriving on Chaos*: but a dozen-and-a-half in a book of 523 pages verges towards the perfunctory. Yet the impact of Japanese methods, directly and indirectly, on management in the 1990s and beyond is likely to be at least as powerful, all over the industrialised world, as that of the Americans was on European management (and Japanese) in the 1950s and 1960s. There's still, however, controversy over the exact nature of Japanese methodology and the extent to which it can be emulated abroad. The debate is entirely phoney – another excuse, conscious or subconscious, for ignoring the obvious.

It's true that cultural and mystical elements exist in Japanese management that can't be found easily, if at all, in the West. Some of these aspects, like the martial arts and philosophy of the *samurai*, have received too much attention in the West; others, like the influence of the delightful and practical philosophy of Zen, have received too little. There are certainly aspects of Japanese management that are foreign to most Western organisations, true, but not because the concepts are esoteric.

The theory that Japanese companies were managed in some very different, non-Western way wasn't much of a comfort, anyway – because if the country's management were truly different, unrepeatable and more effective, the contest would be over: game, set and match to Japan. Increasingly, though, not only have Westerners been looking at Japanese management more objectively, but Japanese companies have begun operating production facilities in the West on a large and expanding scale. Numerous successful cases now exist to show that what works in Japan is truly operative in the West. The benefits of Japanese management are simply not unique to Japan, and it would be astounding if they were.

As Peter Drucker has observed, the three areas where the Japanese have established clear superiority over Western firms are quality control, production control and effective mobilisation of the human energies in the firm. All were learnt initially from American teachers (respectively Deming, John Juran and Drucker himself). The world's most ravenous intellectual magpies, the Japanese, snatch everything that glitters, test it for gold, and keep whatever passes the test.

American managers contemplating the Japanese in their midst are therefore looking at a mirror image of themselves, or rather would be if they had taken any great notice of the Western gurus, absorbed their wisdom, and acted on the same. That points to one enormously relevant and most easily imitated characteristic of Japanese management: it is thorough – 'thorough' meaning not only painstaking, but through-and-through. That's where even some of the best Western competitors fall down.

The thoroughness is shown at the very beginning, in deciding where to locate overseas. One consultant speaks with awe of the Japanese client who even wanted to know how many days' work would be lost to Territorial Army commitments at a UK site. The same thoroughness has led to careful study of all characteristics of potential local employees. Again, the thought that different nationalities need different styles of management is hardly original: the originality of the Japanese is often to act on the obvious. Indeed, that's why they are manufacturing in the West at all.

Observing the world and noting the rise of protectionism in general, and protectionism aimed against the Japanese in particular, the obvious response was to establish a manufacturing presence in important Western markets. The results have become more and more imposing, both in terms of numbers employed and the scale of the enterprises. In scale, the American invasion of overseas markets in the 1950s still looks far more impressive. But where the Japanese astound is in the sheer variety: zippers, cars, batteries, consumer electronics, VCRs, laptops, typewriters, etc.

Their management methods also come in vast variety. The one absolutely common factor, and perhaps the highest one, is insistence on getting results. The small evidence of overseas trial and serious error is a tribute to Japanese thoroughness. Where error occurs, though, the Japanese customarily start the process of thorough diagnosis, prognosis and decision all over again. The difference between Japanese and Western managers isn't that the former make fewer mistakes. Maybe so: but error to a Japanese manager, as to any good manager, is a trigger for action. You seek to rebound from failure to achieve success.

The Japanese expatriate manager, however, would be astounded if personnel policies founded on simple and self-evident truths did fail. 'A company is only as good as the people who work for it', says one expatriate. The matching credo of a top Japanese at the Yuasa battery company's British operation was that 'only good people make a good company'. He added that 'Everyone must enjoy their eight hours of work to enjoy life' – echoing a discovery made and applied long ago by Soichiro Honda, whose passion for lightweight engines powered his company's astonishing rise.

The attitude exemplifies the essential pragmatism of Japanese management, and pragmatism explains why there are so many discrepancies of detail among the Japanese companies operating in the West. For instance, at one Brother plant, nobody assembling the typewriters sits down. Why? 'Our years of experience in making sewing machines and typewriters have taught us that, if they sit down, productivity is lower'. Another company, though, finds its workers are happier and more comfortable (and, presumably, more productive) if they sit on carpets.

Then there's the question of music, or Muzak. The conveyor belts march to music at Brother and Matsushita; not so at Sharp, where silence reigns. Most Japanese companies arriving in the West have decided against instituting compulsory physical exercise, but some newcomers have done just that. The idea shouldn't be so strange: Western schools and the military have long adopted the practice. But the Japanese mostly fear that Westerners will not take easily to what is a national, rather than a corporate, addiction.

The essential pragmatism is shown again when trouble strikes: that's when Japanese management is often at its best, with no inhibitions about getting hands dirty down on the factory floor. That location, insists the video tape company, Maxell, is where all managers must spend half an hour every day, working on the production line – including that in Britain. Anita van de Vliet wrote in *Management Today* that this is 'not so much out of humility as to keep managers in touch with problems and processes of production'. The Maxell boss told her that 'There's no such thing as the Japanese way of management. What we have learned from day-to-day experience is a far cry from sophisticated management theories'.

Even in production management, which, as a local British managing director of Takiron correctly says, is where 'the Japanese have the upper hand, the key is that they keep things simple'. The speaker wasn't Japanese: van de Vliet found very few expats. The more native the workforce and the management, of course, the easier to be sure that you are living up to one Japanese boss's creed (echoed by them all) that 'if you just introduce the Japanese way of doing things, it's no good – you mustn't damage the culture'.

Yet the culture does vary considerably – predictably, given that the uniqueness of each company's culture is vitally important in Japan. It's embedded in corporate slogans like 'Move Forward in Harmony with the World' (Matsushita) or factory banners such as 'Tidiness and Cleanliness Make Quality' (Matsushita again) or 'A Little Better Every Day' (the battery firm, Yuasa). The slogans are not ignored, either, judging by results: the Japanese express general satisfaction with the performance of Western workers and with plant comparisons against Japanese norms.

This isn't mere subjective assessment. Characteristically, the actual objective comparisons in a company like Yuasa are monitored daily. Equally typical is the fact that workers and management share in the comparisons. The point of quality circles, for example, is not just to get detailed suggestions for improvement in products and production, but to involve the workers in their work. Involvement includes subordinate managers, which is by no means always true in the West. The boss's 'way as manager' at Yuasa 'was to ask everyone, so that we could create our own system. It's like a business school, only people are paid to learn'.

One thing they learn is how to cooperate across functions, in contrast to Westerners who keep business compartments resolutely sealed off, not only by the superiors of those inside, but by the inhabitants within. Collaboration is greatly aided by the concept of adaptability, with every manager, every senior professional, an all-round businessman. That has long featured among the four basic Japanese strengths, readily mastered in Western conditions, that explain much of the discrepancy in performance between East and West.

The other three are, first, the removal of all confusion between responsibility and seniority: the best man for the job does the job, the senior man gets the most respect, which doesn't mean that he gets anything else. Second come the fundamental qualities that so impressed Vaughn Beals at Harley-Davidson: persistence, commitment and professionalism. Finally, there is the pursuit of knowledge as business tool: that means more than the product and market know-how, highly important in its own right, which the Japanese search out so assiduously. It also means the knowledge of management itself.

Describing the Japanese approach risks suggesting that everything in their gardens, West and East alike, is lovely, which would, of course, be unreal. Japanese managers, like managers everywhere, not only worry about the day-to-day problems of supply and production, but over long-term issues such as avoiding monotony at the workplace. Like other aspects of corporate performance, though, human relations have proved perfectly amenable, in the West as in the East, to what sounds like a quite ordinary approach to management. But ordinariness is the keystone. Consider this five-point manifesto which van de Vliet extracted from her Anglo-Japanese interviewees:

1. Promote the idea of working as a team, as one 'great big family'.
2. Provide single status for workers and managers.
3. Insist on worker flexibility, with people moving from job to job as circumstances demand.
4. Give prominent importance to the production line – and insist that everybody should work to support it.
5. Provide the highest possible standards of employee welfare.

All five points, naturally, are subservient to the greater good of the company and its progress. The only thing remarkable about that manifesto is that any companies, let alone many, exist which are marked (or cursed) by the opposite: divided allegiances, hierarchical divisions, inflexible workforces, neglected production, inferior standards of employee welfare, and lack of any driving force of corporate purpose. The less-than-best managements have only themselves to blame if (or rather when), in the battle for world markets, they end up among the losers. All the Japanese are teaching is what the best of the West have long practised. What works for the invaders will be just as effective for their hosts.

CHAPTER 57

Motorola: The Impossible Win

The Japanese, as everybody knows, take everything they can find, beg, borrow (and sometimes, alas, steal) from America, refine and adapt it, and then attack the world market with the resulting products. The logical way for America to retaliate is to do precisely the same. And that, according to an article in *Fortune* magazine, is what Motorola has done with a policy described as 'first ignore 'em, then sue 'em, and, finally, learn from 'em'.

The company has an abundant product range – pagers, two-way radios, semiconductors, cellular telephones and computers, military and space electronics, modems, automotive electronics, and that's not all. In most of these, Japanese competition is acute, with the sharpness most evident in microchips. Once, Motorola was world leader. Along with the other US producers, however, it has been swept past by NEC, Toshiba and Hitachi. For a car radio manufacturer to gain pole position in the leading industry of new technology was remarkable in the first place. But losing that lead is evidence enough that Motorola's current tasks are still more imposing.

To meet Japanese standards on quality, speed and innovation, Robert Galvin, the founder's son, led an effort that has 'automated factories, knocked down workplace barriers, and instituted a vast retraining programme covering all 102,000 employees'. That's the well-known formula for success in the new age: speed, quality, innovation, automation, integration, training. The formula doesn't guarantee success: it merely enables success, though 'merely' covers an inordinate amount of grinding hard work and setting (and meeting) the highest standards.

Evidently, Motorola's are higher than those of its major competitors in pagers, for all have succumbed to the Japanese tide. 'If we can supply Motorola', a supplier told *Fortune*, 'we can supply God'.

Quality is about unceasing improvement: Motorola's 1991 pagers, radios and semiconductors were scheduled to have 100th of the faults of the 1987 equivalents. One of the manufacturing directors explained why getting to 99.9997 per cent of perfection is both economic and essential. He made things with 17,000 parts and '144,000 opportunities for someone to make a mistake'. The difference between 99 per cent and 99.9 per cent quality is the reduction in error from a potentially crippling 1,400 errors per product to 144; get to 99.99 per cent and it's only 14.

Small wonder that the *Wall Street Journal* wrote as follows: 'Motorola Inc. enjoys a stellar reputation for high-tech engineering. It fosters that image by trumpeting its Malcolm Baldrige National Quality Award from the US government and Nikkei Prize for manufacturing from Japan'.

But the context of that quote was much less complimentary to Motorola. The *Journal* continued: 'in the booming $2 billion a year market for computer microprocessors, the "brain chips" that run the machines, Motorola is winning booby-prizes. For a decade, the company has trailed arch-rival Intel Corp. Last year it lost more market share *by delaying improvements* on its ageing line of microprocessors'. The italics are mine. Another false step, 'fumbling work on a new speedier chip', meant that Motorola was entering the latest era a full year behind its rivals. In reduced-instruction-set computing, or RISC, the one-time champ is led by far smaller firms: Sun Microsystems and Mips Computer Systems. Motorola, a highly innovative giant, is paying the price, in this one market, for one overriding defect.

Motorola's culture is technology-orientated, or rather dominated. That's why it has moved so readily to the forefront of the total quality movement. Bringing failure rates down to infinitesimal, precisely measured amounts is grist to the mill of the technical perfectionist. But there's no great virtue in delivering a perfect product several months late. The perfectionists will tend to look inwards, at the operations and needs of the company, rather than outwards, to the marketplace which determines all outcomes.

The 'total' in total quality demands precisely the opposite. But the very strong and successful culture of Motorola acted to obstruct essential development in a chip business which not only accounts for 30 per cent of its world-wide revenues, but plays a leading role in its technological prowess – and in its reputation. The circle became vicious, affecting not only fame, but distribution: a chip designer who hadn't worked for Motorola for a decade told the *Journal* that he was 'getting calls from their large customers asking if I knew what Motorola was going to do. I didn't, and I still don't'.

Against this background it's easier to understand how Motorola was outmarketed by Intel when the latter won the contract for IBM's PCs, and why it lost out to Intel's newest 486 microprocessor, too. Intel rushed the latter chip to market: Motorola waited fatally to complete the debugging. That was another major stumble in the series of false steps that brought Motorola down to a 10 per cent market share in PCs. In engineering work-stations, the company, at 28 per cent, lost all but two thirds of its once dominant share.

Will the real Motorola please stand up? Is it the superb company that's spearheading the American drive to retain and regain the high ground in world electronics? Or is it the fumbling force that blew its leadership in microprocessors and muffed its chances to stop the slide, and never mind recapturing the lead? The superb and the fumbler are one and the same. The secret is to let the strengths come through, partly by removing the obstacles that will otherwise block them. After all, Motorola is the company that won the contract to supply mobile phones to Japan's NTT, in competition with the latter's own manufacturing affiliate. A company that can do that can do *anything*.

CHAPTER 58

The Era Of Innovation

'To introduce a new way or process of doing things'. That dictionary definition of the word 'innovation' is a rebuke to managers who wrongly believe that innovators bring only new products into the world. Improved quality like Motorola's depends on new ways, not new products. And new ways also largely explain, for another example, how Japanese car firms have been able to apply pressure on Detroit's corporations, bringing down model development time (to a quarter below America's best effort) and everything else.

It takes 24 months from Japanese prototype to assembly line production: the US time is at least *twice* as long. Some of the new methods, like the techniques of lean manufacture (which economises on all processes to reduce both capital and current costs), depend on novel applications of technical understanding. But all such novelties stem from another innovation, the father of them all, which owes nothing to technology. This is how Nissan managed its 30-month programme for the Maxima model success.

1. The chief executive kept right away from the project, and made everybody else do the same. The decisions were left to the product team, whose leader observed that 'since I have the final authority, I can't have any excuses'.
2. Such leaders always stay with the project from the beginning to the end of its life. So there's no second-guessing, and no job-hopping, either.
3. Everybody had been thinking ahead – components suppliers may be working on wanted parts years before projects start.
4. The team included all the disciplines needed to design, make and market a successful car, working together and

simultaneously, not in separate departments or compartments and not in wasteful sequence, one after the other.
5. The process is constantly improved and tightened. A Nissan man told the *Los Angeles Times* that 'We learned the product development process from the US 30 years ago. But we have been improving on it ever since'.

That new way isn't a production gap or a technology gap, but a management gap. The West knows how to close it. So why isn't it closing? The answer lies in six questions about the innovatory climate in a company. Does it suffer from too much red tape? Lack of funds for innovation? Preoccupation with today at the expense of tomorrow? No innovative thinking? No top management support for innovation? An organisation structure that discourages innovation?

The six questions refer to the six most common barriers to innovation, without which, as 'everybody' knows, firms have no future. For once everybody is right. Only one of the six may be outside management's control: lack of funds. But one audience of senior British executives, answering by operating keypads, included 63 per cent complaining of excessive red tape; the other moans were 44 per cent (funds), 50 per cent (preoccupation with today), 47 per cent (thinking), 34 per cent (top management) and 34 per cent (structure). In other words, on the last two questions, a third of these top people found their firms deficient in areas under their own direct control. That's the management gap. It yawned wide in the case of Motorola's struggling microprocessors.

The *Wall Street Journal* asked the obvious question: 'How could Motorola, one of America's most admired companies and a master maker of other types of chips and of cellular phones, slide into such a predicament?' The answers are all to do, not with innovation, but its management:

1. The extreme emphasis on technological perfection caused critical delays in introducing new products.
2. Internal politics affected the outcome of the debate between the old chip technology and the new: 'We ran into a classic bureaucratic self-preservation reaction', according to a now departed champion of the new.
3. As a result, the state-of-the-art RISC programme was underfinanced and the first chips reached the market a year behind the competition.

HOW TO UNIFY ORGANIC STRENGTH

4. The company didn't give priority to its customers' needs: Hewlett-Packard had to delay a new workstation for six months because of Motorola's late delivery of the 68040 chip. It was a crucial stop-gap: the gap wasn't stopped, and, says an HP executive, 'We can identify hundreds of million of dollars lost'.

Compare those negatives with the five positive points of the Maxima model and you practically delineate the management gap. It lies behind all of business history's sad fishing stories, in which the one that got away is always the biggest. One such fishing story is especially instructive: and the loss immensely large. The very top management, with exemplary foresight, had committed huge resources to a technological leading-edge effort that was likely, if successful, to create magnificent sales. From early days, everything began to go marvellously right among the front-line innovators – the research and development people, whose scientific, conceptual and technological contributions were of unexampled brilliance.

Everything else went wrong. The troubles started to develop when inefficient conduct of the core business generally, and specific trouble with a large and awful acquisition, created problems that took priority over the innovation. That, by no means untypically, lay outside the mainstream business. In the effort to cope with those problems – unrelated to the innovatory effort and its creators – the organisation had mistakenly been changed to a function-based structure that muddled up the innovation and the mainstream products.

To make matters worse, geographical distance yawned between the centre of power and the innovatory centre: they couldn't have been much further apart without leaving US borders altogether. The very top management wasn't paying much heed to innovation, anyway, because the chief executive's attention had been diverted by legal and extramural matters: not to mention the troubles at the acquisition. Five major (and self-defeating) strategic changes followed each other in five years in a forlorn effort to escape from the consequences of that awful buy.

With so much turmoil to sort out, the choice of a numbers-oriented organisation man to reorder the company's affairs seemed natural. But the ingrown inefficiencies in the core business resisted his efforts to control them. And forcing up prices to defend the bottom line only antagonised the customers. They were, anyway, beginning to eye new and effective competition, now appearing in the mainstream market for the first time. That being so, it made redoubled sense, as an internal strategic review urged, to develop a major new business, based on the innovation.

The review's findings were ignored – partly, no doubt, because heavy financing needed for the new product line would have been piled on huge capital needs for the core business. The innovators made this indecision easier for top management because they lacked both business-minded leadership and links with the commercial side, which, anyway, they treated with remarkable arrogance. That only made it even harder for senior managers to grasp the commercial implications of the new technology that was being so superbly (and expensively) created.

The innovators, however, couldn't begin to turn their brilliant achievements into saleable products, for they had no access to product development. That lay with the engineers, headed by yet another numbers man. Top management contained not a single engineer capable either of fully understanding the innovations or of developing an engineering culture that was efficiently organised and geared to taking risks. Instead, the development culture was deeply risk-averse, always preferring to wait until both product and market were fully ripe.

When the company at last ventured into the market sector where the innovators (rightly) saw the future, it didn't use their innovations (which, to make matters and comparisons worse, the centre had inaccurately costed to their disadvantage). An older, established technology was chosen. Too little, and too late, the resulting product flopped in the marketplace. Even if the new technology had been used, the manufacturing plant had been built so far away from the innovators (instead of on their doorstep) that distance, in both senses of the word, would probably have doomed the project.

So would the pressure from the numbers men for immediate results. In all this, the man ostensibly in charge of the corporation's innovatory efforts was an increasingly passive onlooker. He slipped further and further down the corporate totem-pole until his influence on decisions disappeared. The men piled above him were left still more exposed. Unable to understand, as he could, the evolving technology, or to cost it accurately, they simply watched as the market for the innovation exploded all round them.

Finally, the management let the whole wonderful opportunity pass by. The chief executive played no direct part in the project's demise. Yet his had been the very vision, clearly articulated and understood, which had set the innovatory process going in the first place.

HOW TO UNIFY ORGANIC STRENGTH

Ultimately, the blame has to rest where it always must, at the top, which in this case was occupied by one Peter C. McColough: for that's the story, already referred to in Chapter 5, of how Xerox Corporation, under this brilliantly successful chief executive, 'invented, then ignored the personal computer'. That's the sub-title of *Fumbling the Future*, in which Douglas K. Smith and Robert C. Alexander meticulously document the sorry end of what may be the outstanding post-war achievement of American R & D.

Xerox's invention changed the world. It had little impact on Xerox, save to cost a fortune from which others benefited. And as the above account makes clear, it was a management failure entirely. What course of action would have won innovatory success? It turns out to be uncannily similar to the way Nissan got the Maxima out in 30 months.

First, chief executive commitment must be deep and unceasing, even though by definition an innovatory project will be tiny in relation to a sizeable company's sales. That isn't the issue. Almost all great innovations begin small. The real issue is where they are going to finish.

Second, the innovatory team must include business competence as well as scientific and engineering talent. Make it self-contained, but establish a close connection (spiritual and geographic) with an integrated, product-based organisation whose marketing, production and financial arms stay in constant touch, and which will carry the torch when research gives way to development.

Third, ensure that top management includes influential people with enough scientific and engineering background to understand and explain the technologies the company uses, develops and needs. The numbers men, or bean-counters, are invaluable. But they are not employed to take critical strategic decisions about the future. Their role is to help the future to happen.

Fourth, understand that time-scales in innovatory work are extremely difficult to pre-determine. This may well cause delay in getting to market – just as Sony's rivals were well behind with the technology of video-recording. But never innovate merely for the market as is: always aim ahead, like JVC, the pioneer of the rival VHS format, for the market that will be, and you, like JVC, may win the end-game. Don't expect that pay-off to be rapid, but don't expect a pay-off at all unless you're prepared to fund development to the hilt.

Finally, and most important, don't even think of launching a major innovatory programme unless the core business is in splendid shape – and not just when the innovation starts. You need a continuous programme of eradicating inefficiencies, reducing costs and optimising returns, year in, year out. That's often the toughest task for companies riding high on previous success.

Rich cash flows and fat profits disguise a multitude of sins, and make it easy to ignore the internal soothsayers (like the review group in the Xerox case). Never do that. The multitudinous corporate sins are still there, of course, underneath the disguise. They need to be purged by any management which claims to be good: you could add, whether it's innovating or not – except for one thing. If the company isn't innovating, the management can hardly claim goodness, anyway, in a world where competitive advantage depends on new ideas, not only in products, but in the process of everything, including management itself.

Slipping takes only one blunder in one aspect of innovatory management. Companies can't depend on totally avoiding such blunders. Organisations are human and make mistakes, ranging from the minor to the monstrous, and innovation is an innately hazardous process. The remedy is to combine excellent preventive medicine with rapid therapy to cure any outbreaks of illness and, if possible, surge further ahead. The best before-need treatment is summed up in the initials FMEA – or 'failure mode effect analysis'.

FMEA is something which should come naturally to Motorola and other quality leaders, for the phrase and the practice come from quality management. The quality expert looks at the production process and asks a simple question: 'what can go wrong, and if it does, what will be the result?' If the answer is grave, you act to prevent the occurrence with all the craft and intelligence in your power. Apply FMEA to the management of innovation (or anything else) and the management gap will close for ever more.

CHAPTER

59

IBM:
The Biggest Crossroads

The history of International Business Machines in the last decade epitomises the American problem. That's only just and fitting, for IBM is the quintessential company of the half-century now ending. In the unfolding of the Computer Age, which is as good a description as any of those 50 years, IBM left all competition following, mostly feebly, in its wake. The great corporation created by the Thomas Watsons, Senior and Junior, led in technology, marketing, multinationalism, style and sheer success. Like the US economy itself, the IBM of the 1950s and 1960s was a virtually unchallenged giant.

As the 1990s began, a visitor from outer space would have thought that nothing had changed. IBM ended the previous decade with sales of $63.4 billion: as much as the next five computer and office equipment companies (three American and two Japanese) put together. That made the corporation the fifth largest industrial company in the entire world. Its profits of $3.8 billion easily exceeded those of all 17 of the major global contenders in its market, five of whom made losses that year. That net income surpassed the total *sales* of the then still up-and-coming Compaq. No other company in any sector comes even near matching such dominance.

Look at the US macro-economic statistics, and you find a similar picture of extraordinary strength. The country's share of world manufacturing, though well down from 45 per cent in 1953, has long been stable at around a third. That is three times Japan's. Since 1953 Japan has taken its growth out of both the US and Europe, whose share, down from a quarter, is now half that of the Americans'. In exports, with a 13 per cent share, the US is also the largest, just ahead of Germany, well clear of Japan, double Britain. The US has easily the best living standards of the four, and the highest productivity.

In 1988 output per employed American was $41,281, a third higher than Japan, a fifth up on Germany and even further ahead of Britain. By no stretch of the most pessimistic imagination could this be called anything but an enormously strong economy: just as IBM can't be rated as anything other than a company of colossal power and success.

In mainframe computers, the giant's domination over its Western competitors has become more and more overwhelming. At the other end of the scale, IBM is the easy market leader in personal computers, well ahead of any opposition. It enjoys gigantic and immensely profitable operations in semiconductors (mostly for its own use) and software (for its customers). Its technological armoury is the equivalent of that of the US armed services: more copious and advanced than anybody else's. And yet ...

The joker in the pack is dynamism. In 1985, Digital Equipment, the minicomputer phenomenon master-minded by the eccentric and able Ken Olsen, was 13 per cent of IBM's size. Four years later, that ratio was a fifth – even though DEC's mini-market has suffered heavy attack from the PCs and workstations below. In 1985, the combined sales of Apple and Compaq (the latter was then in the *Fortune* 500 for the first time) totalled $2.4 billion, 8 per cent of IBM: in 1989 the proportion was 13 per cent. The Japanese, heading for the majority of hardware sales world-wide, have outgrown IBM even faster.

The macro-economic analogy is with productivity growth. From 1970-88, hourly output in manufacturing grew by 82 per cent in Japan, 52 per cent in Germany, 43 per cent in Britain – and just 16 per cent in the US. The absolute strength of the US economy is not in question; nor is that of IBM. But the loss of macro- and micro-economic dynamism explains the astounding reversal in the relative position of US giants like the computer king. In 1968 world-wide sales of the top ten companies outside the US were only 38 per cent of those of the ten leading US groups; by 1973 the non-American ratio was 51 per cent; by 1989 it was 78 per cent.

The next ten largest non-US companies illustrate the trend even more dramatically. They had half the sales of their US counterparts in 1968; but 21 years later, their sales were 51 per cent higher. The victims (and part-causes) of this relative decline have sometimes seemed almost impervious to their shortcomings. For instance, celebrating a fairly modest, much overdue 9 per cent rise in one quarter's performance, IBM chairman John Akers told *Fortune* proudly that 'Our strategy of listening to our customers and improving the competitiveness of our products and services is working'.

If that chunk of public relations verbiage meant anything (which isn't altogether certain), it implied that the previous IBM strategy was neither to hearken to its customers nor to improve its competitiveness. Very probably, though not creditably, that actually was the case. But how could so great a company, with so splendid a management record and reputation, and such excellent people, have fallen so short? To put the question in closer focus, the same edition reported that IBM has a much more efficient design for its laser printer than Hewlett-Packard, but the latter's 'printers still dominate the market'.

The answer comes back to that literally central issue of capitalising on strengths. The centre can do little to seize dominance of the laser printer market, but can do much to make its printer people also-rans. Note that in 1991 HP, dissatisfied with its performance, engaged in a total re-think (in which the successful printer division was a role model). Yet HP, before the shake-up, had a more decentralised and entrepreneurial culture than IBM, which is well into successor generations of management.

The IBM culture, with the twenty-first century rushing near, still reflected the spirit of post-war decades when corporate managements could rely on an environmental stability that now seems as remote as the three-volume Victorian novel. When IBM gave unprecedented freedom to the group which launched the first PC from Boca Raton, the results were among the most spectacular in the corporation's success-strewn history. When the PC business was hauled back inside the corporate structure, however, its mistakes deserved to become equally legendary.

Well into the new decade, within IBM's savagely cut PC share (down from a monopolistic 80 per cent to under 20 per cent), the off-desktop range included none of the laptops which, outpacing all other PCs, were destined to become the largest sector of the market. In some companies, genuine lack of funds explains such omissions. In groups like IBM, the funds are abundant; but their disposition lies with central management, which creates artificial shortages by allocating capital between businesses, approving this investment project and rejecting that, scaling down and postponing here, going gung-ho for expansion there.

No doubt many of the positive, hell-for-leather decisions are awful: gaffes of that size, though, are easier to hide inside corporate elephants. In absolute terms, the centre's negative decisions may be equally grave, though harder to demonstrate. Hindsight is no help when considering a project that never began. In most cases, nobody outside, and only a few inside, know when an ambitious project has been scuppered by the board; and nobody, of course, can say whether the scuppered project would have paid the handsome dividends foreseen by its disappointed sponsors.

All the same, asking what value top management adds is a fair question – more, it's one that must be asked. At IBM, the quality programme initiated many years ago involved the now well-known device of making user departments assess the internal services they employ. That laudable and sensible approach could usefully include the standard of the service, or addition to value, provided by top management itself. Perpetuation of a hierarchy which reserves all decisions unto itself adds no value.

In late 1991, a year when his company plunged into unprecedented losses, totalling $2.8 billion, Akers seemed to recognise the truth about hierarchy himself, with yet another reorganisation, this time aimed at splitting IBM into separate businesses capable of fending for themselves. Whether they would be allowed to do so remained to be seen – and hoped. For the hierarchy which lets go truly, as IBM did originally with the PC people of Boca Raton, but which does so across the whole corporation, can unleash dynamism that won't just recreate the past, but surpass it.

CHAPTER 60

The Right Management

The greatest challenge to the manager of the future is to make it happen. The challenge is all the greater because organisations themselves are in the firing line. In 1966 Warren Bennis declared roundly that everybody would be participating 'in the end of bureaucracy' within twenty-five to fifty years. The first quarter century has gone by without any clear sign that the prophecy will come true. Bennis stressed the importance of looking 'beyond bureaucracy': but in 1990, as in 1966, the cause of demolishing bureaucracy is still a crusade.

The barbarians still hold the citadel. Plainly, there was something missing in the analysis of bureaucracy's inevitable withering away. Curiously, the Communist state (the ultimate bureaucracy) didn't so much wither away as implode in 1989-90. The regimes that collapsed had lost the consent of the governed. The regimes of the mighty states-within-the-state such as IBM have not. No statues have been toppled, and few heads have rolled. The Western corporate bureaucracies, no matter if their results are disappointing, have kept their legitimacy.

Yet, as summarised by Alvin Toffler in *Future Shock*, everything was against the corpocracies as long ago as the 1960s. They were organisms that thrived on what Bennis described as 'routinised tasks'. He thought that a 'pyramid structure of authority, with power concentrated in the hands of a few ... was, and is, an eminently suitable social arrangement' for such tasks. The change from routine to instability, on this argument, had made bureaucracy obsolete. The very factor that once made bureaucracy indispensable – its ability to handle tasks faster than disorganised methods – now worked against it. Accelerating change had outstepped the maximum speed of bureaucratic response.

Bennis postulated a huge change from settled organisation to 'adaptive, rapidly changing temporary systems'. He pictured continual switching from one *ad hoc* work group and team to another. The only management job remaining from the old systems would be coordinator, bringing together the work of people who were 'differentiated not vertically, according to rank and role, but flexibly and functionally, according to skill and professional training'. This was to be the end of the 'power-laden hierarchy', in Toffler's phrase, of the ' organisation man', and of 'corporate loyalty' – as 'a resurgence of entrepreneurialism within the heart of large organisations' took command.

All this, remember, was published in 1966-70. Yet it bears an uncanny resemblance to futuristic writing about management in 1990, and to much of the argument of this book. All the factors identified by Bennis and Toffler were real and powerful forces. They have only intensified over the many intervening years. Yet the impact on organisations has been strictly limited. Not only have 'power-laden hierarchies' remained in existence; in the 1980s, the hierarchies were using and abusing power with an abandon unmatched since the days of the Robber Barons long ago.

The loyal organisation man, on the other hand, has come nearer to withering away. That he survives at all is a miracle, given the impact on employment of the corporate upheavals dictated by the hierarchies. As the numbers of organisation men have fallen, those of corporate entrepreneurs ('intrapreneurs', in the word made famous by Gifford Pinchot III) have probably increased. But this swing hasn't added up to any resurgence of the vibrant, large-scale capitalist enterprise from which most of today's great companies sprang.

Rather, the large Western organisation has continued to suffer from defects that were identified by Xerox Corporation's Peter C. McColough three years before the Bennis book was published. How much of his 1963 indictment (Chapter 5) still holds true three decades later? Is McColough's cycle of 'emergence, full flower of growth and prestige and then later stagnation and death' truly inevitable? Must the 'heavy hand of custom' stifle venture? Must habit and efficiency drive out flexibility and fresh ideas? And is there no escape from 'the final stage of organisational senility', in which 'there is a rule or precedent for everything'?

The endeavours of top managers like IBM's John Akers to move the clock forward, when internal forces keep on turning it back, show that the problems identified by McColough persist. The halting and slow appearance of the organisational revolution foreseen by

Bennis points to a heavy inertia in the organisation. That drag is deeply rooted in the need of human beings for order, position, permanence, authority, rules, power – all the classic features of bureaucracy. To remove deep roots requires radical action, and that demands radical men and women.

As never before the manager must be a revolutionary, confident that anything and everything can be changed for the better along the whole of the spectrum of technology, distribution and reputation. Those who short-change any of the three do so at their peril. 'Technology' needs to be redefined as the specification and quality of whatever product or service the company offers. Is the offering technically as good as or better than the best competition? Distribution describes the entire process of getting the product or service to the customers. Does it reach the widest possible market as effectively as that same competition – or more so?

Reputation is the sum total of technology, distribution, and promotion. Do all those you need to reach know about the company, and respond well to that knowledge, with a perception which equals or betters the best rival's? Getting the right answers to those three questions lays the foundations of the right business. The recurrent phrase 'the best competition' reflects the realities of modern markets only if your genuinely Unique Selling Proposition is in the same race with others. If it isn't, that's the ultimate in 'competitive advantage'.

It is most unlikely to be timeless. In Compaq's early life uniqueness was achieved by concentrating only on portables. As portables have come down from the barely luggable to the briefcase and even pocket size, Compaq has been forced from sur-petition (in Edward de Bono's word) into competition – and itself lagged well behind Toshiba (still the leader) when the PC moved from lug to lap. The crucial trinity of technology, distribution and reputation needs constant renewal: the continuous re-examination, reassessment, renovation and, if necessary replacement, of parts of the recipe – for today even the best of companies can lose ground, which may be irrecoverable, by one false step.

Missteps are inevitable if a company gets locked into vested technical or marketing interests ('not invented here', 'it will never work', etc.). Let the defence mechanisms win, and you will never exploit the most surefire means of success: achieving the 'impossible'. What enabled Compaq to transform its presence on the desktop – IBM's home ground – was redefining the possible. The 'impossible' beating of IBM to the punch with the 386 chip consolidated the infant company's reputation in the crucial area of technology.

Once reputation has been built, it's a curious commodity. Beyond a certain point, it can't be raised much higher. If you have the high admiration and wide franchise of an IBM or a Motorola, major and sustained efforts are needed to maintain the customer following, let alone augment it. The fact that adverse developments – like those devouring IBM's market share in PCs or Motorola's in microprocessors – took place in a sector involving the highest technology and fastest pace of change is irrelevant. The morals apply to any business.

As noted in Chapter 2, Compaq has asked the 'failure mode effect analysis' question all along the line: what can go wrong and what will be the effect if it does? That careful monitoring is one explanation of its successful run, up to the profit collapse of 1991. That last calamity carries a powerful moral; as the Motorola microprocessor story also tells, the best-managed companies can slip, and the impact of error now rushes upon managements so rapidly.

The buried and unburied mistakes of business haven't been spared in these pages, for they explain the loss of ground among great companies. Some of the major micro-economic blunders which still yawn as traps for firms of any country or size were identified by *Fortune* in April 1990 as:

1. Obsession with direct labour costs. In an age when these seldom amount to more than 15 per cent of total expenses, that's looking at the wrong element of the business system.
2. Abandoning large businesses where low margins are causing problems. That can happen in any business as the product life-cycle develops – but moving out simply hands present and future opportunity to somebody else, often for free.
3. Creating a mismatch between the product and the marketplace. That's the second fundamental going wrong – failing to achieve the right distribution.
4. Using resources to buy other companies (and your own shares) rather than to build established and new operations within the firm. Unless the buy strengthens technology, distribution or reputation, what have you bought?

The magazine cited some awful examples to highlight these errors. (1) A firm making integrated circuits chose a new location for its low labour costs, even though labour was under 5 per cent of the total; it was then crippled by the low literacy standards of the available workforce. (2) Abandoning low-priced mass markets in early applications of solid state electronics (the transistor radio) gave the

Japanese competition unbeatable advantages in later uses like colour television. (3) Raytheon invented the microwave oven, but sold large appliances through traditional outlets. The Japanese sold smaller products through consumer electrical shops.

There's no point in listing (4) the cases of acquisition blunder, because they're endless. Decisions to purchase turnover and sales, instead of building them, often rest on faulty analysis of the same nature as wrong-headed decisions to chase labour costs or drop low-margin products. Making investments pass threshold rates of return, or dropping out of markets (*à la* General Electric) because you can't claim first or second position, isn't strategic thinking, but a tactical knee-jerk. The real issue is the long-run build-up of the company's technical and market strengths.

Motorola's Robert Galvin, one of America's outstanding business leaders (chairman of the executive committee, note, but not chief executive), has isolated the 'biggest problem' in achieving this never-ending crescendo. He describes it as a question of leadership. 'Total customer satisfaction' can't mean the corporation providing only the goods and services it wants to offer, though that has been the prevailing mode since time immemorial. Customers don't want only whatever the company is providing; they also want things that it is *not* providing, either by choice or inadvertence.

Either way, the customer will satisfy those wants somewhere else, and the conventional wisdom will applaud. Businesses are advised to select and focus on what they can do well. Galvin argues, however, that in a generic business, the correct strategy is full-line competition: 'you must offer everything they want'. To follow that strategy, business leaders will have to change their orientation from the knee-jerk cutbacks that, for instance, caused the retreats from mass consumer electronic markets – see (2) above – and Raytheon's persistent reluctance, over many years, to commit corporate body and soul to microwaves (3).

It won't be easy to reverse the contraction and narrowing of the past decade or more. Galvin calls it 'a giant challenge', which only a few companies, two or three handfuls, will meet. Half, in his view, will be US and European; the others will all be Japanese. This merely recognises the fact that Japan's leaders have instinctively followed a full-line policy, partly because of their inhibitions against abandoning businesses, partly because of the competitive reflex that drives them to exploit opportunities identified by others, partly because of their emphasis on building organically on what they have already created in technology and business systems.

Rafael Aguayo has good grounds for his view, looking at the differences of management between Japan and the US, that 'in effect, we have been conducting an experiment since 1950 between two very different styles', which 'is as close as we could possibly come to conducting a controlled experiment on an international scale'. He points out that W. Edwards Deming, the subject of his book, had predicted that 'Japan would prosper while the United States and other nations following other methods wouldn't be able to compete ... The power of Deming's prediction about Japan, which he made in 1950 and which has since proved accurate, is that he made it before the results were known'.

Those results can either be accepted fatalistically, or used as the trigger for renewal, on the classic five-part cycle of crisis, review, restructure, focus and development. To retain strength and momentum, the middle stages of the cycle (review, restructure, focus) should be applied while the development phase is still surging ahead – and on every one of the three dimensions: technology, distribution and reputation. Companies which let this virtuous, overlapping cycle lapse won't need much 'failure mode effect analysis' to discover the likely outcome: it's crisis, and these days crisis comes sooner rather than late.

That is the overriding strategic issue. But the greatest strategy in the world can be ruined by tactical blunders, and tactics in turn depend on basic principles. This book began by examining Operation Desert Storm for its relevance to the West's management problems. That campaign provides two further clues of powerful significance: *Auftragstaktik* and *Beweglichkeit*. The words are German, because they derive from NATO operations in Germany: the first means 'mission-oriented orders'; the second 'battle drill'.

A writer in *The Times* reported that before the Gulf War the British forces in Germany had only recently changed to mission-oriented orders, '*in which commanders are given only objectives*' (my italics). Before this change, the forces had trained with 'detailed written orders, in which every move is plotted'. This truly fundamental change was accompanied by another: 'The battle drills, or standard operating instructions (SOIs), for the liberation of Kuwait were carefully worked out, with simple graphics, to ensure that everyone knew exactly how they would go to war.'

The analogies with business jump out of the page. Work out objectives with sub-unit managers; leave the rest to them; but insist that they in turn ensure that all their people know what they're doing, why and how, and are encouraged and enabled to do it their way, as best as they know how. That sounds much simpler, even simplistic, compared to the ten highly demanding principles I have sought to elucidate and illustrate in this book. But reducing the complex to simple, intelligible, intelligent terms is the well-established route to success in any field.

Looking at the future of management in the mid-1970s, I wrote that 'The future only holds terrors for those who are mismanaging the present'. To put that truth another way, the right management with the right stuff will create the future it wants through a present of which it can be proud. That's the essence, and the task, of the Superchief.

Epilogue: Winning In The Global Market

This book is testimony to the power of individual managers, working in concert with like-minded fellows, to win victories for themselves and their businesses against any competition. It began with an analogy between war and commerce. While the differences between the two states are immense, the similarities have enlarged for two reasons: the military have become far more sophisticated, and world markets much more combative. One author, indeed, even believes that the Third World War is looming in the shape of a conflict for global markets between Japan and the US.

The argument may be farfetched, but the reality is worrying enough: for the first time since it launched the Industrial Revolution, the West has lost its quasi-monopoly over its domestic and international markets, and has seen a Japanese quasi-monopoly take its place in many sectors. Some people argue that this is less serious than it sounds, since global marketing has produced global products and components, so widely sourced that the ultimate label – American, Japanese, German or whatever – hardly matters; and the argument obviously has truth.

The overwhelming odds, though, are that far more non-Western parts (and whole assemblies) are found in Western goods than *vice versa*. Nor can anybody doubt that the world's fastest-growing economy by far is now the Japanese economy outside Japan. That presents a greater challenge than Western managers have ever faced in the past. While British employment provides British jobs, no matter where head office lies, that doesn't end the debate. How many hundreds of millions of extra profit, for example, would British car firms now be generating if Japanese rivals hadn't scooped so much of their domestic market – and their potential exports?

But would Britain's managers have used those millions well? In Britain as in the US, difficulties in world markets, and increasingly in domestic ones, have been caused by under-investment in products and services, equipment, R & D, and worker training, under the direction of men who are themselves under-prepared for the task because they lack continuing education. They operate top-heavy command and control (and communication) structures in which subordinates are constantly second-guessed or stultified. The leaders have no incentive to amend any of these defects, because their rewards are large, win or lose.

In the US, for 'large' read 'enormous'. The average 'compensation' of US chief executives was $1.86 million in 1989. That's nine times the income of Desert Storm's highest paid executive, President Bush. Of course, Bush entered the White House as a multi-millionaire, while Schwarzkopf (57 at the time of his triumph) was able to become one effortlessly on his then imminent retirement – which raises another highly significant point. The new breed of able and talented military leader leaves the scene at the age when, quite typically, people get appointed to run a major company. Is there any doubt which is the better policy – either on remuneration or retirement?

Many objections can be made to these comparisons, and to praise of the success of Desert Storm. Financial constraints didn't enter the picture (although the US stood to turn a handy direct profit on the conflict, after voluntary contributions, let alone the indirect gains). The competition proved to be weak – but that didn't appear to be the case when the world's fourth largest army took the field. The Western allies massed overwhelming force to overwhelm. But in business that's the whole meaning of 'competitive advantage'. You don't want to leave the opposition any chance of outmaking or outmarketing you: that's what all Japan's investment, information, planning and build-up are intended to achieve.

And there's another, powerful analogy in the multinational network of alliances that won the war. Alliances are integral to today's global competition in the civilian markets. Rosabeth Moss Kanter, the editor of the *Harvard Business Review*, is prominent among those placing great emphasis on these new joint ventures and collaborations. It's the final F in her four F essentials for the modern business: Focused, Fast, Flexible and Friendly. Without question, the ability to work with other companies, even competitors, as customers, suppliers and collaborators has become a new and mandatory requirement for success in global and national markets.

But even more important is the ability to collaborate within the corporate frontiers. Not only must the corporation become 'focused, fast, flexible and friendly', so must each manager – concentrating on defined tasks that will achieve desired results, working to eliminate the bottlenecks, barriers and misconceptions that waste time, using an open mind to seek and accept new ideas and methods, and (most important of all) doing all this as a key member of changing groups of associates who will never be equal in age, rank, reward or talent, but who are always equal in their ability to contribute to the group's performance.

This represents a decisive reversal of the big business faults summarised above. The way ahead demands heavy investment in products and services, equipment, R & D, and worker training, under the direction of people who are thoroughly prepared for the task because they believe in and obtain continuing education. They will have to operate light command and control (and communication) structures in which subordinates are not subordinated and take their own decisions on their own initiative. Their dominant incentive will not be money, but (like that of all great business founders down the ages) the urge to create, build and consolidate – and never to stop.

This raises the final analogy with the military victory of 1991. After the event (and with much meretricious hindsight), America was heavily criticised for stopping short, for not pressing home its triumphant force to eliminate the Iraqi president and the rump of his army. Whether that criticism is right or wrong, Western business has certainly suffered from stopping short: from not using one success (like the wonderful creations of the micro-electronic engineers) to build another (like the consumer electronics empire which passed, instead, to the Japanese). Britain has become especially notorious for innovative pathfinding which left others to turn the paths into marketing highways.

Inside Japan, the search for new success is never-ending because of the almost monthly evidence that he who hesitates is lost; in 1991 even the great Toyota lost its apparently eternal lead in new car sales to a product from the relatively insignificant Daihatsu. Outside Japan, that ceaselessness has become a potent weapon against Western competitors who, after triumph, rest on their laurels, count their rewards (including the personal ones), and wait complacently for their rivals to catch up. This book has been full of cautionary tales that spell out the unpleasant results all too painfully.

HOW TO UNIFY ORGANIC STRENGTH

Institutional reforms, for example, affecting the availability and cost of finance, the relative powers of shareholders and top managements, and the latter's rewards, may be needed. They haven't been the subject of this book, because more than enough cases exist (again, many in its pages) to show that the solution lies in the hands of determined individuals. In a world where Superchiefs jostle across frontiers, there's no point in uttering that traditional British cry of fair play, 'May the best man win'. He will.

Bibliography

I am extremely grateful to a host of authors, and their publishers, for the contributions made by their books to my knowledge and thinking. But I should like to express special thanks for the following books, most of them quoted in the text, without which this book of mine would not have been possible.

Aguayo, Rafael, *Dr. Deming: The American Who Taught the Japanese About Quality*, London: Mercury Books, 1990.
    An excellent account by an ex-banker who adds powerful thoughts of his own to a wholly convincing description of the Deming philosophy

Ansoff, Igor, *Implanting Strategic Management*, England: Penguin Books, 1987.
    Since the appearance of the classic *Corporate Strategy* in 1965, Ansoff has made this crucial subject his own: this latest work breaks new ground

Belasco, James A., *Teaching the Elephant to Dance*, London: Hutchinson Business Books Ltd, 1990.
    Amid a welter of valuable ideas, this book is notable for its documentation of how large companies seek to emulate the agility of the small

Burrough, Bryan and Helyar, John, *Barbarians at the Gate*, London: Jonathan Cape, 1990.
    A brilliant, fly-on-the-wall account of the fight for RJR Nabisco, which exposes the greed culture of the 1980s in all its vulgarity

Campbell, Andrew, Devine, Marion and Young, David, *A Sense of Mission*, London: The Economist Books Ltd Hutchinson, 1991.
    Exceptionally well-researched investigation of the realities and the results that lie behind and follow after corporate mission statements

Deal, Terrence and Kennedy, Allen, *Corporate Cultures: The Rites and Rituals of Corporate Life*, New York: Addison Wesley, 1982.
    Much too little has been written about the culture of the corporation: this stimulating study puts the issue in excellent perspective

BIBLIOGRAPHY

Drucker, Peter F., *The New Realities*, England: Heinemann Professional Publishing Ltd, 1989.
Like all this great thinker's work, this collection throws searching light on contemporary issues while setting out lasting and invaluable truths

Goold, Michael and Campbell, Andrew, *Strategies and Styles: The Role of the Centre in Managing Diversified Corporations*, Oxford: Basil Blackwell Ltd, 1987.
By analysing companies into three styles of central management, the authors greatly clarified the issue of combining strategy and control

Goold, Michael and Quinn, John J., *Strategic Control: Milestones for Long-Term Performance*, London: The Economist Books Ltd/Hutchinson, 1990.
A pathbreaking investigation of how companies actually practise what everybody preaches – the development and control of business strategy

Harvey-Jones Sir John, *Making It Happen*, London: Collins, 1988.
A clear-headed, practical investigation, based on a remarkable leadership performance at ICI, into how large companies can be led effectively

Heller, Robert, *The Complete Guide to Modern Management*, London: Mercury Books, 1991.
The authors in this encyclopaedic collection cover virtually all the many and varied management techniques and philosopies that CEOs must know

Heller, Robert, *Culture Shock*, London: Hodder & Stoughton, 1991.
Most managers don't want to know how the IT revolution is going to change management itself: this book explains why they must know – and act

Houlden, Brian, *Understanding Company Strategy: An Introduction to Thinking and Acting Strategically*, Cambridge, Mass: Basil Blackwell, 1990.
A clear and practical strategic primer that tells managers what strategy is and shows them how to use its tools to the best advantage

Kanter, Rosabeth Moss, *When Giants Learn to Dance: Mastering the Challenges of Strategy, Management and Careers in the 1990s*, London: Simon & Schuster, 1989
Wide-ranging, deeply humane and highly informed, this book shows just why its author is the most popular exponent of the new management

Lewis, Michael, *Liar's Poker: Rising Through the Wreckage on Wall Street*, Sevenoaks: Hodder & Stoughton, 1989.
Any doubts over the veracity of this spirited account of high jinks and low morals in Salomon Bros were blown away by the scandals of 1991

Morita, Akio, *Made in Japan*, London: Fontana, 1988.
More autobiographical than managerial, the Sony co-founder's book provides important insights into the Japanese mentality that has reshaped the world economy

BIBLIOGRAPHY

Nayak, P. Ranganath and Ketteringham, John M, *Breakthroughs!*, London, Mercury Books, 1987.
Arthur D. Little fathered this unmatched series of studies in innovation, important for understanding both the negative and positive problems

Ohmae, Kenichi, *The Borderless World: Power and Strategy in the Interlinked Economy*, London: Collins, 1990.
McKinsey's Tokyo head ranges far afield into the future of the interlinked world economy, but offers sharp insights into the business necessities

Peters, Tom, *Thriving on Chaos: Handbook for a Management Revolution*, London: Pan Books, 1989.
Much longer, and more overflowing with ideas, than *Excellence*, this is a stimulating survey of what the new management really means for firms

Smith, Douglas K. and Alexander, Robert C., *Fumbling the Future: How Xerox Invented, Then Ignored, the First Personal Computer*, New York: William Morrow & Company Inc., 1988.
A case study of almost unexampled brilliance into the strange way in which a great R&D achievement became a total write-off for its owners

Sonnenfeld, Jeffrey, *The Hero's Farewell: What Happens When CEOs Retire*, Oxford University Press, 1991.
Management succession, obviously a key determinant of performance, had won too little attention before this intelligent and witty study

Stalk, George, Jr and Thomas, M. Hout, *Competing Against Time*, Free Press, 1990.
A superbly researched book on a key issue – time as a competitive weapon – that managers in goods and services alike must learn to master

Tasker, Peter, *Inside Japan: Wealth, Work and Power in the New Japanese Empire*, London: Penguin Books, 1989.
Among the multitude of books trying to explain the Japanese to the West, this one stands out for perceptiveness, perspective and conciseness

Toffler, Alvin, *Future Shock*, Bodley Head, 1970.
The granddaddy of futurology best-sellers still reads well today, when the misses, as well as the hits, among its forecasts can be taken into account

Walton, Mary, *The Deming Management Method*, London: Mercury Books, 1989.
Almost a step-by-step introduction to the philosophy which has animated far more managers in the East than the West - to the latter's great loss

Waterman, Jr., Robert H., *The Renewal Factor*, London: Transworld Publishers, 1988.
The other half of *In Search of Excellence* has contributed a powerful study of what corporations must do to seize opportunities - and resist threats

Index

accounting, financial, 61
  see also financial control companies
achievement, and motivation, 267
Ackerman, Roger, 239
Adidas, 197
aggressiveness, strategic, 30–1, 104
Aguayo, Rafael, 47, 54–5, 63, 64, 113, 188, 189, 210, 268, 302
Akers, John, 294–5, 296, 298
Alexander, Robert C., 28, 291
Allaire, Paul, 250
Allen, Ronald, 102
alliances, 305
American Express, 221
American Home Products, 178–9
Amheuser-Busch, 181
andon, 277
Annenberg, Walter, 255
Ansoff, Igor, 30, 31, 32–3, 34, 98
Apple Corporation, 7, 9, 10, 28, 112, 123, 221, 245–7, 294
armies, xiv–xv, 302
Asahi Breweries, 78
assembly lines, 275–7
AT&T, 162, 198, 219
Atari, 78
authority, 218–29
  and responsibility, 252–3, 271
automation, 275–7
automobile industry, 62, 190–2, 201
  Japan, 190, 275–7, 287–8, 306
Ayer, N.W., Advertising, 17

Baldrige, Malcolm, National Quality Award, 189, 191
Bank of England, 5
Barbarians at the Gate, 15–16, 17, 139–40

Bartlett, Christopher A., 39, 147–9, 152, 156
BAT Industries, 169
Baumann, Bob, 122
Beals, Vaughn, 233
Bean, L.L., 191
Beecham Group, 116, 122, 179
Bekaert, 134, 190, 193, 201
Belasco, James A., 38, 221
benchmarking, 169
Bennis, Warren, 297–9
Bergsma, Ennius E., 101–2
Berkshire Hathaway, 173–5, 178, 179
Berry, Tony, 100–1
Black, Sir James, 264
Black & Decker, 195, 197
Blue Arrow, 100–1, 229
BMW, 197
board of directors:
  and CEs, 118–23, 136–7
  non-executive directors, 138–43
Body Shop, 260
Boeing, 245
Boesky, Ivan, 135
Bond, Alan, 237
bonds market, 21–2
Bonoma, Thomas V., 41
Borderless World, The, 144, 145, 146
borrowing, 237
Bosch, Robert, 62, 185–7, 188, 209
Boston Consulting Group (BCG), 31, 82, 83, 86, 89
Bower, Joseph L., 276
Bradlee, Ben, 256
brands, 194–9
Brazil, 110
Breakthroughs!, 106–7, 275, 276–7
Bristol-Myers, 181

INDEX

British Airways, 67–9
Brooks, Mel, 43
Brooks Brothers, 237, 238
Brown, Helen Gurley, 259
Brown, Tina, 259
Bruck, Connie, 224, 225–6
budgeting, 61
Buffett, Warren, 173–5, 179
Bullitt, Dorothy Stimson, 255
bureaucracy, 7, 52–3, 102, 218, 297–8
Burrough, Brian, 15
Bush, George, 305
Business, 264–5, 269, 270
business schools, 68, 70–2, 102
  and women, 261
business system management, 79, 81
Business Week, xii, 10, 12, 37, 45, 78, 97, 100, 102, 117, 123, 140, 143, 192, 215, 225–6, 228, 247, 254
buyouts, 41–4
  see also takeovers and mergers

Cahners magazine group, 133
Caldwell, Philip, 118, 128
Camels, 16–17
Campbell, Andrew, 57, 58, 207, 211
Campbell's, 97–9, 197
Campeau, Robert, 237, 238
Canion, Rod, 9, 11, 13, 15
Canon, 119
Car magazine, 192
Car & Truck Dealer, 201
Carlson, Chester, 27
Carlzon, Jan, 202
Carrier Corporation, 215–16, 230
Caterpillar Tractor, 50, 245
change:
  and CE, xi–xii, 33–4, 219–20
  markets, 74, 163
  and organisation, 31–2, 220–3
  resistance to, 51–2
'channel warfare', 80–1
chaos, 15–16
Chesebrough-Ponds, 46
chief executive (CE), 100–5
  age of, 102, 113
  and board of directors, 118–23, 136–7
  and change, xi–xii, 33–4, 219–20
  and delegation, 5, 20, 106–7, 111–12, 222
  departure and replacement of, 120–2, 127
  ego of, 115–16, 118
  Japan, 106–8, 111, 113–14
  motivation of, 113–14

'Nine-Yes Answer', 109–10, 114
  pay of, 6, 117, 140, 225–6, 269, 305
  style, 103–4
  women, 254–62
chief operating officer (COO), 123
Chrysler, 115, 116–17, 123, 236
Citicorp, 178
Citizen Watch, 12
Claiborne, Liz, 254
Clark Equipment, 86
Coca-Cola, 178–9, 181, 194–6, 197
collaboration, 305–6
communications, xi–xii
Compaq Computer, 9–14, 61, 119, 123, 245–6, 247, 294, 299–300
Competing Against Time, 82–3
competition, 62–4, 76
'competitive advantage', 74–5
  and time, 81–2, 287
competitive effectiveness, 30
complaints, dealing with, 198–9, 201
ConAgra, 115
consensus, 5–6, 170
  decision-making, 6, 165
continuous improvement, 276–7
Copley, Helen, 255
Corning group, 239
Corporate Cultures, 146
Cosmopolitan, 259
cost, 82
cost cutting ('cost down'), 60
  Japan, 61, 239
crisis, 227–32, 302
Crocker National Bank, 228
Crystal, Graef S., 6, 225
Culture Shock, 92
customers, 301
  complaints, 198–9, 201
  'delight', 201
  information, 83

Daihatsu, 306
Dana, 185, 211
Daniell, Bob, 215–17
data, 50
  see also information
Deal, Terrence, 146
de Bono, Edward, 80, 299
decentralisation, 147–9, 251
decision-making, consensus, 6, 165
delegation, 20, 252–3
  CE, 5, 106–7, 111–12, 222
Delta Air Lines, 240
Deluxe Cheque Printers, 179, 181, 200

312

INDEX

Deming, W. Edwards, 4, 47–9, 50, 63, 64, 73, 97, 189, 210, 268, 280, 302
Deming cycle, 48–9
Deming Prize, 48, 188
Dentsu agency, 205
Deutsch, Morton, 268
development:
  new products, 51
  staff, 67–9
Devine, Marion, 207, 211
differentiation, 199–200
Digital Equipment, 294
directors:
  board and CE, 118–23, 136–7
  non-executive, 138–43
Disney, Walt, 225–6
Disney Corporation, 197
Distillers, 135–7
Dorrance family, 97–9
Dover, 179
Dow Chemical, 228, 245
Dow Jones, 179, 181
Drexel Burnham Lambert Inc., 18, 21
Drucker, Peter, 21, 69, 72, 74–5, 190, 267, 279–80
Dunlop, 230
Du Pont, 258, 265

earnings per share (eps), 132, 134, 137, 174–81, 175–7
Eastern Airlines, 115
Eastman Kodak, 79–80, 195, 197, 221, 245
education:
  business schools, 68, 70–2, 102
  Japan, 72–3
effectiveness:
  competitive, 30
  and efficiency, 190
Egan, Sir John, 191–2
Eisner, Michael D., 226
Eli Lilly, 264
EMI, 31–2
'empowerment', 37, 203
entrepreneur, corporate, 29–34
equity, return on, 132, 134, 137, 174–81
error, 52–3, 224, 280, 292, 300–1
Europe:
  manufacturing, 293–4
  market, xii
  quality, 189–90, 192
European Quality Award, 190
executive *see* chief executive (CE); management
executive information systems (EISs), 141
experience, 150–1

'4 F', 305–6
failure mode effect analysis (FMEA), 9, 292, 300
family businesses, 98–9, 136–7
financial control companies, 57–8, 161
Financial Times, The, 41, 43, 101, 155, 163, 166, 209
financial year, 61
Fisher, George, 119
flexibility, 25–6, 73, 305–6
Fluor, 229
Ford, Henry, II, 115, 118, 127, 129
Ford Motor Company, 38, 81, 127–9, 134, 190–1, 198, 202
Fortune, 4, 6, 20, 41, 77, 85, 101, 119, 127, 177, 178–9, 189, 191, 237, 239, 263–4, 265, 267, 269, 284, 294–5, 300–1
  500 list, 10, 16, 38, 56, 177, 180, 194, 195, 225, 226, 294
Fumbling the Future, 28, 291
Future Shock, 297, 298

Galvin, Robert W., 119, 284, 301
Gates, Bill, 70
Gatorade, 228
Geneen, Harold S., 119–20, 121
General Electric, 37–40, 41, 164, 228
General Foods, 85–7
General Motors, 101, 127, 143, 179–80, 198, 202
Ghoshal, Sumantra, 39, 147–9, 152, 156
Gilbert, Xavier, 76–7
Gillette, 79–80, 190
Glaxo, 116, 264
globalisation, 144–6, 245–7, 251–2
  see also multinationals
Goizueta, Roberto C., 194
Goldsmith, Sir James, 23, 44–5, 46, 169
Goold, Michael, 57, 58, 59–60, 165, 166, 167–8, 169, 170–1
Grace, J. Peter, 6
Graham, Katherine, 254, 255–6
Grand Metropolitan, 228, 230
Gray, Harry J., 120–1, 215
Green, Adolphus, 17
Greeniaus, John, 18
growth:
  after crisis, 227–32
  measurement of, 175–81
  share prices and earnings, 132, 134, 137, 174–81
  sustaining, 9–10
Guinness, 135–7, 140
Gulf War, xv, 68, 240, 302, 305
Gutfreund, John, 174

313

INDEX

Haas, Robert, 204, 205
Haloid Company, 27
Handy, Charles, 69
Hanson, James, Lord, 23, 46, 56–7, 121
Hanson Industries, 56–8, 60, 121
Harley-Davidson, 233–5, 240
Harper, Mike, 115
Harper, Peter, 58
Harvard Business Review, 37, 39, 61, 82, 147, 156, 201, 204, 205, 206, 229, 276
Harvey-Jones, Sir John, 109–10, 111, 114, 116, 119, 145
Hayden, William J., 192
Heinz, 98–9
Helyar, John, 15
Henderson, Bruce, 82
Hero's Farewell, The, 121–2
Hershey, 197
Heublein, 228, 230
Hewlett, Bill, 209
Hewlett-Packard, 188, 208–9, 245, 289, 295
hierarchy, 6–7, 21, 37, 112, 218–23, 267, 275, 297
Higuchi, Hirotaro, 78
Hitachi, 164
Hobby, Oveta Culp, 255
Honda, Soichiro, 122, 128, 222–3, 281
Honda, 233, 234–5
Houlden, Brian, 167, 168, 170
Hout, Thomas M., 82–3, 276
'humanistic management', 73–4

Iacocca, Lee, 115, 116–17, 123
IBM, 10, 12, 33, 52, 179, 191, 197, 238, 257, 286, 293–6, 299–300
Ibuka, Masaru, 162
Icahn, Carl, 23, 138
ICI, 46, 58, 80, 109, 116, 119, 145
improvement, continuous, 276–7
In Search of Excellence, 70, 73, 97, 168, 195, 221, 278
incentives, and targets, 57–8
Index Alliance, 80–1
inertia, xi, 7, 25–6, 52, 102
inflation, 177
information, xiii–xiv, 21–2, 50
 and CEs, 104
 customer, 83
 executive information systems (EISs), 141
 interpretation of, 85–7
 networked PCs, 88–93
 and technology, 141, 161–2
innovation, 287–92
Insead, 261

Inside Japan, 53, 71–2, 108
Intel Corporation, 285, 286
'intrapreneurs', 97
intuition, 150–1
investment, 57, 173–5
ITT, 119

Jaguar Cars, 129, 168–9, 191–2
Japan, 4–5, 7–8
 business education, 71–2, 72–3
 CEs, 106–8, 111, 113–14
 continuous improvement, 276–7
 cost cutting, 61, 239
 and Deming, 47–9, 73, 302
 management attributes, 279–83
 manufacturing, 293–4
 people management, 234
 philosophy, 61–2, 165
 quality, 47–8, 188
 slogans, 282
 strategic planning, 164–6, 170–1
 training, 73
 value statements, 207
 women, 262
Jell-O, 85–7
Jews, 257–8
jidoka, 277
Jobs, Steve, 28, 70, 245, 246
Johnson, F. Ross, 15–16, 17–18, 19–20, 101, 120, 139–40
Johnson & Johnson, 264, 265
Juran, John, 280
just-in-time (JIT), 239–40, 277

Kaiser Cement, 57
kaizen, 276–7
Kaku, Ryuzaburo, 118–19
Kalchas Group, 132, 133, 175, 176, 178, 227–8, 229
kanban, 276
Kanter, Rosabeth Moss, 37–8, 221–2, 305
Kellogg's, 99, 179, 180, 197
Kennedy, Allen, 146
Kepner-Tregoe, 51, 54
Ketteringham, John M., 106, 275, 276–7
Kiam, Victor, 116
Kidde, 57
KLM, 191
'knowledge industry', 21–2
Kodak, *see* Eastman Kodak
Komatsu, 50
Korn/Ferry International, 102, 103, 112
Kravis, Henry, 41
Kravis, Kohlberg, Robert (KKR), 41–2
Kreps, Juanita, 139–40
Kroc, Ray, 145, 146

314

INDEX

Kume, Yutaka, 108
Kuroki, Yasuo, 106–7

LaMothe, William Edward, 99
Landor Associates, 194, 197–8
Lane, Chris, 67
Lazell, Leslie, 116, 122
Leber, Richard W., 229–30
Levi Strauss, 203–5, 209
Levitt, Theodore, 75, 201
Lewis, Michael, 174
Liar's Poker, 174
Liebling, A. J., 255
Little, Royal D., 42, 121
London Business School, 108
Long Range Planning, 150–1
Loomis, Carol J., 179
Los Angeles Times, The, 108, 288

McCaw, Craig, 140
McColough, Peter C., 25–8, 291, 298
McCormick, Charles P., Jr, 99
McDonald's, 144–6, 197, 200
McDonough, 56
McGovern, R. Gordon, 97
McGregor, Douglas, 74, 266
McKernan, Leo, 86
McKinsey & Co., 127, 139, 144, 229
Made in Japan, 107
Maisonrouge, Jacques, 252
Making It Happen, 119
Maljers, Floris, 150–1
management:
 attributes of, 278–83
 business system, 79, 81
 buyouts (MBOs), 42–4, 46
 changes in, 130–2
 'competitive advantage', 74–5
 by fits and starts, 129, 132–4
 'humanistic', 73–4
 of innovation, 287–92
 measurement of, 176–81
 motivation of managers, 266–71
 multinational, 248–53
 by objectives, 75, 159–60
 and ownership, 46
 philosophy, 73–5
 production, 275–7, 281
 quality, 79, 81, 186–93
 out of recession, 236–41
 'scientific', 73
 'Stalinist', 6–7
 time-based, 79, 81, 83–4
 traditional, 21
 training, 67–9
 and values, 206–11
Management Today, 56, 234, 281

Manger, Hansjörg, 185–7
Manpower Inc., 101, 229
markets:
 change, 74, 163
 European, xii
 fragmentation of, 84
 information, 161–2
 leaders, 198
Marks, Simon, 209
Marks & Spencer, 62, 208–9, 211, 237, 238
Marshall, Sir Colin, 67, 71, 201
Matsushita, Konosuke, 51, 164, 207, 211
Matsushita Electric, 164, 253, 282
Maxell, 281
Mayer, Richard, 85–6
Maytag, 179, 181
Mazda, 239
measurement, of growth, 175–81
media business, 224–6, 255, 259
Mercedes-Benz, 62, 197
Merck Inc., 178–9, 180–1, 195, 245, 263–5, 268–9, 270–1
mergers, *see* takeovers and mergers
Metromedia, 228
Midland Bank, 228
Milken, Michael, 21, 42, 45
Miller, Merton H., 177
Miller, Neil, 206, 210, 266, 267, 268, 270
Miller/Ginsburg, 210
Minolta, 30–1
MIPS Computer Systems, 172, 285
mission statement, 54
Mitchell Energy, 179
Mitsubishi Bank, 207, 211
mobility of managers, 49
Montgomery of Alamein, Bernard Law, Viscount, 71, 231
morale, 6, 53
Morita, Akio, xiii, 106–7, 162
motivation:
 of CEs, 113–14
 of managers, 266–71
Motorola Inc., 119, 284–6, 288–9
moves, company, 116
multinationals, 144–6, 248–53
Murdoch, Rupert, 121, 228, 237, 255

Naked Manager, The, 5
Nalco Chemical, 179, 181
National Airlines, 229
National Biscuit Company, 17
Nayak, P. Ranganath, 106, 275, 276–7
NBC, 197
Nebraska Furniture Mart, 173, 181
'neo-democracy', 112

315

INDEX

Nestlé, 197
networking, personal computers, 88–93
New Realities, The, 74–5
New Yorker magazine, 102, 224
Nicholas, Nicholas, 224
Nike, 7
Nintendo, 76–8
Nissan, 108, 287–8
Nivea, 197
non-executive directors, 138–43
Norburn, David, 101, 141–2
NTT, 286

Ohmae, Kenichi, 144, 145, 146, 253
Ohno, Taiichi, 275–7
Olsen, Ken, 294
'OODA Loop', 83
O'Reilly, Tony, 98–9
organisation, 217–23
    bureaucracy, 7, 52–3, 102, 218, 297–8
    and change, 31–2, 220–3
    hierarchy, 6–7, 21, 37, 112, 218–23, 267, 275, 297
    matrix, 147–52
    structure of, 112–13, 114
Otis Elevator, 81, 200
ownership, and management, 46

Packard, Dave, 209
Palo Alto Research Center (PARC), 28
Pan Am, 121, 228, 229
Pantry Pride, 45
partnerships, 112
pay:
    CEs, 6, 117, 140, 225–6, 269, 305
    managers, 268–9
PepsiCo, Pepsi-Cola, 16, 194, 197
Perdue, Frank, 116
Perelman, Ronald, 45
performance, measurement of, 83–4, 176–81
Performance Research Associates (PRA), 198–9, 201
Perot, H. Ross, 143
personal computers (PCs), 10, 28, 90–1
    networking, 88–93
Peskett, Tony, 15, 20
Peters, Thomas J., 25, 70, 73, 113, 168, 195, 278, 279
Petersen, Donald, 127, 128–9, 134
Pfeiffer, Eckhard, 11–12, 246, 247
pharmaceutical industry, 263–5
Philip Morris, 16, 17, 85, 179, 180–1
Philips Electrical, 148, 155–7, 163, 197, 221

philosophy:
    Japan, 61–2, 165
    management, 73–5
    Western, 59
Pickens, T. Boone, 23
Pillsbury, 221
Pinchot, Gifford, III, 97, 298
planning, xiii–xiv
    see also strategy
Plastow, Sir David, 71
Pope, Alexander, 167
Porsche, 197
Porter, Michael E., 74, 91, 199–200
portfolio strategy, 31, 85–6
power sharing, 5, 20, 37, 53–4
Pratt & Whitney, 215
prejudice, 257–9
pricing, competitive, 62–3
Pritzker family, 72
Procter & Gamble, 64
production management, 275–7, 281
profit, 211
    as target, 57–60
progress, continual, 127–9, 133–4

Quaker Oats, 228
quality:
    Deming, 47–9
    Europe, 189–90, 192
    Japan, 47–8, 188
    total quality management, 79, 81, 186–93
Quinn, John J., 59–60, 165, 166, 167–8, 169, 170–1

racism, 257–8
raiders, corporate, 23, 44–6
Rank, 231
Raytheon, 301
RCA, 38, 40, 41, 51, 228
recession, management out of, 236–41
Reed, John, 178
Reed International, 133, 134
Reedpack, 133
Rehfeld, John E., 61
Remington, 116
Renewal Factor, The, 279
reporting systems, 158–63
reputation, 299–300
response rate, 82–4
responsibility, and authority, 252–3, 271
responsiveness, strategic, 30
restructuring, 149, 158, 227, 231
Revlon, 45
Reynolds, R.J., 16–17
RJR Nabisco, 15–18, 19, 41, 101, 119, 120, 139–40, 228, 237

INDEX

Robert Bosch, 62, 185–7, 188, 209
Roddick, Anita, 260
Rogers, Buck, 33
Rolls-Royce, 177
Rolm, 211
Rosen, Benjamin, 9, 10, 11, 13, 119
Ross, Steve, 224, 225, 226, 269
rotation, job, 150
Rousseau, Jean-Jacques, 158
Rowntree, 196
Royal Dutch-Shell, 238

Saatchi & Saatchi, 250
Sahl, Mort, 19
Sainsburys, 62
Sakai, Kuniyasu, 205
sale of businesses, 43–4, 46, 56–7, 132–3
Salomon Inc., 174
Sampras, Pete, 12
SAS, 202
Saunders, Ernest, 135, 137, 140
'scenario' planning, 238
Schwarzkopf, General Norman, xv, 305
'scientific management', 73
SCM, 56
Scolnick, Ed, 270
Sculley, John, 112, 245, 246
Seiko, 61
Semler, Ricardo, 111, 112
Sense of Mission, A, 207–8, 211
service, 199, 201–2
sexism, 257–9
Shapiro, Irving S., 258
share prices and earnings, 132, 134, 137, 174–81
'shareholder value analysis' (SVA), 229–30
Shewhart cycle, 48–9
Shotuko, Prince of Japan, 53
Shugrue, Martin, 115
Sieff, Israel, 209
Silver, Michael de Kare, 228
Sloan, Alfred P., 127, 267
Sloane, Nat, 229
slogans, 282
SMILE, 253
Smith, Douglas K., 28, 291
Smith, Roger B., 101
Smith Corona, 60
SmithKline Beecham (*formerly* Smith Kline & French), 116, 122, 179, 264
Sohio, 229
Sonnenfeld, Jeffrey, 120–2
Sony, xiii, 106–7, 162, 197, 247, 291
Spartan rules, 204–5
Spindler, Michael H., 245, 247

'Stalinist' management, 6–7
Stalk, George, Jr, 82–3
Stauffer Chemical, 46
Stella Artois, 80
Stern, Joel, 177
Stoy Hayward, 98
Strategic Control: Milestones for Long-Term Performance, 59–60, 165, 166, 167–8, 169, 170–1
Strategies and Styles, 57, 58
strategy, corporate, 167–72
 control companies, 57
 development of, 53–4
 implementation of, 150–1
 planning companies, 57
 planning, Japan, 164–6, 170–1
 responsiveness, 30
 and turbulence, 30–4, 98
success:
 Japanese philosophy, 61–2
 Western philosophy, 59
Suchard, 196
Sugar, Alan, 70
Sumitomo, 165
Sun Microsystems, 245, 285
sunk cost, 52
Supermanagers, The, 30
suppliers, 63
'sur-petition', 80, 299
Swatch, 77

tactics, 167
Tagamet, 116, 264–5
takeovers and mergers, 23, 44–6, 56–8, 133
 and brands, 196
 partial, 228–30
Takiron, 281
Tambrands, 181
targets, 159–61
 and incentives, 57–8
Tasker, Peter, 53, 71–2, 108
Teaching the Elephant to Dance, 38, 221
teamwork, 283
 see also consensus; empowerment
technology, 22
 information (*q.v.*), 141, 161–2
 networking, 88–93
 and new product development, 51
Texaco, 138
Texas Instruments, 13, 14
Textron, 42, 121
Thatcher, Margaret, 56, 60, 261
Theory X and Theory Y, 266–7
thoroughness, 280
Thriving on Chaos, 25, 279
thrust, direction of, 130–4

317

INDEX

time-based management, 79, 81, 83–4
Time-Warner, 224–6, 269
Times, The, 225
Timmer, Jan, 163
Timmons, Geoffrey A., 29–30
Timotei, 151
TMI, 67
Toffler, Alvin, 297, 298
Toshiba, 60, 61, 164–6, 170–1
total quality management (TQM), 79, 81, 186–93
Touche Ross, 90
Toyoda, Shoichiro, 276
Toyota, 190, 197, 241, 275–7, 306
training, 67–9
  Japan, 73
  see also education
transnationals, 144–6, 248–53
Tregoe, Ben, 51, 54
Trippe, Juan, 121
Trotman, Alex, 128
Trouble-Shooter, The, 109–11, 114
Trump, Donald, 237
Tupperware, 80–1
turbulence, 29–30, 98
Turning the Tables, 111
turnrounds, 19–20, 24

Understanding Company Strategy, 167, 168, 170
Unilever, 46, 149–51
United Airlines, 228
United Kingdom (UK):
  CEs, 102
  Toshiba, 165–6
United States of America (USA):
  CEs, 102–3
  electrical industry, 164
  manufacturing, 293–4
United Technologies, 121, 215–17
US Industries, 56

Vagelos, Roy, 264, 265, 269, 270
value, 62, 206–11
  of brands, 196
  of companies, 177–8
  statements, 207

van de Vliet, Anita, 281, 283
Vanity Fair, 259
Vasotec, 264–5
versatility, 73
Vinck, Karel, 193, 201
Volkswagen, 197

Walkman, Sony, 106–7
Wall Street Journal, The, 45, 179, 285–6, 288–9
Walton, Mary, 47, 97
Walton, Tony, 225
Warhol, Andy, 21
Warner Communications, 224–6
Washington Post Inc., 181, 254–6
Waterman, Robert H., Jr, 70, 73, 139, 142, 168, 195, 278, 279
Watson, Thomas, Jr, 121, 293
Watson, Thomas, Sr, 293
Welch, Jack, 37–40
Well Made in America, 233
Wells, Frank G., 226
Wells Fargo, 228
Wenner, David L., 229–30
What Car magazine, 190–1
When Giants Learn to Dance, 37–8, 221–2
White, Gordon, Lord, 23, 46, 56–7, 121
Whitney, John, 157
Wilson, Joe, 27
Wolfe, Tom, 21
women CEs, 254–62
Worthington Industries, 179
Wozniak, Steven, 246
Wrigley, William, 99

Xerox Corporation, 25–8, 34, 79–80, 169, 188–9, 231, 250, 291, 298

Yamauchi, Hiroshi, 76, 77
Yanmar, 220
Yoshida, Hideo, 205
Young, David, 207, 211
Young, John, 209
Yuasa, 281, 282

Zemke, Ron, 199, 200